PIXIE DUST

A Memoir

Bronwyn MacRitchie

Pixie Dust

Copyright © 2020 Bronwyn MacRitchie

All rights reserved. No part of this book may be reproduced or transmitted in any form or by any means without written permission from the author.

This book is a work of non-fiction based on the memories and recollections of the author.
Some names have been changed and time lines consolidated.

ISBN 978-0-646-81775-0
ISBN 978-0-646-81776-7 ebook

A Catalogue record for this work is available from the National Library of Australia

Cover photo by giselaate
Cover by Bronwyn MacRitchie and Rebecca Trowbridge
Text and typesetting by Bronwyn MacRitchie

Printed in Australia by Lightning Source

For Tippy

and in memory of my siblings Keith, Ross, and Zilla

'Since the dawn of time there have been those among us who have been willing to go to extraordinary lengths to gain access to that domain normally reserved for birds, angels, and madmen.'
Steven Beach

DIFFICULT ENCOUNTER

'Why anyone wants to live in the big smoke girlie, is a puzzle,' said Dad. 'Nothing but noisy cars, large crowds and ... where the blazes is the number?'

We stood on the kerb in Crown Street, Surry Hills and gazed at the contrasting array of awnings, facades and doorways. I was drawn to the striped canvas above the butcher shop as it fluttered and flapped. In the window below, a teenager in a stained white apron leaned in and placed a tray of sausages into the display of meats, then surveyed both sides of the street. He spotted me staring and smiled. The freckled cheeks and sandy hair turned back to the counter as my shyness was revealed by a red face and trembling knees.

'Ah, here we are,' said Dad, as I reached twelve in my crack-counting distraction. 'Ready?'

I straightened the skirt on my home-made dress, wiped the tips of my shoes on the back of my socks and nodded.

I was there because he said I was not to be trusted on my own. I was fifteen, rebellious and hard to handle. Dad had given me two choices as a career - nurse or secretary. Betty would train me as a secretary to work in the family business but the thought was unbearable, so nursing was my escape from the suffocation and isolation of a small bush town.

'You can do nursing in Sydney and your mother will keep an eye on you,' Dad had said. 'It's time she took some responsibility. Besides, she's a nurse.'

This was the first time he'd spoken of my mother. The confirmation that she was a nurse provided a connection I hadn't known was there. Naturally I was curious. I was also excited, nervous and scared at seeing her after all these years.

The cream brick building we entered was three storeys high and divided into flats. I followed Dad through a brown wooden door and down two sets of stairs to a sub-basement. We stopped in front of a door with a brass '8' in the middle. My mother lived here and she was a stranger to me.

'I'll be going now.'

'Please, Dad. Do you have to leave?' My dress was scrunched into a ball in my sweating palm.

'You'll be fine.'

But I was not fine. I remembered a vivid image from ten years ago. The back of my mother's floral dress, Tippy looking over her shoulder, his curls bouncing with each step as she walked away from us. He was clutching a strand of her red hair in his tiny fingers. Zilla stood beside the car door waiting to get in. She jumped in and kneeled on the seat looking at us through the rear window, her eyes wide, glancing back and forth from Ross to me. One hand pressed so hard on the back window it showed white fingertips through the glass. My mother sat beside her and looked straight ahead. Then the car drove down the hill. We waited for her to turn around and wave, because they were going on holiday without us. Tippy and Zilla watched us as the car wove down the hill to the main road. Ross and I stood until we couldn't see them anymore. We stood long after the dust trail drifted through the trees and faded.

'You and your mother need some time together,' Dad said as I tried to shake the memory. He turned to leave but the door opened and there she was. My mother. She looked up at Dad and I stared at her.

'Hello, Ben.'

'Hello, Mary. Bonnie, this is your mother.'

'Hello.' The squeak didn't sound like my voice. She gave me a quick look, then stepped closer. I was hoping for a hug but she took my hand. Her cold fingers gave it an abrupt shake. I was uncertain how to respond. I wanted her to cup her hands around my face and say what a beautiful young woman I had become, to look me up and down with tenderness.

'Hello, Bonnie.' Her voice was throaty. Not the soft, melodic sound I'd stored in my mind. But the resemblance between us left no doubt this was my mother. I had her bumpy nose and fair, freckled skin. I was taller and inclined to be round shouldered. Betty had criticized me for my hunched stance and had put a shortened broom handle down my back, tying my arms together. My mother's dowager's hump caused me to straighten my back to improve my posture. The red hair from so long ago, was now silver-grey, cut short and permed. She wore a starched white apron over the pale blue uniform of Crown Street Women's Hospital, with nylon stockings and black shoes. On the bib was a nurse's watch and badge. My uniform was similar.

'Come in,' she said.

A gentleman appeared behind her.

'This is my friend, Gerald,' my mother said. Gerald stretched out his hand and gave me a firm handshake, squashing my fingers. He was the same height as my mother. Both were short compared to Dad, who was six feet tall.

'Hello, Bonnie. Pleased to meet you.' He spoke with a posh British accent. He had pudgy cheeks, large brown bespectacled eyes and thick grey hair. A dark red waistcoat strained at the buttonholes, stretched over his considerable paunch. A maroon cravat gave him the appearance of lord of the manor. He greeted me with a wide welcoming smile that eased my nerves a little.

'Gerald,' said Dad.

'Ben, how are you?' They shook hands. I could tell Dad didn't like him much because he didn't answer but it seemed like they knew each other.

We stood in the doorway in awkward silence. A toilet upstairs flushed and the sound of clambering footsteps broke the moment.

'Can't stay, Mary, business to attend to. I'll be back in a couple of hours to drop you off at the hospital, Bonnie. Tat-tah.' He gave me a quick kiss on the cheek, turned and left. I listened to his footsteps fade until the front door closed.

'Come in,' said my mother. 'Let's sit down.'

I followed them into a large room and noticed we'd entered through the only door. Two brown vinyl divans faced each other and the large gold lamps on side tables at each end spread a pale, yellow glow, highlighting the checked throw rugs stretched across the back of the divans.

'Why don't you sit there.' She pointed to one and they sat opposite. I looked around the room to avoid staring at them both. Against the wall beside the sink was a polished wooden fold-up table covered with a white lace tablecloth. Sitting on top was a tray with cups, saucers and a plate of biscuits. Lace curtains on the small window matched the green on the cupboard doors. The four canisters sitting on top were in perfect alignment. At the other end of the room was a large, two-door, dark wooden wardrobe. I noticed the ceiling was very high and everything was clean, tidy and dust free. A gaudy gold-framed painting hung on one wall. On the opposite wall was a photo of the Queen. The pathway between each piece of furniture was narrow and the absence of photographs created a mood lacking coziness; no framed ones on the side tables, none on the walls. We didn't have them at the Mount Hope house either.

'Have you checked into the Prince of Wales yet?' asked my mother.

'Yes, I did that yesterday.'

'When do you start work?'

'Tomorrow. I'll be living in the nurses' quarters.'

'Did your father ever talk about me?' she asked suddenly, tilting her head and pressing two fingers into her chin. She looked at me, large eyes blinking behind the thick lenses of her spectacles. Her tone was flat, lacking warmth.

'No, he didn't talk about you.' Maybe she thought I knew more than I did or was she curious about Dad's opinion of her? I knew nothing of her relationship with Dad as no-one talked about her. I had stopped asking about her as my questions were ignored or the subject changed, until I ceased to be curious. No reminders or photographs. No bits of information. A name not to be mentioned, she became a distant, faded memory as daily activities secured our focus.

Gerald was staring at a spot on the wall to my left as if it needed immediate attention and I tried not to turn around to see what it was. My mother's expression was difficult to read and I wondered if her tightly clasped hands meant she too was feeling uncomfortable. I was pleased Gerald was there. Being alone with my mother would have been difficult. He took an enormous hanky from his trouser pocket and gave his nose a vigorous blow. My mother leaned into the cushions and I crossed and uncrossed my legs and tried to think of something to say.

There were raised voices outside the door. A man and woman exchanged words in Italian. I didn't understand what they were saying, but it sounded like an argument. It stirred memories from Dubbo – memories of Dad home after weeks away at the mine, laughing and playing with us and at night, angry voices in the kitchen. Each time he left, my mother cried and drank sherry, so we kept out of the way. I tried to recall hugs, sweet kisses on my cheeks or encouraging words from her, but couldn't. Facing her now, I'd hoped to be overwhelmed and excited, but she was a stranger. The instantaneous connection I'd expected, hadn't happened. Still, I longed for us to be friends, not troubled by moments that happened so long ago.

'I've been in touch with him from time to time to enquire about you all, see how you're doing, that sort of thing,' she said, puncturing my thoughts.

Hearing that was a shock. I had yearned for contact, for knowledge to fill the ache left by her desertion, for a photograph or letter, anything, and all this time he had known and she knew, but we hadn't. I felt cheated.

'Really? He never said anything to us.' I crossed my arms and leant back against the clammy vinyl, thinking she was more interested in Dad than me.

'Were you in touch with Keith, too?' I asked. 'He was living in Sydney before he died.'

'Yes,' she chewed her bottom lip and for the first time her voice faltered. 'He often visited us here.'

I'd upset her by mentioning my elder brother who'd died in a car accident the previous year. I was jealous and hurt over secrets my Dad and brother kept. Gerald reached over and gently took hold of her hand. She pulled away so he dragged out his hankie and blew his nose again.

'Would you like a cup of tea?' she asked.

She lifted her chin again and rubbed her lips together. This was my mother. My actual, real mother sitting across from me. I wanted to drop my guard and give her a big hug but shyness glued me to the couch and I didn't know how to behave, so my questions had to wait.

'Yes, please.' What should I call her? I hadn't' called anyone Mum since I was five. I could not reconcile this mum with my fictional one, but was desperate for her to like me and, despite my confusion, I sought the approval neither Dad or Betty could give.

'I'll make the tea, Mary, you two can talk.' Gerald went over to the sink, put the kettle on the stove and added three scoops of tea to the teapot on the tray. I could see he was trying not to make a noise by the slow, deliberate way he moved, but his hands shook as the spoon hit the side of the teapot. Tea leaves scattered across the bench.

'Why have you chosen nursing?' she asked.

Should I tell her that I didn't know? Should I tell her what a dreadful woman Betty was and I couldn't wait to get away? Should I say it was because I couldn't stand the gossip of a small town? That Dad thought I was having an affair with a man who was married with five children – a man over a hundred miles away whom I'd never met. Should I tell her that Dad preferred the gossip? Should I say I was not certain of my choice?

'I want to look after sick people,' I said. 'Like you do.'

THE ARRIVAL

In my earliest memories, Dubbo was our home. Then in 1951, Keith returned to Bathurst for his third year at boarding school and Mum wept when the *For Sale* sign was hammered into the front yard of our four bedroom house. Dad loaded up the car, packed us all into the Oldsmobile and set off.

We travelled into the night. Headlights burrowed through the darkness that threw up the ghostly shapes of trees, whose limbs reached for us as we drove past. Dust from our wheels tumbled and turned as my friends and home in Dubbo vanished.

My brother, Ross, was sleeping in the well between the back and front seats, his head rested on the hump in the middle. My sister, Zilla, was lying on the back seat with me, her feet on top of my chest, grinding her teeth. Tippy's gentle snore came from Mum's lap in the front.

'Where are we?' I asked, half asleep, squinting over the back seat through the front window at the road ahead shadowed in darkness. A kangaroo sprang out, its eyes glowing red, then swerved to avoid the car.

'Trangie,' said Dad. 'Go back to sleep, Bonnie.'

I snuggled down in the seat, pulled the blanket around my shoulders and drifted back into the rhythms of corrugations, the rumble of the motor and the comfort of my sister's feet.

'Wake up, girlie,' said Dad. 'Mount Hope's just down the road. Thought you'd like to see our new town.'

'Hmph,' said Mum.

'Zilla spewed all over Dad's shoes while you were asleep,' said Ross.

'I was car sick,' said Zilla.

It was daytime. Dad pointed to the right at a small three-sided tin shed with a missing roof. In front was a line of fence posts in varying stages of decay, enclosing a circular track dotted with small bushes.

'That's the racecourse.'

'Doesn't look much like a racecourse, Dad.'

'When did you see a racecourse, Ross?' I said.

'I've seen plenty.'

'Bwack birdie,' Tippy pointed to a crow sitting on top of the shed, watching us as we passed.

'Are we here?' said Zilla, twisting around to peer through the now dusty back window.

Our car slowed as we approached a bend in the road. We hadn't seen any houses yet. On top of a post was a faded, lopsided sign. It read MOUNT HOPE.

'Look. We're here, we're here,' we all chanted.

'Where are all the people?' asked Zilla.

'There are none,' Mum muttered, holding Tippy close. 'We're in the middle of nowhere.'

'They're working,' Dad said as we drove around a bend and saw a scattering of houses. Dirt tracks weaved in seemingly pointless directions. A short strip of bitumen curved up the hill and disappeared. Perched on the top of the rise was a long, flat-roofed building with mud-coated trucks, dented utes and old cars parked randomly out front.

We turned off the main road and drove in first gear up a bumpy, winding track beside a huge slag dump. The sun glinted on the roof of a tin shed, the walls of which were concealed by an enormous piece of machinery. The bumper scraped on the uneven surface as we bounced our way up the steep hill. There were tracks everywhere. Animal tracks criss-crossed the top of the hill and into the scrubby bush. Deep-grooved tyre tracks were either side of grassy tufts in a centre ridge. The one we were on led to the top of the hill where there were a couple of trucks and a generator chugging louder than our revving engine.

Dad turned onto a wide plateau about halfway up where there were two houses, a short distance from each other.

'Is this our house?' I asked.

'No, Bonnie. That's Halfords. Ours is over there.' He pointed to a Nissen hut. It looked like a giant water tank lying on its side, half buried in the dirt. The same shape as the army buildings across the road from us in Dubbo.

'It's not finished,' said Mum. 'There's rubbish everywhere.'

'It'll all be done in a couple of weeks Mary.'

A man appeared around the side of our house as we tumbled out of the car pushing and jostling each other. His striped shirt was hanging out of the sides of his overalls, a leather belt with a pouch in front had a hammer dangling from the side.

'Who's that, Dad?' I asked.

'Say hello to Nick. He's building our house.'

'Sorrys Mr 'Clern'n ... Oi's jest finish goes to Cobar ... see youse Monday. This you femily?' His words tumbled out in such a gallop, I didn't understand them.

'Yes. This is my family.'

Nick removed his hat and a dark mass of corkscrew curls sprang from underneath – he was immediately three inches taller. His head bobbed up and down and, as he pumped Dad's hand, his curls beat time. We all nodded together.

'Pleases to meet youse. I goes now.'

He positioned the hat, jammed the curls back under, strode over to his ute, got in and rattled down the hill.

'Bonza bloke,' said Dad.

'He talks funny,' said Zilla.

'Like the man from the cafe in Dubbo,' said Ross.

'The Par ... Parthe ...'

'The Parthenon, Bonnie,' said Mum.

'Why is our house round?' I asked.

'Air flow. Now, out you lot. Have a look around but don't go far, I can't stand here gas-bagging all day. Gotta see a man about a dog.'

'What dog?' said Ross.

'It's an expression,' said Mum. 'It means he needs to talk to someone.'

While Dad went up the hill to the mine where he would work, Ross, Zilla and I ran to a large boulder and sat near the unfinished porch amongst scraps of wood and piles of rubble. A work table covered with a paint-splotched tarpaulin held down by a couple of bricks was out front. On the slag dump below were haphazard clumps of gum, pepper and wattle trees.

As we looked down the hill we saw the entire town. Unlike Dubbo, where our house was in a street, the scattered houses were so far apart from each other, we'd need to ride bikes to get between them. Below us, scattered around an open plain, the patchwork of buildings had no symmetry. At the centre, a neglected tennis court and cricket pitch rested behind a series of dirt roads strung out in all directions. One led to a house with a jumble of car bodies in various states of decay and another to the single strip of bitumen on the main road that crossed in front of a building with a sign on top – MOUNT HOPE ROYAL HOTEL.

At the back of the hotel, four pigs scrounged about a muddy pen that bordered another dirt road. It forked into several different directions, one leading past a structure with *Store* the only readable word on the dilapidated sign where a roof poked out above two enormous pepper trees. Another road led to a white house with large steps leading to a covered verandah. On the opposite side of the road an unpainted schoolhouse sat in the middle of a small rise, boards weathered and grey, a bell dangled from a pole inside the fenced yard.

'Do you think we'll go to school here?' I said.

'Maybe, 'spose so,' said Ross.

'I can't see any kids. I wonder where they are?' said Zilla.

'Dad said there's not many people living in the town. The rest live out on properties,' said Ross. 'Only a few kids go to school.'

'Gosh. There were twenty-five kids in my Transition class in Dubbo,' I said.

'And I just started Kindergarten,' said Zilla.

'We'll probably be in the same class,' I said.

'Gosh, I hope not,' said Ross.

Dad came down to get us. 'Come on, kids. Help unpack the car.'

'Can we get an ice-cream Dad, please?'

'Steady on, Bonnie.'

'But it's Saturday and we always have ice-cream on Saturday.'

In Dubbo, Dad's sister, Aunty Ethel owned the corner shop. It was a block down the road from our house and she lived out the back with her three children, Cecil, Beatrice and Melville. On Saturday mornings we spent our pocket money there. We ogled the mouthwatering content of the gigantic screw top jars kept high up on the top shelf. The ladder reached to the ceiling and was attached to a track on the top shelf. We envied Aunty as she zipped back and forth plucking goods from each level and placing them in a cane basket hooked onto the side of the ladder. When she stretched to reach the top shelf, her dress would rise up to reveal stockings held up with bits of elastic and we caught a glimpse of her fleshy thighs. We'd point, then change our minds, sending her on a roundabout of indecision, the ladder zoomed back and forth until she became cranky. Sometimes she sent us home with nothing.

It was her strawberry ice-cream I loved though. A creamy mound perched on top of a cone, dribbles melting down the sides and over our hands, tongues sweeping around the wafer to gather every drop. A few days before we left, Ross had gone to the shop to buy us both an ice-cream. When he returned he handed me an empty cone.

'I dropped yours,' he said as I stared at his probing tongue curling around his.

'How'd you know it was mine?'

'Because I'm eating mine, silly.'

When Dad told her we were moving to Mount Hope, Aunty sold the shop and moved back to Western Australia.

'Yumm, ice-cream,' said Zilla.

'Me ice-cweam,' said Tippy.

'You could try Cobar,' said Mum. 'You'll be able to buy an ice-cream there. It's only a hundred miles away.'

'Can we go to Cobar, Dad?'

'Give it up, lass,' said Dad, as he walked up the side of the house to the back door.

'It's so far from anywhere,' said Mum. 'Not a blade of grass in sight. What happens if one of the children gets sick?'

'They'll be fine, Mary.'

'Everything is dusty. It's in my mouth already.'

'There's a kennel,' said Ross, 'but we don't have a dog.'

'Ah, here comes Mr Halford,' said Dad.

Mr Halford walked down the hill. Trotting beside him was a small white dog with a dark brown splotch across the back, its brown ears sticking straight up, twitching back and forth, backside and tail wagging.

'Come here, girl,' said Dad. 'She's only a pup.'

'What's her name?' asked Ross as we all squatted down to pat a dog as excited as we were. She jumped, licking our faces.

'We've never had a dog before ...'

'She's cute ...'

'Pup-pee ...'

'Now I don't hold with any of that licking nonsense,' said Dad. 'Never know where that tongue's been.'

'Can we call her Lassie?' Ross asked. We all nodded in agreement.

'Good a name as any,' said Dad. 'How about you take her for a run?'

HOUSE MUSIC

We unpacked the car and rushed through the house listening to the echo of footsteps and voices in empty rooms. The front door was closed because of the unfinished verandah, and the lounge room was packed with suitcases, mattresses, Tippy's scattered building blocks and our colouring pencils. The kitchen was operational and uncluttered with table, chairs and easy access for traffic.

Mum launched into a frenzy of cleaning and began baking. When Ross and I poked our fingers into the mixing bowl for the third time she shooed us outside.

'Go, play,' she said. 'Never get anything done with you two underfoot.'

We were sitting among the sawdust, bent nails and wood off-cuts under the front verandah of the round house, with Lassie perched between us, when Dad poked his head in.

'What are you flamin' kids doing here? Have you been pestering Nick again?'

'We're chasing Martians,' said Ross. He reached across Lassie and thumped me.

'Yeah. We saw one sneak under the house,' I said, understanding the message.

The truth was, Lassie had chased a brown snake from there a short while ago. She'd turned out to be an excellent watchdog. Her brown ears and white tail had shot up, she'd stood rigid, and barked in the direction of the snake, legs dancing, not venturing too close. Dad had told us, 'They won't hurt you, if you don't hurt them, but steer clear, just the same.' He said that about spiders too, but it didn't make me feel any better.

'What does this Martian look like?' he said, eyebrows raised.

'It was pretty fast,' said Ross, 'but we saw antennae and it had one eye.'

'Yeah. One eye. A big one.'

Dad bent down and looked under the house. There were blobs of dried concrete among the rocks and wood, but no alien.

'It must've climbed out while we were talking,' said Dad. 'Now skedaddle. This part of the house is a work site and no place for kids. Besides, I saw a brown snake around here earlier.'

'It's alright, Dad, Lassie chased it away.'

'That damn dog'll get itself killed, one day. You kids steer clear. I can remember when I was a boy ... '

We took off down the hill before one of Dad's lectures about the dangers of the bush trapped us for longer than our concentration could last. Lassie trotted in front as we scrambled towards the clump of pepper trees in a race to be first. We'd already established our favourite spots on the slag dump, a three-minute run from the house, as well as the best climbing trees, hiding spots and forbidden shafts that tempted further scrutiny. We met two of the local kids who also played on the dump. They showed us where the dry dump was and the best bike riding tracks. Paddo was the same height as Ross, with curly black hair and dark skin. Chris was blond and fair. We were all around the same age and despite us being the newcomers, Ross established the role of leadership from the beginning, taking charge of the slag dump as if it was his personal domain and we were his servants.

Dad had built a chook pen out the back. Lassie sniffed and growled at it with uncertainty since it was situated in the middle of one of her walking trails. We loved collecting the eggs and eating the delicious cakes Mum baked. Dad also built us a tree house from a wooden packing box in the gum tree at the side of the house, complete with a ladder attached to the trunk. A boy's bicycle was shared between the three of us. Zilla and I found the bar that ran from the handlebars to the seat too high to swing our leg over to reach the pedals, so we'd stick our leg between the bar and the pedals and ride hanging out one side. Ross had claimed it as his, so we had to book riding times. Zilla wasn't interested in the tree house or climbing trees. Tippy spent most of the time inside with Mum, but Ross, Lassie and I loved the freedom of our extended back yard and explored the hill, the slag dump and the dry tip at every opportunity. We were enjoying ourselves outside, but Mum wouldn't let Zilla stray far from the back door, so most of the day she sat at the kitchen table drawing and colouring in. We were having fun, but not Mum.

'It's not even a proper house. It's a Nissen hut. I half expect the Army to storm in and inspect their quarters.' Mum muttered at the sink after we'd been in the house for a few weeks. 'Four bedrooms, we had once. The children even had a playroom.'

Dad pushed back his chair and walked out the back door without speaking because Mum had taken to grumbling about the harsh conditions whenever he sat at the kitchen table. Nick had almost finished our house, however. I was fascinated by the strands of abundant, black chest hair that escaped from the top of his shirt. He lived with his family in Cobar and stayed at the pub during the week, going home on weekends. Because of Nick's limited English, Dad's body language increased when delivering instructions. He became frustrated with his inability to convey his ideas, so he sketched them on torn bits of brown paper, which Nick kept under rocks, bricks or nailed to a piece of wood. Paper fluttered like trapped, brown butterflies trying to escape. Sometimes Ross and I switched them around and watched Nick scratch his head wondering about the mix-up.

Nick was adding a timber verandah to the front of the house. Half of it was to be enclosed for our bedroom. Mum and Dad already had their room and while we waited for ours to be finished, we slept on the lounge room floor. During the day, the heavy kapok mattresses were propped against a wall. We played behind them in the tunnel created by the curve, and often knocked them over with our boisterous play. We couldn't lift them back because they were too heavy.

'When will this house be finished?' Mum asked Dad each night at dinner.

Dad's answer was short. 'Soon.'

'I can't stand the mess. The children's clothes are filthy all the time, they have nowhere inside to play, I can't open the front door because of the dust and Tippy could fall off the verandah. All I can hear is Nick hammering. And his dreadful singing.'

I liked his singing, even if I couldn't understand the words. Nick sang as he drilled, sawed and hammered. It wasn't the same as Slim Dusty or Bing Crosby that Dad liked. Ross and I sat in the tall pepper tree and listened to his voice drift down the hill. At smoko, he collected his lunchbox from the back of the ute, sat on a large rock in the shade, then removed a sandwich prepared by the pub cook. He poured his coffee from a flask, stretched out his legs and sighed. The routine was the same every day.

When he finished eating, he returned to the ute, packed the thermos into his bag and picked up a long, thin leather case. He released the clips, opened the lid, took out a violin bow, then looked directly at us and smiled. Two fingers wiggled us forward until we were crouched close in front of him.

'What will you play today, Nick?' None of the tunes he played were familiar, but I asked anyway.

'Youse listen,' he said, 'youse know song.' He showed me the screw at the end of the bow and began to turn it, pointing to the hair as it tightened.

He rubbed along the hair with a hard lump of bees wax then, with a special cloth, cleaned the saw he'd been working with all day. He gripped the wooden handle between his knees with the teeth pointing toward his chest and with his left hand, bent the metal over his left leg. He drew the bow up and down across the outer edge with his other hand, the sound lowered when he straightened the metal, and rose higher when he bent it more. I was captivated by his slow careful movements. I recognised the tune as *Beautiful Dreamer*.

'It's Dad's favourite song.' I jumped and clapped. 'Bing someone – he's got the record.'

'He's got millions of records of him,' said Ross. 'He sings this one all the time at the mine.'

Dad had rigged a shower in an old concrete storeroom up at the mine. When he finished work, his voice reverberated around the concrete and rang down the hill and around the town as he belted out Bing Crosby songs.

'I learn from listen,' said Nick. 'He sing louder than motor.'

Nick winked at me and I watched the quivering saw as the bow moved back and forth, making the sounds of a wobbly violin. It wasn't long before one of the publican's dogs joined in howling. Soon all the dogs were bellowing an out of tune chorus. He stopped playing and they stopped. When he started again, the tune was unfamiliar, but the dogs didn't care. When the publican yelled SHUDDUP we laughed.

'Here,' he said, turning the bow toward me. He gave me a nudge. 'You try, yes?'

I took the bow in my right hand and he showed me how to hold it with my fingers around the end. Then he guided my arm, moving it back and forth. I held the saw between my knees like he did, but my short arms couldn't bend the steel.

'Ross?' I turned to see if Ross wanted a go, but he had abandoned music, preferring to throw sticks for Lassie to chase.

'I hold saw,' said Nick, 'you play.'

I stroked the bow against the steel, but got a terrible screech. This sent the dogs at the pub crazy. They howled long and loud so, too shy to persist, I returned the bow to Nick.

'You play, I watch,' I said.

On Friday afternoon, Dad got out his twenty button concertina, fifteen buttons at one end and five at the other. He and Nick sat side by side sheltered by the trees. When Dad started playing, Nick joined in with his saw. Dad pulled and pushed, his fingers danced over the buttons while his legs bounced up and down, beating time. When they harmonised, their voices rang out down the hill, Dad strong and deep and Nick a higher tenor. Not only did the dogs join in with their howling, but the blokes sitting on the pub verandah enjoying a beer would shout out comments.

'Gonna whip the hat round for a few bob, Ben.'

'Don't ya know any other tunes, we heard those last week.'

'Crikey. You two are scaring away the customers.'

'I hear they're looking for a duo for the Euabalong dances.'

I liked listening to their playing. They laughed, had fun and didn't mind us crowding them. The house was finished, so Nick would be returning to Cobar with his saw. He'd be missed. I decided I wanted to play music because it made people happy.

* * *

We missed the Friday singalong with Dad and Nick. The town dogs returned to announcing strangers' cars as they drove into town. The building rubble had been removed and Dad had created a sloping dirt bank from the verandah around the steps, concealing the underneath. Mum spent her mornings cleaning and baking. Biscuits for smoko and cakes for dinner, roasts when Dad came home with some lamb. She clanged about in the kitchen, rarely venturing beyond the back door.

Zilla and Tippy spent their time with her, while each day Ross and I found new and exciting adventures outside. We didn't go to school, but each afternoon, when the youngest napped, Mum brought our writing books out and taught us writing and sums at the kitchen table. Every night Dad read all of us a story, alternating between girls' and boys' preferences. Once a month we'd leave before daylight and drive to Cobar to purchase groceries, returning the same day.

Sometimes the routine changed.

'Doing some blasting underground this morning, so stay close to the house and DO NOT come up the hill,' Dad said at breakfast one morning. 'Remember the sirens, there's five minutes between the warnings before we push the plunger. You lot mind your Mum, okay?'

'Yes, Dad.'

'Is it dangerous? Will we be safe?'

'I know what I'm doing, Mary. I've been at it a long time. You'll all be fine.'

Mum stirred and scraped, baking a series of cakes as if expecting a mob of visitors. The kitchen table was covered in small cakes, square cakes and round cakes. She walked back and forth from the back door, flapping the tea towel, checking the hill, checking us.

'I want to be able to see you at all times,' she said, wiping her hands on her apron then whipping up another batch of mixture.

At ten o'clock we heard the first warning. A long, loud siren followed by another of equal length. Even though Dad had warned us, it was still alarming. Dogs barked. An egg dropped from my hand and smashed on the ground. The chooks squarked and flapped around me, surging forward at this unexpected treat. Ross was attaching pram wheels to a wooden crate. He glanced up, ignored the siren and resumed concentrating on his task, impatient to finish putting it together.

'We've loads of time,' he said. 'Five minutes.'

Ross continued, screwdriver held in one hand, tongue poked out over his top lip as he set the wheels over the pencil markings for his billycart. Beside him, Lassie leapt to her feet and dived into her kennel in the corner.

Tippy poked his chubby two-year-old fingers through the holes in the wire mat at the back door, reaching to retrieve a fallen bottle top stuck underneath. Zilla sat on a log with her colouring book, brows furrowed, lips pursed forward, as her pencil wriggled back and forth in concentration. She and Ross had thick, dark, curly hair that bounced whenever they moved. I wished I had hair like that instead of wispy, blond waves.

Mum burst out the back door, narrowly avoiding Tippy, 'Inside, kids. NOW.'

Eyes searched from the hill to us. She jammed Tippy on her hip, held the back door open with the other hand as her eyes flicked back and forth, anxious and alarmed. Zilla grabbed her book but I hesitated, basket poised, wondering if I should mention the dropped egg. Ross was still working beside the kennel. Lassie's ears and eyes moved back and forth as she backed further into her kennel, sensing Mum's alarm.

'Dog stays out,' Mum said.

'But Mum, she's frightened,' said Ross. 'Can't I stay with her?'

One-minute siren warning. A series of short wails.

'You will do no such thing. Get inside.'

'Sorry Lassie,' he said, drooped his head and shuffled past Mum into the kitchen.

'Bonnie?' She swung the back door as I ran past her. The siren stopped as the door slammed shut and breathless puffing filled the kitchen. A fresh-baked cake sat in the middle of the table under a tea-towel cover. Its buttery smell fused with smoky wood and room warmth. I placed the basket of eggs on the kitchen table, not wishing to be responsible for any more breakages.

The floor trembled. Our bodies inched closer to each other. Dust trickled from the ceiling in puffs as Zilla clutched Ross and he realised he still held the pram wheels. Tippy buried his head in Mum's chest, arms tight around her neck as we huddled.

At first, the sound was a muffled groan, then the canisters on the kitchen shelf vibrated, tapping against each other, threatening to topple over. Cutlery jangled inside the kitchen drawer. Dirt on the floor bounced in tiny pockets on the masonite and a marble rolled past us under the kitchen dresser.

'My pencils,' cried Zilla.

'Zilla, no.' I turned, not quick enough. As she ran out the back, the earth erupted. Mum slammed Tippy down on the floor and whipped past me, face pale. She stretched, clasped Zilla's arm and yanked, hauling them both back into the protection of the kitchen.

With a thunderous boom, a burst of dust and stones hurtled into the air from the other side of the hill. They seemed small as they disappeared through a cloud of red-brown dust and hovered in the sky as we watched from the safety of the house. When they fell, a thousand hammers pounded the roof's tin. We covered our ears. Zilla cried about her pencils and Mum breathed in short pants as she patted her chest.

'Look,' said Ross, our faces pressed against the window watching the dramatic display, eyes wide, mouths open. Outside, it was raining rocks. Some rolled and stopped, others tumbled down the hill in a haphazard race as they bounced and jumped over each other. One huge boulder smacked the top of the hill then zig-zagged, changing direction with each bounce, growing in size and speed.

'Jings,' said Ross, 'It's as big as an elephant.'

'Big as a cow,' said Zilla.

'Big as a donkey,' I said.

'Quick, come and look, Mum.' We watched, spell-bound, our breath clouding the glass as our fingers clutched the lip at the bottom of the frame.

Mum peered through the top pane of the window. 'Oh my. It's heading straight for the house.'

'Bang, bang,' said Tippy, pounding his fist on the floor.

'Into the front room, all of you,' Mum said, shoving us ahead of her. Tippy was about to close his fingers around the marble, when she scooped him up and ran to the front room.

One long siren sounded the all clear warning as the clock on top of the glass cabinet chimed.

I watched the cloud of dust move across the front window as it dispersed and swept past, floating over the town. The clattering gradually subsided, bringing stillness and relief to our ringing ears.

'Can we go outside now?' asked Ross.

'No.' said Mum picking up a book. 'Come and sit down.'

'But we want to see the boulder,' said Ross dropping onto the couch and crossing his arms.

Mum began to read but Tippy was the only one interested. *'The Mole had been working very hard all the morning, … '*

The back door slammed.

'Ahoy there. Anyone home?' Dad shouted. 'What are all the cakes for?'

'Boy, Dad that was great,' said Ross, rushing to meet him. 'Did you see that big boulder ...?'

'Boulder? What boulder?

'It bounced down the hill ...'

'... really fast.'

'... big as an elephant.'

'... gigantic.'

'Hang on, kids. Don't all talk at once. Where's your mother?'

'In there.' We all pointed.

'Is it over?' Mum's voice came from the front room.

Tippy bounced up and down, arms reaching towards Dad. 'Come here, little man.'

'Didn't you hear the last siren?'

'Yes, but how do I know it's safe? I don't feel safe. The children ...'

'It's safe. Now come on kids, let's check out this boulder, then we'll get stuck into those cakes, eh?'

CUT DEEP

The explosions were not restricted to outside.

'You're going to see her, aren't you?

'No, Mary. I will be in Sydney to see the accountant.'

'I know you're seeing her, Ben. It's been going on since Dubbo.'

'Give it up, Mary.'

'Why don't you give her up.'

The arguing hadn't stopped since we left Dubbo. It spilled out from the bedroom to the kitchen. Every night was the same. We nosedived into our meals to avoid eye contact. Chores became a welcome escape and we longed for laughter, tickles and cuddles.

It was my turn to tie up the dog and I was trapped outside the kitchen doorway, listening to their after dinner bickering.

'We should have stayed in Dubbo. I miss Maree,' said Mum.

'You can't have a maid out here. You'll have to manage without.'

'There's no-one to talk to. I've no friends here.'

'You've got to make an effort, Mary.'

'Oh, you mean go to the pub, Ben? Sit in the ladies bar and drink sherry while people who have lived here all their lives discuss things I know nothing about?'

'People are not like that.'

'Oh yes they are. I even miss Ethel. That's how bad it is.'

Mum scraped the vegetable scraps onto an enamel plate so I took a quick look around the corner and saw Dad leaning on the end of the table, arms folded. Mum's lips were squeezed tight and I knew that expression. Dad would be lucky if he got another word out of her for a week. She grabbed the plate of scraps and headed straight for me. The carving knife swished back and forth in time with her footsteps. Even though I was standing in the doorway, she didn't seem to notice me. Her gaze was fixed beyond the opening to the night sky and the look on her face scared me. I pressed into the wood to make myself as small as possible. As she passed through the doorway on her way to give the scraps to the chooks, I lifted my hand to scratch my nose and felt a sharp sting.

When I looked down, blood was flowing from my finger, down my other arm, spilling over my new nightie. Through the parted flesh I saw the bone of my first finger. I looked from my finger to Mum and then to Dad as I realised what had happened. My wailing hit the room with the volume of an ambulance siren. Mum dropped the plate and knife to the floor and the scraps scattered on the mesh doormat. Dad scooped me up, laid me on the table then took my cut finger and squeezed the sliced ends together while Mum looked on, horrified. The pain intensified. I tried to free myself from Dad's grip but, even though I fought with the fierceness of a trapped wild cat, I couldn't move against his strong arms. Mum's hand was across her mouth.

'Mary, don't just stand there. Get the flour.'

Mum moved swiftly. She grabbed the tin, wrenched out the packet of flour and tipped it all over my hand. It felt cool, and for a moment I forgot my finger as above me, the kitchen bulb swayed back and forth disturbing the wafting clouds of flour.

'Whatever possessed you to use the carving knife on the scraps?' Dad said. 'She's only five. She could lose her finger.'

That's right, I'm five I thought. I'd had a birthday in March and Ross would be seven in May. He wouldn't do all this hollering and crying: even when Dad belted him with the strap, he didn't cry. I should be braver.

'Yes, and here we are, Ben. No doctor, no hospital and no friends.'

'Give it a rest, Mary.'

Their heads moved in and out in a silent ritual, stirring the haze and blocking the light. My finger pounded and I knew this wasn't Mum's fault. I'd been in the wrong place and now I just wanted them to stop bickering.

'I got blood on my nightie.'

'Don't worry about your nightie,' said Dad. 'The blood will come out.'

'I need a hankie.'

Mum pulled one out of her pocket and wiped my snotty nose. Without saying a word, she moved to the stove, poured warm water into a metal bowl and lifted the first aid kit out of the cupboard. She gently brushed the congealed flour away from my hand and was careful not to touch the open wound. The water attacked my cut as it drizzled down over Dad's fingers, past my elbow and splashed onto the floor. I whimpered with the fresh sting each dribble brought. Mum repeated it until the bleeding lessened.

I leant against Dad's chest, limp and drained of energy. His heartbeat was strong and fast, out of sync with my throbbing finger. Mum pulled a large wad of gauze and a white bandage from the kit and wrapped it around my wound. The entire kitchen, including us, was coated in a fine layer of flour. Through the descending veil, I noticed Ross standing in the doorway twirling the curls on his forehead. He gave me a quick nod I found comforting.

Dad stroked my hair and whispered, 'It's alright, Bonnie. You're okay.'

When Mum finished tying the bandage, he gently lifted me off the table.

'Hop in the bath and clean up. Ross'll give you a hand, won't you fella?' Ross nodded. 'I'll bring you in a fresh nightie, then it's early to bed tonight. Your mother and I need to clean up the kitchen. You've caused quite a stir, young lady.'

The mood in the kitchen followed us to the bathroom. Ross teased me about how if I wasn't careful my finger would rot and then Dad would have to chop it off with the axe. But we both knew it was not my finger that was worrying us.

'It's my fault. I shouldn't have come inside.'

'Don't worry about it, sis. They'll be fine in the morning.'

'It's getting worse. Do you think they hate each other?'

'I dunno.'

'They've never argued like that.'

But their quarrels had escalated following that first dynamite explosion. Mum was edgy. A tapped arm caused a jumpy reaction. She'd dropped a few things when we'd approached her from behind.

'Come on, get that off. There's blood everywhere,' said Ross.

'I don't want to get it wet. It hurts.'

'Nearly done?' said Dad through the doorway. He handed Ross my fresh nightie. 'Get a wriggle on, we're almost finished out here.'

I wondered whether Mum was going to come in, but she must have been too busy cleaning.

When I was dressed, we went back to the kitchen. The haze had disappeared and the blood was gone. The lingering aroma from Mum's chicken casserole was replaced with the scent of disinfectant. Dad was leaning against the table rubbing his hand across the back of the chair and Mum stood at the sink wiping it clean of invisible specks.

'Swallow this,' she said, handing me a small cup with clear liquid in it. 'It will take away the pain and help you sleep.'

'Is it gin?' said Ross, leaning on the table with his hand under his chin.

'Don't be cheeky, young man,' said Dad. 'Now both of you, off to bed.'

It tasted like bitter peppermint and when I handed the cup back, I put my arm around Mum's waist and gave her a cuddle.

'Night Mum.'

'Night,' she said, giving me a brief glance as she continued cleaning, each wipe delivered a faint whiff of Dettol and bleach. 'See you in the morning.'

I pushed Zilla's legs over to the other side and climbed into bed. The springs squeaked as she squirmed and stretched before settling into a new position without waking. The hollow in the middle from the drooping springs caused us to roll into each other during the night, so I was glad to have the end that allowed my wounded hand to dangle over the edge. I lay on my back, closed my eyes and slept.

'Bon, Bon. Are you awake?'

'Yeah.' When I opened my eyes, Ross was sitting on his bed, gazing out the window.

'How's your finger?'

'Sore.' The throbbing returned when I bumped my hand turning over trying to avoid Zilla's legs. The volume of discussion in the kitchen was intense. 'How long have they been fighting?'

'Ages, but I can't hear what they're saying.'

'It's my fault.'

'It's not your fault.'

The back door slammed, then the ute engine rumbled and gravel crunched as it made a hasty departure.

'That's Dad, off to the pub.'

It was rare for Dad to slam a door. His anger was usually restrained, his words regulated and his actions measured. He was predictable. We could read his mood and adapt. Mum was the opposite. Her moods changed so frequently, we never quite knew what to think.

'Mum's crying,' I said. 'She's in the lounge room.'

'That's Bing Crosby,' said Ross. 'She's playing his records.'

Dad's record collection was special. They were kept in the cabinet underneath the record player in the lounge room and we were forbidden to touch them or the record player. I'd seen Mum and Dad dancing to them in Dubbo. The needle dropped, scratching across the vinyl as the instruments began the introduction for *Beautiful Dreamer*.

'Something's wrong,' said Ross.

'Yeah.'

'Come on, let's take a look.'

We tiptoed across the verandah, hugging the wall, until we could see through the lounge room window. The doors of the record cabinet were open and Mum was sitting on the floor with her back to us, records spread around her. Most of them were broken. She grabbed the neck of a sherry bottle sitting on the floor beside her and took a gulp. She pulled a record from its sleeve and smashed it on the floor. The black vinyl shattered and sprayed everywhere. I heard her sobbing and muttering to herself. I covered my mouth and held my breath so I wouldn't cry out. She repeated the process several times. Ross grabbed my arm and we tiptoed back to our room.

'She's in so much trouble,' Ross said, 'Dad's going to be furious.'

'Why is she doing it?' I asked.

'She must be really angry.'

'Really, really angry. I don't like this.'

'Let's go back to bed. It'll be okay tomorrow.'

'How do you know?'

'Cause that's what Dad always says.'

'Do you think we'll have to go back to Dubbo?'

'I dunno, hope so.'

'I'm scared,' I said. 'Can I come over and sleep with you?'

'Oh, alright.'

We lay together without speaking and fell asleep to the sound of Mum's destruction. I wondered what Dad would do when he got home.

In the morning, neither of us wanted to go into the lounge room. An urgent need for the loo changed our mind, but we decided to go together. We crept in through the front door to the lounge room. The smashed vinyl and torn record covers were gone. Everything had been cleaned. Plates clattered and voices chattered in the kitchen. Tippy and Zilla were having breakfast with Mum and Dad.

'Morning you two,' said Dad. 'You had a bit of a sleep in this morning.'

'We didn't mean to, Dad,' said Ross.

'It's all right. How's your finger, little lady?'

'Sore.'

'I'll change the bandage and check the cut,' said Mum.

Ross and I looked at one another then at Mum and Dad. They were acting like they did every morning. Tippy was trying to pick up soggy cornflakes in his fingers and milk dribbled down his chin.

'What'd you do to your finger?' asked Zilla, chewing a mouthful of cornflakes.

'I cut it,' I said.

She stared at me. 'That was silly.'

Mum sucked in her breath as she removed the bandage from my finger.

'Ow. That hurts.' My finger was swollen and a craggy red line snaked across my first knuckle.

'Give us a look,' said Ross.

'Sit down and eat your breakfast, young man,' said Dad.

'All finished,' Mum said. 'You can eat with your left hand.'

After breakfast, Mum told us to play in our room. She took Zilla and Tippy into the bedroom and we heard the drawers opening and closing and the wardrobe door banging.

'What's she doing?'

'Tidying up,' said Ross.

Dad went up to the mine but returned a short time later. It was the first sign things weren't normal.

'I can hear Bert's ute coming up the hill,' said Ross.

'How do you know?'

'It's his motor.'

Ross knew the sound of everyone's cars.

'Maybe he's going up to the mine.'

'Nope, he's coming here.'

We kneeled on Ross's bed and looked out the window. Dad came out and tossed a couple of suitcases into the back. Mum came next holding Tippy, Zilla walked behind. She turned, smiled and waved at us. Tippy was sucking his thumb and tugging his ear. Ross and I scrambled off the bed, rushed through the kitchen and crashed into Dad.

'Where's Mum going, Dad? said Ross.

'She's going on a holiday for a while,' he said.

'Why can't we go?' I said.

'Because I need you here.'

'But Zilla and Tippy are going.'

Dad gave us the look which meant don't ask any more questions. This was adult business.

I pushed at his legs to get outside. 'She hasn't said goodbye. She has to say goodbye.'

Dad stepped aside and we tore down to the ute. Mum had her back to us and was getting into the front passenger seat. Tippy looked over her shoulder clutching a strand of Mum's red hair in his tiny fingers.

'Mum, where are you going?' said Ross.

Mum didn't turn, she didn't answer.

'Mum,' I asked, 'can we come?'

She still didn't answer. She sat in the car and stared straight ahead. Bert was in the driver's seat with the engine running.

Zilla kneeled on the seat in the middle and looked out through the rear window. Her dark, curly hair shook, her eyes wide, looking between Ross and me. One of her hands was pressed so hard on the back window, her fingertips were white.

The ute drove off down the hill. Mum didn't look back. We waited for her to turn around. They were going on holiday without us. Tippy and Zilla watched us as the ute weaved down the hill to the main road. We stood until we couldn't see them anymore, until long after the dust trail drifted through the trees and faded. Until Dad came out and took us inside.

'She didn't even wave goodbye,' said Ross.

'Why didn't she wave goodbye, Dad?' I asked.

* * *

When Ross and I entered the kitchen the following morning for breakfast, Mrs Halford was setting the table. She wore a brightly coloured apron over her skirt and blouse and her handbag was sitting on the sink. Even when there was nowhere to go shopping, Mrs Halford carried a handbag.

'Good morning, children,' she said.

'Where's Dad?' I asked. 'When's Mum coming back?'

'Your Dad is at the mine. He asked me to look after you while your Mum is away,' she said, placing the milk jug on the table and giving it an extra stir to distribute the lumps of powder.

'Wow,' said Ross. 'Are we having visitors?'

'Mum doesn't use the tablecloth for meals,' I said. 'Only guests.'

'Oh. Mr Halford and I use a tablecloth all the time,' she said. 'Sit down and have some breakfast.'

We tucked into cereal and toast while Mrs Halford pottered around wiping the stove, stacking dishes on the sink and re-organising the fridge.

'When you're finished you can wash the breakfast dishes and do your chores,' she said.

'I can't wash up. I've got a cut finger. Look.' I held up my bandaged finger as proof.

'I'm sure it's not that bad. Ross can wash and you can wipe.'

'It's pretty bad,' said Ross.

'When you've finished everything, come on over. I'll be in my kitchen. Oh, and bring your writing books,' Mrs Halford said, as she picked up her bag. 'Don't forget to clear the table and mind you don't spill anything on the cloth,' she added, pausing before closing the back door.

'I always thought she was a nice lady,' I said.

'It's going to be a long holiday,' said Ross.

Mrs Halford didn't allow us the freedom to roam around the slag dump or climb our favourite trees.

'Until the school gets going again,' she said, 'we'll carry on with your school work.'

After breakfast and chores, we sat at her kitchen table practicing our reading, writing and sums, even though I found it hard to write with my sore finger. We had lunch with Dad, then an afternoon nap, which we spent mucking around in our room. We loved stretching out on the single beds without the kicking legs of our siblings. Their toys were packed into a suitcase and stored underneath my bed, so without Tippy's strewn across the floor, we had walking room. Ross's bits and pieces straggled from under the bed, constantly threatening to invade what I now considered to be my half of the room.

***

One afternoon, unbeknown to Dad, Ross and I were lying on the floor of the tree house – our pirate ship and jungle hut.

Mum had been away for three weeks.

'Hal, I need a favour from you and the missus.' We could hear Dad who was standing by the chook pen out the back with Mr Halford. Lassie sat beside him, chin on paws, waiting. Dad slapped his hat on his leg, fiddled with the brim and looked around.

'What is it?'

Ross and I exchanged glances.

'Can you take the kids for a few days?'

'Sure, Ben. We don't mind helping out while Mary's on holiday.'

'Thing is, Hal. Mary's ah ... she's shot through and left Zilla and Tippy with Ethel.'

I grabbed Ross's arm. Ross clamped his hand over my mouth, put a finger on his lips and added a silent, 'Shh.' We rolled over slowly to avoid creaking the boards and peeked through a gap in the floor.

'Cripes Ben, when did this happen?' Mr Halford removed his hat, then repositioned it on his head.

Dad pulled a pouch from his top pocket and rolled a cigarette. Tobacco shook loose as he tried to control his trembling hands.

'I just got a call from Ethel. Mary said she was going shopping and would be back to collect them before dark. That was yesterday.'

'Maybe she's had an accident.'

'No. She finally got hold of Mary's brother, Ted. He said she's not coming back. No reason.'

'That's rough.'

'The kids'll be confused. I'm heading off in the morning to bring them home. Can Ross and Bonnie stay with you until I get back?'

'Of course.'

'I'm not sure how long I'll be away. By the way, where are those two?'

'I saw them hanging out of a tree a short while ago.'

'Good-oh. They've taken it pretty hard that she's gone away without them, even if it was only for a holiday. I have no idea what I'm gonna tell them now.'

Dad gave Mr Halford a slap on the shoulder, turned and walked up the hill to the mine. His shoulders sagged, he stepped deliberately, as if climbing stairs. He picked up a rock and said, 'Bugger, bugger, bugger,' then hurled it as far as possible. Lassie took off in full pelt in pursuit of the stone.

'For cryin' out loud, git back, Lassie. Git back to the house.' Dad shrugged and kept walking. 'Bloody dog.' Lassie skidded to a stop, crept to the tank stand in disappointment, and flopped down with a big sigh.

She resumed watching, offering small snorts and occasional grunts of displeasure.

Mr Halford stood alone. He patted Lassie and watched Dad walk up the hill. He shook his head and strolled to his house. Ross and I stayed frozen until both were out of sight.

'Why would Mum do that?' My mind was a muddle of half phrased questions.

'I dunno, but we can't say anything. It has to be our secret. Right?'

'That means she's not coming back, doesn't it?' I sniffed.

'We've gotta get out of here. Dad thinks we're at the slag dump.'

'Why? Why would she leave us?' I began to cry.

'I dunno, Bonnie. Come on, let's go.' He grabbed my arms and stared into my eyes. 'We can't let on we heard anything,' he said, squeezing hard.

We both knew the consequences of listening in to adult conversations.

'Okay, okay. Let go, you're hurting me.'

'Just remember what I said.'

We clambered down and wandered to the clump of pepper trees on the slag dump and a good place to talk about secrets. Lassie followed us and poked her head through the branches.

'Here Lassie.' Her presence was a comfort. She sat between us offering the occasional lick, which we avoided, but recognised as her way of giving assurance.

'We gotta pretend we don't know anything, right Bonnie?'

'Yeah, I know, I heard you the first time.'

'Ya gotta stop snivelling.'

'I will, I will. It's just …'

'Yeah, I know, but you can't, you just can't. We shouldn't have heard.'

'Yeah, but we did and I wish we hadn't.'

I buried my head in Lassie's fur. It smelt dusty, but clean. She licked my tears as Ross chucked stones at the tree trunk. Dad's voice called us for dinner.

'You right?' Ross wiped his nose on his sleeve.

'Yeah. Good.' We walked up the hill. It seemed much further than usual. Even Lassie had no bounce in her step.

When we arrived at the Halfords for dinner, Mrs Halford glanced in our direction frequently but we smiled and pretended not to notice, chewing each mouthful, mindful of the need to keep silent.

After dinner we walked back home. In the kitchen, Dad sat me on his knee and tousled Ross's hair. He cleared his throat, scratched his head.

'I'm going away for a few days so you two'll be staying next door. You'll be on your best behaviour and I need you both to look after the chooks and feed Lassie for me. Be good kids for the Halfords.'

'But Dad ...' I started to cry.

'It's alright Bonnie, I'll be back before you know it.'

'Are you going on holiday too? Why can't we come? Because when ...'

'I'm not going on holiday. I'm coming back with Zilla and Tippy. Your Mum's not well.'

'What's wrong?' said Ross before I blurted out we'd heard him talking to Mr Halford.

'She's staying in Western Australia for a while. What's important is – I'm coming back.'

'How long will you be away?'

'I'll be back before you know it. Now, clean your teeth and put on your pyjamas and we'll walk over to the Halfords. I'm setting out early in the morning so I'll be in to say good night before you go to bed.'

'It's not fair,' said Ross.

'Yes, son, sometimes life's not fair.'

ABANDONED

'What's the problem, love?' Mrs Halford sat on the bed and stroked my forehead. Her voice hushed and tender.

'I want my Dad.' I hugged my doll tight and stroked my fingers across the split in the back of her head. She was a Christmas present and I'd dropped her that same day while being chased through the house by my oldest brother, Keith, who was still away at boarding school. I felt broken, like my doll.

'Are we going to be sent to boarding school, with Keith?'

'Keith is at a boys' school. Anyway, your Dad will be back soon with Zilla and Tippy. Won't it be fun to have them back?'

"Spose.'

'They'll be home before you know it. How about you get some sleep before you wake your brother, hmmm?'

'I'm not asleep,' said Ross, his voice muffled beneath the blankets at the other end of the bed.

'Oh dear,' said Mrs Halford. 'Let's go and make some cocoa.'

The kitchen was cosy and warm. Mrs Halford made cocoa and we sat at the table sipping in silence.

'Do you think Mum doesn't love us anymore?' said Ross.

'Now don't you go thinking that,' said Mrs Halford, adjusting the belt on her dressing gown. 'Of course she loves you.'

'Then why did she leave?' he said.

'She didn't say goodbye,' I said. 'Dad said she's sick.'

'What's wrong with her?' said Ross. 'She can come home. We can look after her.'

'What does 'shot through' mean?' I said.

Mrs Halford spluttered into her cocoa. 'Ah, well now ... I think perhaps some things are best answered by your father,' she said. 'Now it's time for bed. Everything will look better in the morning.'

'You're such a blabber mouth,' said Ross when we were back in bed.

'I didn't mean to. It just slipped out.'

'If Dad finds out ...'

'Maybe she'll forget about it.'

In the morning after breakfast with the Halfords, Ross and I walked across to the house to change out of our pyjamas. All the photos on the wall had been removed. Ross opened the cabinet doors and we both looked inside.

'We're not supposed to look in there. What are you looking for?'

The photograph album had also been removed from the cabinet where three Bing Crosby records sat in torn sleeves, a reminder of Mum's tantrum.

'I don't care. Who's going to stop me?' His anger softened and when he looked at me and I saw he was scared like me. 'I thought Dad might've put the photos in here.'

Ross banged the door shut. 'He must've burnt them.'

'Mum's gone with Zilla and Tippy and now Dad's gone and ...'

'You're not going to cry again.'

'I'll cry if I want,' I said as I wandered into Mum and Dad's bedroom.

The dresser was empty of its photos, doilies and the glass bowls that held her rings and bobby pins. All that remained was the irregular, dusty imprints on the dark surface. Gone was the photo with all of us grouped in front of the new Oldsmobile. Dad had had it for two days when Keith and Ross burnt a hole in the leather upholstery and the event was published in the Tottenham newspaper. Also gone were the photos of the five of us, dressed in our Sunday clothes, standing on the lawn with the sun in our eyes peering into the camera lens as the next door neighbour waved his hand about getting us to smile. Tippy was only six months old.

'I wish Zilla and Tippy were here,' I said running my fingers through the dust, rubbing out the rectangular marks wanting to erase the pain I felt.

'I wish Keith was here too.'

'Do you think he knows ... about Mum?'

'Dunno. Maybe. I've heard Dad talking to him on the phone.'

'Do you think Dad's coming back?' I asked Ross as he opened the dressing table drawers and looked at the empty shelves.

'How would I know?'

'If he doesn't, we'll have to stay with the Halfords forever.'

'Yoo-hoo, children.' Mrs Halford's cheerful voice bounced down the hallway catching us by surprise.

'Good heavens. Are you still in your pyjamas?' She glanced into the room catching us at the open drawers.

'We ... we ...' Ross stammered.

'It's alright,' she said. 'Pansy phoned with a message from your Dad. He's with Aunty Ethel and says he will call back in fifteen minutes.'

'Is he coming home?' Ross asked.

'You can ask him when he calls. Let's go and wait.'

Pansy ran the Post Office and Telephone Exchange from her house down the hill past the pub. Each house was on a party line with everyone having their own ring.

'Why doesn't he phone here?' I asked.

'I'm sure there's a good reason, Bonnie, but if we don't go now we will miss the call.'

The phone rang as we walked in through the back door. It was in the kitchen, high on the wall. Ross and I couldn't reach the mouthpiece, so we needed to stand on a chair, and fight over who should speak first. Mrs Halford decided. Oldest first.

'Dad, when are you coming home?' Ross asked.

'What did he say?'

'Shush, I'm trying to listen. Stop pulling my arm.'

'Bonnie, let your brother talk, then you can have a go,' said Mrs Halford.

'But I want to know when they're coming home.'

I plonked down at the kitchen table, folded my arms across my chest and sulked, listening as Ross said, 'Yes, Dad,' every now and then. He held out the phone to me and I climbed on the chair. 'He wants to talk to you,' he said.

'Hello Dad,' I said into the mouthpiece, the earpiece pressed hard against my head.

'Hello Bonnie,' said Dad. 'Are you being a good girl for Mrs Halford?'

'Yes, Dad. Dad, when are you coming home? Are Zilla and Tippy there? Are they coming back too? … '

'Hang on girlie, one question at a time. We'll be home … '

'Dad? Hello Dad?' The line crackled and Dad's words broke into pieces and faded. 'Dad, I can't hear you. Mrs Halford, the phone's gone funny.'

Mrs Halford took the phone and listened. 'Sometimes it does that. Can't do anything about it. Your Dad will phone back when he can.'

'What did he say to you?' I asked Ross.

'Nothing much. Asked if I was behaving myself.'

'Me too. When's he coming home, Mrs Halford?'

'I don't know, child.'

'It's not fair. He should be here.'

'You're not going to cry again, are you?' said Ross.

'I'll cry if I want.' I stormed out, slamming the back door and heard Mrs Halford say to Ross, 'Give her a few minutes. She'll be fine.'

I went into Mum and Dad's room and lay on the bed, hugging the pillow. Ross came in moments later, climbed up and lay beside me.

'Don't tell me it's gonna be okay,' I said between sniffs, 'because it's not.'

'I miss them too,' said Ross.

'It's not the same, with them. She pulls my hair when she's brushing it and I try to remember my manners and not speak with my mouth full but ...'

'She's okay. Dad'll be back soon.'

'How do you know?'

'Cause he owns the mine, silly,' he said looking around the room.

Ross stood up and balanced on the narrow bedhead.

'You'll get into trouble if you climb up there.'

He climbed up to the top of the wardrobe. It wobbled as he turned and sat and a sheet of dust drifted down and settled on the pillows and bedspread.

'Get outta the way. I'm gonna jump,' he said, as he shifted to a crouch.

'It's too high. Don't.'

'Course it isn't. I've done this before.'

'You have not. You'll cop it if you jump.'

I climbed off the bed and stood near the doorway, leaning against the frame. There were many spots for testing our jumping skills. Concrete blocks and old mine machinery were favourites but jumping off furniture inside the house invited punishment by strap and Mum and Dad's room was always out of bounds.

'Who's gonna stop me?'

Ross positioned himself on the edge and with tongue poking out, pushed off the wardrobe. He landed on the bed with a plop. The springs groaned. As he bounced above the bedspread, his knees hit his chin with a smack and he rolled off the bed with a shriek. Blood dribbled through his fingers as he clasped his hand over his mouth.

Mrs Halford came running through the kitchen and threw Ross over her shoulder.

'Go fetch Mr Halford from the mine, Bonnie,' she shouted. 'He'll be in the office.' Over her pounding footsteps, Ross groaned and his head bounced up and down leaving sprinklings of blood on the masonite floor.

When I returned with Mr Halford, Ross was on the bench in the kitchen holding a bloody cloth, while Mrs Halford shone a torch into his open mouth.

'Looks like the lower incisors have penetrated the mucosa,' Mrs Halford said. 'Have a look, Mr Halford,' she said as she stepped aside. 'Do you think he'll need a doctor?'

The closest was Lake Cargelligo, sixty miles away.

'Is he going to die?' I asked. 'Can I have a look, too?'

'Good job you've lost a couple of bottom teeth,' said Mr Halford, 'or it could have been serious. Best not jump off the wardrobe again, young fella.'

'The mouth is very good at healing quickly,' said Mrs Halford, patting Ross on the shoulder.

'He'll be fine in a few days,' said Mr Halford. 'No need to fuss.'

Ross wriggled his jaw back and forth and touched his tongue. 'Do we have to tell Dad?' he said. Despite the fingers in his mouth, we understood.

'We'll see,' said Mr Halford.

'Come on, you two,' said Mrs Halford. 'We've got a mess to clean up.'

* * *

'They're back,' yelled Ross as Lassie barked at the sound of Dad's ute coming up the hill.

Although Dad had been away for two weeks, it felt much longer. Zilla and Tippy had been gone for four weeks. We tore out of Halfords back door and dashed around to the front as Dad pulled up outside the house. He lifted Zilla and Tippy out as Aunty Ethel stepped from the passenger door, arms wide ready to give Ross and me a hug. My face squashed against her large bosom. I was happy to see her, but she wasn't Mum.

'Where are Cecil and Beat and Mel?' asked Ross.

'Aunty Dell is looking after them while I'm away,' she said.

Aunty had three children. Mel was the youngest and the same age as Keith. Cecil and Beat were older, still living at home but working. Aunty Dell had one daughter, Pat.

'Are you going to open a shop here, Aunty? I asked. 'We miss your ice-cream.'

'No,' she said releasing me from a bear hug. 'I've come to look after you.'

'Are you staying forever?' asked Ross.

'For a little while,' she said. 'Who would look after my children if I stayed here?'

'Aunty's got a cow,' said Zilla. 'We had fresh milk every morning.'

'Can we get a cow too, Dad?' I asked, thinking about the lump-free milk.

'No, we are not getting a cow,' he said. 'Now, we're all a bit tired from the trip, so how about helping your brother and sister unpack, while I get Aunty settled.'

'I had my own bed,' said Zilla when we were back in our room.

'Did you see Mum?' I asked.

'No, but Dad told us not to talk about it.'

'Do you know where she is?'

'Dad said she's on holiday.'

'We've got a tree-house now,' I said. 'You wanna see?'

'Yeah.'

Now Zilla and Tippy were home again, it was as if they'd never left. Back to shared beds, messy room and sibling squabbles. Aunty must've spoken to Mrs Halford, because each morning after breakfast we sat at the kitchen table doing school work, while Tippy played on the floor with his toys. Dad walked up the hill to work each morning, and came home for morning smoko, lunch and dinner. He didn't sing in the shower anymore and slept on a camp bed in the lounge room so Aunty could sleep in his bed. The connecting door from our sleep-out to her room was kept permanently locked.

'Aunty,' I said as we sat at the table writing times tables. 'When's Mum coming back?'

Aunty cracked the eggs into the bowl and began to beat them in double time.

'I don't know,' she said. 'Maybe you can ask your father.'

When I asked Dad what happened to Mum his body stiffened and he glared at me over the rim of his glasses.

'Your Mother's not here,' was all he said.

I wasn't going to push it. Whenever Dad had enough of our questions, the look on his face became fierce. After that he would threaten us with the strap for being a nuisance.

We had more freedom to play on the slag dump, in the treehouse and around the hill with Aunty there. She didn't worry about us getting hurt or wandering too far. We heard her booming voice wherever we were. If we ignored her, she'd stand in the doorway with her hands on her hips then remove one of her shoes and tap it on the side of her leg. We learned fast because she hit hard and a whack from her shoe stung.

She baked cakes, cooked stews with dumplings and added loads of vegetables. She grumbled about having to use powdered milk but baked fresh pies and sponges that tasted delicious. But she wasn't Mum. Aunty Ethel's cooking meant our chooks had trouble keeping up the supply of eggs, so Dad bought three more bantams from Mr Taylor which increased our brood to six. All gave us eggs except one.

The chooks were kept in a large enclosed pen with plenty of room for scratching and running. They were locked in the roosting box at night, safe from foxes and feral cats and the wire was small enough to prevent snakes from getting through. If I complained about the size in comparison to our bedroom, Dad said I could go and live with the chooks, if I preferred.

One Sunday morning Dad grabbed the axe, slung it over his shoulder and opened the pen door. 'That old boiler's going today. Ross and Bonnie, time you knew how to kill and pluck a chook.'

I stood with the egg basket in my hand and stared at him.

'Wow, this'll be great,' said Ross.

'I'm not so sure,' I said. 'What about Zilla?'

'She can help with the plucking.'

We gathered around the chopping block outside the pen ready for the lesson in chook-killing to begin. My job was to feed them and collect the eggs. I didn't chase them, trim their wings or pick one up. Lice crawled all over them, their tiny eyes glared, and sharp beaks and clawed feet were implements of torture certain to rip me apart.

'Come on, grab the brown and bring her over here.' Dad pointed to the hen in the corner, the one that hadn't been laying any eggs. 'The rest are locked in the roosting box. It upsets them seeing their mates getting their heads chopped off.'

Dad thought my participation in this activity would toughen me. I disagreed.

Ross sauntered over, picked up the docile chook and plonked her on the chopping block. She gazed at him as a chick would to a mother.

'How'd you do that?' I said.

'Dad gave her a drop of whisky this morning,' said Ross.

'Wanted her to be calm for the big event,' said Dad.

'She's drunk,' said Ross.

'Just groggy,' said Dad.

Dad placed a thin rope around the neck and another around the feet while Ross held her down.

'Right. This one's for dinner tonight, so let's get cracking. Bonnie, hold the rope around her feet, here.'

I reached for the rope trying not to notice the distance between her claws and my hands.

'A bit closer, lass. Her brain's the size of a pea, she won't bite.' He laughed at his joke.

'Please Dad, do I have to?'

'Listen girlie. When I was a boy, 'bout your age, I was up at the crack of dawn, feeding animals and doing chores. I could ride a horse, rope a cow and kill a chook. I didn't have a bike because we couldn't afford it and I certainly didn't have things as good as this. You'll thank me one day. You eat chicken, don't you?'

'Yes Dad. Sorry Dad.'

Ross grinned at me so I poked my tongue out.

'Ross, you hold the head here.'

The top of the block was scrubbed clean but buried deep in the cracks I noticed a mix of dried blood and feathers. I shuddered at the thought of what was about to happen.

'Ready?'

Dad raised the axe. The legs twitched so I let go.

'What'd you do that for? said Dad, axe suspended above his head.

'It moved,' I said.

The chook flapped and squarked, found traction on the block, so Ross let go as well. It gave a strangled squeak, flew off the block and stumbled into the pen.

'That's torn it,' said Dad. 'What's your excuse, Ross?'

'It slipped,' said Ross.

'Well girlie,' he said to me, 'Off you go – catch her. You're lucky I trimmed her wings a couple of days ago.'

I approached the doorway with dread. My inability to think of a decent excuse to avoid contact with the darting creature clouded my brain.

Ten minutes of uncoordinated floundering later, Dad said, 'Damn thing will die from stress if you don't catch it soon.'

Ross took the bait and threw himself across the dirt in a nimble cricket lunge and grabbed a leg.

With the chook back on the block, Ross and I were positioned as before.

'Mum wouldn't make us do this,' I said.

Dad didn't wait. One swing of the axe and with a crunch and crack, the head was severed. I screamed, threw my hands in the air and backed against the tank. Blood spurted as the headless chook stood, flew a brief distance, landed with feet pumping and zigzagged across the yard, a fountain of spray erupting from its thin, flabby neck. The ghastly brute was heading for me.

'Holy cow,' said Ross.

'Once had one running about like that for a couple of days before it dropped dead,' said Dad.

'Funniest thing.'

'It's not funny,' I yelled. 'Get away.' I stood on the tap of the tank, as the chook hit the concrete pad beneath my feet and stumbled in the opposite direction.

'Can't hear you,' said Dad. 'I chopped off its ears.' He slapped the axe on the block and roared with laughter.

'It's not funny, Dad.' I said.

'Wish I had my camera.'

The chook began a drunken seesaw towards Ross. I'd seen similar movements from folks doing the chicken dance.

'Dad?' he said, arms above his head as if about to be attacked. He stepped back. 'Dad?' alarm in his voice.

'Ha, ha. Your turn,' I said from the safety of my two-foot high perch.

The chook stopped at Ross's feet, spun around and dropped dead.

'Must've run out of breath,' said Dad, still laughing. 'Okay, kids. Entertaining as that was, we're not finished. Get your sister, Bonnie, time to pluck this chook. Fetch the wash tub and boil the kettle.'

'Do we put the chook in boiling water?'

'Yep,' Dad said. 'Then it's time for smoko, I need a cuppa.'

SMOKE AND MIRRORS

'Mary's only been gone a couple of months and you're already planning to bring her here?'

Aunty and Dad were in the kitchen and Ross and I were building a teepee underneath the treehouse. We'd used old blankets and a tree branch for the centre post but were having a problem securing it to the hard ground. Zilla and Tippy sat on the edges, holding them down for us.

'How long is this going to take?' asked Zilla.

'Keep your voice down, Ethel,' said Dad, 'the children will hear.'

'Shush, Zilla,' said Ross.

'When's she coming?' said Aunty.

'On Friday,' Dad said, 'and there will be no more talk about it.'

'This is boring,' said Zilla.

'Will you shush, Zilla,' I said.

With our hands holding the branch upright, we stopped what we were doing and listened.

'Then you don't need me anymore,' said Aunty. 'I'll catch the Thursday train to Sydney then fly back to Perth.'

'At least wait until she gets here,'

'Who's *she?'* I asked Ross.

'Dunno.'

"I'm bored. I'm going inside,' said Zilla. 'Come on Tip, let's go.'

Zilla and Tip stood, a gust of wind pulled at the blankets and our teepee collapsed on top of us.

'Good one, Zilla,' said Ross.

We gathered up the blankets and abandoned the teepee. Aunty called us to go inside, wash up and set the table for tea. Dad sat drinking a glass of beer.

During dinner Aunty said, 'I'll be leaving in a couple of days.' She glanced at Dad, then us. 'Time for me to go.'

'Why?' asked Ross. 'Who's going to look after us.'

'Your Dad has sorted out something,' she said. 'I need to get back home. Aunty Dell's been looking after everything for me while I'm here.'

'Will you come back?'

'Maybe for Christmas, Bonnie. We'll see.'

'But you haven't been here long,' said Zilla.

'Two months is quite a long time to be away Zilla,' said Aunty. 'Now eat up, I've baked a custard tart for pudding.'

'We'll miss you, Aunty,' said Ross.

In the two days before Aunty left, she had us sweeping outside, cleaning the bathroom and dragging baskets of washing out to the clothesline. The beds had clean sheets and even the cobwebs were removed from all the hiding places we could reach.

When Thursday came, we said a tearful goodbye to Aunty, then she left with Bert to catch the train to Sydney.

After Friday lunch, Dad showered, shaved and put on his good trousers.

'Are you going to the pub, Dad?' asked Ross.

'I'm collecting someone from the train,' Dad said.

'Can we come? I asked.

'Not this time,' said Dad. 'I need to get a wriggle on, so stay inside until I get back. I'll only be half an hour.'

We were in the middle of building paper aeroplanes when Lassie barked and Ross yelled, 'Dad's coming up the hill,' so we scrambled to the front door, all squashed against the door frame and watched him open the car door. A strange lady stepped out, stood and brushed her hand across her hair, then smoothed her dress. As they walked up the steps, we backed into the lounge room and stared through the opened door.

The woman who approached was younger than Dad but almost as tall. Her dark brown hair was pulled back into rolls held with bobby pins. A wide elastic belt with a silver clasp was stretched tight around her slim waist. She wore a striped nylon dress and underneath I could see her lace petticoat. A black handbag draped over her left arm and, in her right hand, a cigarette was held away from her face. Lassie put two front paws on the top step and delivered her warning bark.

'Cut that out, Lassie. Kids,' said Dad. 'there's someone I'd like you to meet.'

Lassie circled Betty, then plonked on the ground with a series of low grunts. We stood clumped together in our front room, jostling each other, wondering who this strange woman was. Tippy sat on the floor, drawing lines in the dust blown into the hallway from the open door.

'This is Betty,' said Dad. 'These are my children. That's Ross, this is Bonnie ...'

'Hello children,' she said. Her voice was deep and croaky, her smile stretched thin as her eyes swept over each of us in turn. 'My, what a lot of hair you have,' she said to Zilla. As her gaze returned to my father, the smile deepened to show smudged red lipstick across her top teeth.

'Betty has come to live with us,' said Dad.

'Why?' said Ross. 'There isn't any room.'

'Are you our new housekeeper?' I asked. Maybe this could shorten my list of chores.

'No,' said Dad. 'She'll be looking after the shop.'

'What shop?' said Ross.

'We don't have a spare room,' Zilla had her hands on her hips, and I could tell she was not happy with the comment about her hair. She had deep red curls the same as Mum, unlike mine – blond, thin and wispy.

'Sharing with Ross and Tippy is bad enough, they're messy ...' I said, wondering where we would fit another bed since our room was so small. Two beds, a chest of drawers and a box for books and toys. There was no extra room.

'I'm not sharing with any more girls,' said Ross.

'Nothing's changing,' said Dad.

'But where will she ...?'

'Don't you worry about that. Betty will be in the big room.'

'She could stay at the pub,' I said. 'There's lots of room there.'

'Where will you sleep, Dad?' Ross was twirling the curl on his forehead, a sign he was anxious.

'Never you mind. Betty'll put her things away then head down to the shop. We'll talk tonight at dinner. I've got more important things to do than stand here gasbagging with you lot.'

His voice deepened, each word was pronounced with care, the signal to stop asking questions. We remained in the hallway blocking the entry, uncertain of what to do when Tippy toddled up to Betty and reached for her leg but clutched a hand full of stocking instead.

'Mummy,' he dribbled, gazing at the stretching nylon threatening to topple him. He leaned backwards as the stockings stretched in his gripping fingers and grabbed her petticoat which, along with him, descended to the floor.

'I'm not your mummy.' Betty lifted her foot as if to shake off a bug, then stepped back when Dad bent down.

'Come on Tip, my boy.' Dad untangled his fingers from her petticoat and lifted him into his arms. 'Say hello to Betty.' Tippy's eyes widened. He inhaled.

'Cover your ears,' said Zilla.

Tippy launched a penetrating wail at the ceiling in the realisation that this woman was not Mummy. He buried his head in Dad's shoulder while Betty ignored the drooping petticoat and wrinkled stockings. She sucked on her cigarette and blew into the air, then dropped it on the verandah and crushed it with her foot. We observed this breach of the rules, but Dad said nothing.

'It's been a long day. I'd like to unpack please Ben.'

Dad grabbed her suitcase with his spare hand and carried it into the bedroom. We crowded around the doorway, watching. As she walked past us, sweet smelling perfume and lingering cigarette smoke followed her into the room.

'The children?' said Betty.

Dad placed Tippy on the floor, patted him on the backside and pushed him towards us.

'I'd prefer them not coming into the room, if you don't mind,' she said.

She placed her handbag on the dresser, extracted a packet of *Craven A* cigarettes, turned, looked straight at us and raised one eyebrow as Dad walked out the door. She strode to the door linking our rooms together and locked it closed.

'Come on kids, let's give Betty time to unpack.' He ruffled Zilla's hair and steered us outside to the verandah and into our bedroom. 'You be good,' said Dad. 'I'm going back to work.'

'She's got no chin.' I lay across the bed, bouncing Tip up and down in time with the squeaking springs. I loved hearing his pop-gun giggles, it was fast and catching.

'Gosh, she's tall,' said Zilla.

'I wonder how long she's staying.' Ross was still twirling the front of his hair.

'She wears a petticoat.' Zilla said. 'Tippy showed us most of it, didn't you Tip.'

'Do you think that's *her*,' I whispered to Ross. 'You know. The *she* Aunty was talking about?'

'Don't know. I don't like her. She's weird,' said Ross. 'Get off my bed, Zilla.'

'I don't think she likes us,' Zilla whispered as we walked out to the front verandah and through the front door into the lounge room.

'I don't think I like her either,' I said.

Dad's bedroom door was open. Scattered across the bed were dresses, cardigans and shoe boxes. Coat hangers clinked as she bunched them together and hung them in the empty part of the wardrobe. Mum's side. Her suitcase was covered in colourful labels overlapping each other. Some were faded, cities were printed on others. I was turning my head to read one when she glanced in the mirror on the dresser. The side mirrors were open and I remembered Mum dragging the pearl handled brush through her hair, adjusting the mirrors so she could see the back of her head. The vision faded and I was left with Betty fixing her bobby pins. Her eyes met mine. On the end of the dresser was an ashtray where a lit cigarette weaved twisting patterns of smoke across her face. As the threads zigzagged upwards, she raised both eyebrows and glared at me through her distorted reflection in the mirror.

* * *

Mum and Aunty had both been whizzes in the kitchen. The regular whirr of the mixmaster during the morning was a sign something delicious and sweet was being prepared. It was also the signal for us to rush into the kitchen because both of them would leave large blobs of raw mixture on the beaters for the four us to lick clean. Baking smells filled the house. The kitchen table was layered with racks of biscuits and cakes and the sink heaped with tins and bowls. Small fingers couldn't resist a nip from the side of a cake fresh from the oven but it also brought a light-hearted flick of the tea towel on our backside.

It soon became evident that Betty was not interested in cooking. The Mixmaster was removed from the bench and put in the far corner of the bottom cupboard. Packets of Sao, Ginger Nut and Milk Arrowroot biscuits filled the emptied tins when Aunty's supply of biscuits and cakes ran out. Benches were cleared of canisters and the kitchen became cold and clean. The table had a permanent plastic cover instead of a linen tablecloth and new salt and pepper shakers sat in the middle beside the sugar bowl and a glass ashtray. The aroma of fresh baking was replaced with the stink of stale cigarettes.

We were entranced with Betty's ability to peel a potato in one long, thin strip without breaking and she could cut a tomato thin enough to have two slices each on six plates. When a shiny new meat slicer, with its razor-edged blade arrived and sat on the bench in the kitchen, the devon portions became even thinner.

The milk on our cereal was diluted as the scoops of powdered milk were reduced and eggs and toast were reserved for the adults.

'I'm still hungry,' Ross said one breakfast after Dad had gone to work.

'Really,' said Betty.

'Me too,' said Zilla.

'Me too,' said Tippy with half a bowl of uneaten cereal.

'And me,' I said.

'Haven't you had enough breakfast?' Betty asked.

Timid heads shook.

'Could we have eggs?' Ross asked.

'We have chooks,' I said.

'Yes. I do know that, Bonnie.'

She broke a slice of burnt toast into four squares then handed each of us a piece. 'Here,' she said, 'starving children in Africa would love to eat breakfast.'

'Where's Africa?' asked Zilla.

'Mum would've let us have eggs,' said Ross.

'I want Mummy,' Tippy banged his spoon on the table. 'I want Mummy.'

'Stop that this minute, you silly child.' said Betty.

'Don't you speak to my brother like that,' said Zilla.

'He's not silly,' I said. 'You're silly.'

'You're not our mother,' Ross said, putting an arm around Tippy. 'You can't tell us what to do.'

'You should go back to Sydney,' I said. 'We don't like you.'

Betty sucked in her breath as she grabbed the dirty plates and put them on the bench. She opened a cabinet door above the sink and pulled out a small yellow box labelled *Vincents Powders*. Flipping open the box she removed a white envelope, spread the edges to form a V-shape and tipped the powder into her mouth.

'What's that stuff for?' I asked.

'Headaches. Now whose turn is it to wash up?' She swivelled on her heel and left the kitchen.

'We'll cop it for sure when Dad gets home,' said Zilla.

As the portion sizes on our plates shrank so did our time with Dad.

Each morning when we came in for breakfast he'd be sitting on the chair at the back door putting on his boots.

'Bye kids,' he said as he left. 'Remember, Betty's in charge.'

At night he came home after showering at the mine and Betty grabbed him as soon as he came through the back door.

'Ben, we need to talk.' She'd lead him into the bedroom and close the door.

'What do you think they're talking about?' I asked Ross as we stood waiting in the kitchen to find out Dad's mood when the door opened.

'Probably about us being cheeky to Betty again,' he said.

'I can't help it. I don't like her.'

'She's always cranky.'

'Probably those headache powders she's always taking.'

'Well, I think we'll be getting the strap again.'

When the door opened Dad came back out but not Betty.

'Yep,' said Ross. 'It's the strap for you and me again.'

'Outside you two,' said Dad, pointing to Ross and me.

'But Dad ...'

'Don't *but Dad* me,' he lifted the belt from behind the door and stood back to wave us through.

From the lounge room, Scottish bagpipes shrieked from the gramophone player. It had become permanently associated with beltings.

'This is going to hurt me more than you,' he said. 'Now bend over Bonnie.'

'Dad, I promise I'll be good. I will. I promise. Please Dad.' *Whack, whack.*

'Your turn, young man.' *Whack, whack.*

'Now you two. You will not give Betty any more cheek,' he flicked the strap as if it was a whip.

'But Dad, she's ...'

'No buts, Bonnie.' He rolled the strap around his hands. 'It's up to you two to set an example to the younger ones.'

'Yes, Dad.'

'Off you go,' he said. 'No more nonsense.'

Conversation at the dinner table felt awkward with Betty there. We didn't know her. At least Mum asked about our day and even Aunty Ethel was interested in our chatter about the new adventures we'd dreamed up, or the discovery of a critter we'd never seen before. Things we had learned. But now the discussions related to the shop, the news or the weather and they spoke to each other as if we weren't there.

Instead of doing school studies, our days became regimented with chores written on torn tabs from cardboard boxes or the back of old business letters. A new list appeared on the kitchen table each morning under the salt and pepper shakers and if the chores were unfinished or incomplete, the following day it would be written in capitals and underlined several times.

TODAYS CHORES

Make beds, tidy room. Torn clothes in mending basket
Dirty clothes in laundry basket
Clean room
Feed chooks
Collect eggs
Feed dog
Fill salt and pepper shakers
Clean bath
Chop wood - Ross and Bonnie
Stack wood for stove
Put wood in stove. DO NOT LET GO OUT
Sweep around back door
Cut newspaper for toilet

We learned from Betty about the importance of thrift, especially when cutting squares of newspaper for the toilet.

'Too big,' she said, examining the uneven sizes we tore.

She folded the paper over several times, using one of my Golden Books as a template, cut and handed each of us a sheet along with rulers and pencils so the sheets were all the same size.

'Dad likes big bits,' said Zilla.

'I think I know what your father likes,' said Betty.

'But he ...' I kicked Zilla under the table.

She had begun to speak for Dad. Not only had we lost our Mum but we were losing Dad as well.

TRACKS

Sunday afternoon became nap time. Betty and Dad went to their bedroom for a couple of hours, with the fan humming behind the closed door. Our instructions were to stay on our beds and be quiet until they came out. Tippy was sleeping and the others were reading. I didn't want to follow the rules anymore.

'What are you doing? We're not supposed to go out,' said Ross.

'I can't sleep.'

'I can't either, but we have to stay in our room.'

'I'm going out to play.'

'You'll cop it.'

'I don't care,' I said as I put on my shoes and walked onto the verandah.

It was unusual for me to rebel. I didn't like to upset anyone but Betty was taking Dad away from us.

I walked next door to see if Gai Halford would play with me. She was twelve and we didn't see her much because she was usually away at boarding school. Their back door was closed and there was no answer when I knocked. I ached for Mum. I knew she would understand how awful Betty was and how she was taking Dad away from us so I decided to walk to Perth to find her.

On Sunday afternoons the town was quiet. The pub was closed, the mine was silent and even the dogs dozed in the warm sun on porches and verandahs as the sound of generators, each with its own rhythmic throb, pumped over the plain.

When I reached the bottom of the hill, I looked across to the General Store. The bowsers out front were padlocked and the doors closed. The shop was opening next week and it was already Betty's realm, despite the board on top with Dad's name written on it. The Mount Hope sign was just around the bend in the other direction and I thought if I got to Cobar, Perth wasn't far away. Mum would be surprised.

I strode down the road, past the dry tip, past the racecourse, and past the place where there were lots of Christmas trees. The road was powdery and I was glad I'd worn my sandshoes. The trees on the side of the road rustled and swished as the breeze moved in and out of the branches. I imagined strange beasts weaving in and out of them, sharpening their claws on the trunks ready to frighten me when I slept. I shifted to the middle of the road and told myself it was safer ground. Nothing could harm me there.

I'd been walking for what seemed an age and decided it had been mistake not to bring water. I ran my tongue around the inside of my mouth and longed to put it under the garden tap to lick the drips. Then I remembered Dad told us how he used to dig for water when he was in the bush, so I braved the tree beasts, climbed through the fence and looked for something to help me dig for water. I wasn't certain how to tackle this and tried to remember one of Dad's bush lessons.

I searched for a place to start. A kangaroo sat in a small clearing, staring. He leaned back on his tail, twisted his head, then twitched his ears, scratched a leg and took a short hop in my direction. I bolted to the nearest tree, climbed as high as I could, pulled my legs up over the branch and hugged my knees wishing Ross was with me. He wouldn't be scared. This was harder than I thought. The kangaroo hopped away and I waited a long time before climbing down. I returned to the road, abandoning my search for water, to re-commence my journey.

When I reached the two-mile marker on the side of the road, I heard my name bouncing through the treetops. It was like an echo inside my head so thought it must've been my imagination. I looked around, but saw no-one. There it was again, a muffled *Bo-nn--ieee ... Bo-nn-ieeee ...* drifting across the plain. I turned towards Mount Hope and squinted at the silhouette of a man on top of the mine water tank, calling my name. I recognised my father's shape.

I wasn't going to answer because I was on my way to Perth to see my mother. She'd gone away without taking me and now there was this horrible lady in our house in the bedroom with Dad. She said things like, 'I'll have to ask your father,' or 'Wait 'till I tell your father,' or 'I don't think your father would allow that.' I hated her. I kicked the stones on the surface of the road, selected a few and pitched them into the scrub, disturbing birds residing in the branches.

I continued walking in the centre of the road, but my tears made me feel less confident and more alone. Behind me, I heard the engine of a truck approaching and thought this may be my chance to get a lift. It'd be quicker than walking.

The truck pulled up beside me and Dad poked his head out of the window as it kept pace with my walking.

'Where are you off to, Bonnie?'

'I'm going to Perth.'

'Right. Why Perth?'

'I want to see Mum.'

'Oh, I see. It's a long trip and you must be thirsty by now.' He stretched his arm down and held out a tin mug. 'Why don't you get yourself a drink from the waterbag.'

Dad stayed inside the truck while I unscrewed the cap on the waterbag hanging from the front bumper. The heat from the motor brushed over my arms as I poured water into the cup and took a drink, grateful I didn't have to dig it out of the ground. I handed the cup back.

'Thanks Dad. I'll be going now.' I was determined to get to Perth before nightfall and began walking again.

'Maybe you're hungry as well,' he said, once again keeping a slow pace with the truck. 'Why don't you come home and have a feed and a bath then you can set off in the morning when you're nice and fresh.'

It seemed sensible. I thought about it for a moment and decided a feed and a bath would be good. If I left in the morning, I could bring my cardigan and water. I'd have loads of time to get to Perth.

Dad reached over and opened the passenger door.

'Hop in,' he said.

I climbed in, yanked the door shut and checked the scratches on the dashboard rather than look at Dad. My legs hurt and my tummy rumbled. I needed to re-think my plan to find Mum.

'You okay?' Dad asked, as the gears grated and the truck turned back towards home.

'Yes,' I mumbled.

'Do you want to talk about it?'

'No.'

When we arrived back at the house, Lassie greeted me with a jump and a lick at the back door, and I heard splashing and laughter coming from the bathroom.

'How about you have a bath with the others?' said Dad. 'By then dinner will be ready.'

'Where you been?' Zilla asked.

'Looking for Mum.'

'Did you find her?' asked Ross.

'No.'

Tippy put his hands in the air, indicating he was finished. I lifted him out of the bath, wrapped a towel around him and gave him a big hug. He squeezed his skinny, wet legs around my waist and hugged back, planting sloppy wet kisses on my cheeks. It felt good.

'Come on Bon,' said Zilla. 'Get in before it gets too cold.'

'How come the bath is so full?' I asked. 'It's usually just enough for our backsides to sit in.'

'Dunno,' said Ross. 'Betty filled the boiler and topped it up after she and Dad each had a bath.'

Sunday night was bath time, with oldest to youngest the order. By the time Tippy got to have a bath, the water was as brown as the dam.

We had my favourite at dinner that night – baked beans on toast. Betty was at the shop checking that everything was ready for the opening. I was glad, because it was just Dad and us kids.

After Dad had said goodnight, I snuggled in bed, feeling the cozy warmth of my sister's feet as we jostled for space in the ever-deepening dip in the middle. Tippy was asleep on his small bed in the corner, backside in the air, arms stretched above his head breathing in little puffs.

'I've got minties under my pillow,' said Ross as we all scrambled to feel under each of ours.

'Me too,' said Zilla.

We had three minties each.

'I'm going to save mine,' said Zilla, who could make a musk stick last ten minutes. She chewed everything twenty times.

'Well, I might have one now,' said Ross, who always managed to fill his mouth to capacity before chewing.

'I think I'll save mine,' I said.

I heard the back door close and Dad's footsteps crunching up the hill to turn the generator off. The house creaked and the leaves of the gum tree swept against the corrugated iron in the swelling wind. As I closed my eyes and huddled into the comfort and safety of my bed, I felt the brush of Dad's lips on my forehead.

'Goodnight Bonnie,' he whispered.

* * *

Dad announced at breakfast the following morning we could have a billy cart race the following Sunday.

'Can Paddo and Chris come?' asked Ross.

'Wouldn't be a race without a few mates,' said Dad.

Paddo was scrawny and dark-skinned, with a mass of tangled black hair. His words came out in a long, slow drawl with exaggerated arm movements and everything was a competition. He and Ross were the same age. Chris was my age. He lived at the Post Office and was taller than Paddo. His straight blond hair stuck up at his forehead and like Ross and Paddo, was competitive.

Dad helped us with our carts and we'd help him prepare the track. We'd ridden our bikes down the hill but had never managed to finish the carts to be good enough for racing. We scrounged spare bits and pieces from the dry tip, scrambling over the discarded washing machines and broken bicycles in search of the prized pram wheels.

With an illustration from a Ginger Meggs cartoon, we fashioned our carts to his design: flat board for sitting; wheels fastened to pieces of wood back and front. The back wheels were fixed and the front wheels turned left and right from a rope attached to each end and held in our hands. This, along with our feet wedged against the edge of the wood, controlled the steering. When braking was needed, we jammed our sandshoes on the wheels and it was common to have flaps of rubber peeling off our Dunlops from frequent use.

On Saturday afternoon, Paddo arrived first. He'd dragged his billy cart, hammered together with scraps of wood, through the scrub and up the slag dump from his home, half a mile away. Chris turned up with his billy cart in the back of his dad's ute. It was painted with black splotches of paint and looked like a damaged cow. Ross's was the same as mine – a packing box set on small pram wheels – except his had a painted skull and crossbones on the side. I'd tried to scratch my name into the wood. It looked like woodworm had attacked it, so I gave up.

Ross had the brilliant idea that if he used Tippy's child restraint harness and attached it to Lassie, he'd get her to pull the billy cart up the hill for him. Lassie sniffed it, then as if knowing her fate, darted under the Halfords' house. She wasn't interested in being a passenger either, and sought refuge behind Zilla, who shared Lassie's lack of interest in anything to do with building or racing billy carts but offered advice on the general design.

'Track's great Mr McLernon,' said Paddo as he walked back with Chris from their inspection. Dad had scraped and shovelled with the loader, removing jagged rocks and deep ditches to make the track less hazardous. Coloured streamers nailed to trees on the side were warning signs for sharp bends, dips in the track or rough areas. Zilla and I had made a flag for the finish line. Crooked lettering and splashed paint on a torn pillowcase flapped at the bottom of the hill.

Betty declared no interest in racing of any kind and walked down to the shop after breakfast with headache powders in one pocket and cigarettes in the other.

The start was a line in the dirt at the end of Halfords' house with Mr Halford as the unbiased judge. Our four carts were lined up ready to race. It was his job to check out design, construction and safety, making sure it complied with the code, whatever that was. His deputy was Zilla. They walked around the carts examining each with all the seriousness of Formula One officials, checking them against a book with the handwritten title OFFICIAL CODES FOR BILLY CART RACING. He did question the size of Chris's wheels as they were bigger than everyone else's. He, Dad and Zilla huddled as he flipped through his book and discussed the possibility of disqualification. Slapping against his leg was the starter pistol, a cap gun.

'Doesn't specify pram wheel size,' Mr Halford said to us. 'Pram wheels is pram wheels,' he nodded at Zilla.

'LET THE RACE BEGIN,' she shouted, jumping up and down, grinning and waving a brown and white scarf tied to a stick. The image of a leopard crossed my mind and I looked into the scrub hoping it was only my imagination.

'That's for the finish,' said Ross.

'Oh, sorry,' said Zilla, grabbing the green scarf from Tippy, who was sitting on his dinkey making engine noises and turning an imaginary steering wheel.

'You can do it again for the official start to the race,' said Dad.

'But I've got to be at the finish line to wave the other flag,'

'Tell you what,' said Mr Halford. 'I'll do the start and you can do the finish. How's that sound?'

'All right,' said Zilla.

'Now, who's got the stopwatch?'

'Check,' said Dad. 'When the starter's pistol fires, I'll start timing.'

'Good. Now then. Bonnie, Chris, Ross and Paddo. Man your carts.'

Dad, Zilla and Tippy climbed into the ute and drove down to the finish line while we all stood behind our carts ready to push.

The track was a curve past the Halford's house and around to the junction of the mine road. A small pothole before the steep descent could send a cart in the wrong direction. However, it was the large ditch at the end, we called *The Big Dipper,* that caused the most problems. Hitting the far bank caused carts to become airborne and sail over the finish line at the junction of the main road where landing could be dangerous. It was fortunate traffic was rare.

When Dad shouted from the bottom of the hill, Mr Halford fired the gun and we began pushing to get a fast start. With rattling metal, crunching stones and pounding feet we took off. Paddo rounded the bend first, still running beside his cart. With his mouth grimacing in concentration, he leaped onto the flat board and grabbed the rope. He bounced on the downhill slope and leaned forward, feet poised, ready to operate the brakes. Ross and Chris were half a wheel behind, already seated, focused on the track, bent in determination. When I took off, I saw them all hit the first dip, breathing through clenched teeth, backsides and carts in the air together, flying along. I could hear Paddo hissing like a jockey from my rear position.

We yelled at each other as we hurtled down the rough road. Birds scattered and the undergrowth shook. Ross shot ahead while Paddo grappled with getting his feet into position to steer the cart. Chris was having a hard time steering and he became the first casualty. He hit a rock and took off. A wobbly wheel and missing shoe slammed into a wattle bush. The rest of us jolted and shuddered towards the Big Dipper. Zilla and Tippy were screaming as I pulled ahead of Paddo and Ross going so fast, I gripped the rope and wedged myself against the board, hoping I wouldn't crash. For a moment, I was an aeroplane on a runway ready to take flight. The wind whipped my hair across my eyes as I realised the cart was speeding out of control. I clenched my jaw to conquer emerging terror and resisted the temptation to close my eyes.

My bony backside was smacking against the board and the rope burned my hands but I felt smug being first, beating the boys. Previous attempts at the Big Dipper on the bike flashed across my mind – bent wheel, grazed hands and knees but – I could win. The cart was rocketing down the track and I couldn't control the steering so I jammed my feet on the wheel to slow it down. I shot to the left and crashed into a pile of dirt as Ross and Paddo tore past, clattering over the bumps and charging down the hill at a daring speed.

Paddo turned to Ross with a smirk and I heard him shout, 'You haven't won yet!'

He realised his mistake when he hit the Big Dipper side on. The cart, instead of becoming airborne, hit the bank with a thud. One wheel dislodged, flew into the air, bounced off the roof of the ute then across the road to disappear into the scrub. Paddo landed face down underneath his cart surrounded by splintered pine boards with his feet sticking out the back.

Ross hit the brakes and pushed hard, death grip on the rope, counting on there being enough time to avoid crashing into Paddo as he swooped into the Big Dipper, zoomed off the bank and sailed over the finish line, landing with a thump and a skid beside the ute parked at the bottom of the road.

Zilla jumped up and down, waving the leopard scarf from the back of the ute, shouting 'AND THE WINNER IS ...' but Ross jumped off his cart and ran over to Paddo.

The sprawled shape on the ground wasn't moving.

'You okay, young man,' said Dad, lifting the demolished cart from around Paddo's body.

Paddo groaned, then rolled over and found he was surrounded by a sea of dusty, worried faces. His arms and face were grazed, his pants torn and knees bleeding.

'Broke the first rule of racing,' he puffed as Ross extended his hand to help him up. 'Keep your eyes ahead and never look at the other driver,' we all chanted.

'Beaut race,' said Paddo. 'Can we do that again sometime?'

'Yeah. That was fun,' said Chris.

'Yeah,' I said.

'I think we've had enough excitement for one day,' said Dad.

THE CRIME

'When can we see inside the shop?' Ross asked Dad one morning.

'I don't see why you can't see it before we open on Wednesday,' said Dad. 'It's been a mess until now, but we've finished painting all the shelves so you can give Betty a hand to fill them, eh Bet?'

'Maybe for a little while. I don't want them getting in the way.'

'We won't get in the way,' we chorused.

'You can come with me after breakfast,' she said.

We'd caught glimpses of the inside through the open door, but the ladders, wood and paint tins made it difficult to see what it was going to be like. I wondered if there would be a ladder on a rail, like Aunty Ethel had in the shop in Dubbo. She had rows of multi-coloured lolly jars on the top shelf and we didn't know it was called *confectionery* until Betty brought in the labelled boxes for the shop and put them in a suitcase under the bed.

We drove down to the shop with the meat slicer sitting on the front seat and us in the back perched on a tyre. When we pulled up, Dad was nailing the sign with *'B.McLERNON GENERAL STORE'* on the roof. Betty stopped between the two bowsers out the front, climbed out and went around to the side door. We heard her footsteps as they approached the front door, the bolt dragged across the metal inside then she opened it.

'You can come in and sit on the floor until I sort out what you're doing,' she said, reaching to the front seat of the ute and lifting out the meat slicer.

I felt as if we were walking into the wicked stepmother's lair. We grouped inside the doorway, half afraid, half curious and I was terrified there was an oven in the back where she would turn us into stew.

'Well, in you come,' she said. 'We've got work to do.'

We shuffled in and sat in the middle of the green linoleum covering a square of floor about the size of our kitchen. The only place with no counter was at the front door. Narrow shelves reached from top to bottom on our left and right and were filled with tins and packets. The side door had a kerosene fridge on one side and on the wall on the other side, a telephone. Betty walked through a gap in the counter in front of us and went behind a row of screw-top jars filled with all manner of lollies. She placed the meat slicer on the counter beside a stack of newspapers and magazines, then picked up a bunch of papers held together with a bulldog clip. We stared drooling at the mint leaves, musk sticks and boxes whose open flaps read *Wrigley's Chewing Gum.*

Dad came through the side door, unscrewed a jar and lifted out a musk stick.

'Nice and fresh,' he said popping it into his mouth.

'Dad,' I said. 'You're not allowed to do that.'

We looked at Betty. She stared back, her hand resting on the handle of the meat slicer.

'I'm just eating my share,' he said. 'Sign's up, I'm off,' he said to Betty. 'Bye kids.'

'Here is your list of jobs,' said Betty, flapping a piece of paper at us. 'This way.'

We passed through the gap and followed her around a partition into the storeroom. Wooden boxes lined the walls, stacked high to the roof. Tea chests filled with salt and tea leaves sat in the middle along with bags of sugar, boxes of tomatoes, pumpkin, carrots, potatoes, onions, swede and turnip.

'I could climb up there,' said Ross.

'You will do no such thing,' said Betty. 'You are here to work, not play.'

I pulled Tippy close.

'Unpack these cartons. Zilla and Tippy can pass the tins while Bonnie and Ross stack them into the labelled wooden boxes. Here is the list.' She jammed the note on a nail sticking out of the wall just inside the opening. 'There are the boxes,' she pointed to a line in the middle. 'Start with the peas. I'll come in and check on you later.'

STOREROOM.

16oz tins. Peas, beans, beetroot, carrots,
mix veg, sweet corn, tomatoes.
32oz tins beetroot, tomatoes

'We'll be here all day,' said Ross.
'Yeah,' I said.
'We'd better get started,' said Zilla.

'Here we go Tip. You pass to Ross and Zilla can pass it to me,' I said.

It didn't take long for the boredom to set in. We'd stacked the peas, but halfway through the beans, Tippy dropped a can and it rolled down to the back wall.

'All right Tip,' said Ross. 'I've got an idea.'

He looked at the can in his hand and rolled it down the concrete. It hit the wall with a thump. We froze, waited for a moment before each grabbing a tin of beans.

'Let's have a race,' said Ross. 'First to the back wall wins.'

We stood in the walkway facing the back wall.

'Bonnie. Pick up those two down there then we can ...'

'Then you can what?' said Betty, standing behind us.

'Oh crikey,' I said, putting the can on the shelf.

'I take it you have finished?' said Betty, hands on hips.

'Well, no,' said Ross. 'We're taking a break.'

'Finish with that box, then you can go.'

'Can we have a lolly?' I asked.

'I think not.' She walked behind the partition and said over her shoulder. 'Anyway, you'll be going to school next week. Your father will tell you about it tonight.'

***

'Betty said we're going to school next week,' said Ross at dinner.

'Teacher arrives on the weekend, so you'll all be going,' said Dad.

'Wow, that's great,' I said. 'I loved school in Dubbo.'

'Who will be going?' said Ross.

'Town kids, I expect,' said Betty.

'Muttons, Pattersons, Lloyds. You'll see,' said Dad.

'What about Tippy?' said Ross. 'He's only three and Zilla's four. They don't go to school yet.'

'Zilla and Tippy will be going back to WA with Aunty Ethel in a couple of weeks. Until then they'll both go to school with you.'

'Why can't they stay here?' I said.

'That's the end of it, Bonnie.'

I wanted my little brother and sister to stay with us.

On our first day we all walked down the hill dressed in our day clothes. We didn't have a special uniform or shoes and it felt weird walking to school without a case filled with pencils and books. Apart from lessons with Mum, Aunty Ethel and Mrs Halford, it had been six months since we left school in Dubbo.

We walked past the shop where we could see Betty through the window putting change into the till, past the empty house beside the shop to the back of the pub where we greeted the publican's pigs as they snorted around their pen, then up the track to the school. The schoolhouse had been scrubbed inside, the yard cleared and a bell hung from the top of a thick post with the rope dangling from the clapper.

The new teacher stood on the front verandah.

'Hello,' he said to each as we arrived. 'I'm Mr Burwell.'

Most of the kids were older than me and there seemed to be lots more at the school than we'd seen before. We'd met Johnny Paterson and Chris Mutton on the slag dump when we first arrived because we were around the same age. There were the Lloyd kids, Janice, Marie, Brian and Kevin then Chris's sister, Noleen, Johnny's brother, Melvin, George Schneider and Alan Harrison.

There were fourteen students including us, aged from four to fourteen. I was in a class with the other six-year-old Chris, and there were three aged seven in Ross's class. The rest ranged from fourth to sixth class and high school. Mr Burwell's desk sat in front of the huge blackboard stretching across the wall behind. In the corner, a pot belly stove prepared with kindling and paper was ready for cold mornings. On one wall spread above a row of coat hooks were a map of the world and several times-table charts. Everyone was in the same room and each desk seated two students. Names etched into the wood and abstract ink-stained patterns across the lid pointed to previous use.

Mr Burwell was tall, young and enthusiastic. We were outside exploring rocks, bugs and insects as well as inside, learning maths, reading and history. I loved going to school because we were out of the house most of the day, and Mr Burwell made learning fun. I shared a desk with Chris Mutton. Johnny Patterson with Zilla, and Tippy sat at one on his own at the front. They left a few weeks later to live with Aunty Ethel.

Even though the shop was open and most of the goods were stacked in the storeroom, Betty still kept a few things at the house. We went off to school each weekday and when we came home there would be boxes lining the hallway, and we were fascinated by the coloured labels of cigarettes, tobacco and confectionery. Betty would take some of them down to the shop on Sunday morning and stay for a couple of hours catching up on paperwork. It was at one of those times that Ross signalled me into the lounge room.

'Under the bed,' Ross said. 'I saw Betty checking it when they arrived on Friday. She emptied all the boxes, put them into a suitcase and shoved it under there.' Ross pointed to the brown suitcase under the bed in Dad and Betty's room. 'See it?'

'What's in there?' I asked.

'Lollies for the shop. I'm going to have a look. Stay here and keep watch, if you hear anyone or anything, call me.'

'Wait a minute. This is going to get us into big trouble.'

'It'll be okay. She won't know if we're quick,' he said.

'I don't know. You know what she's like.'

'Yeah, well Dad said we all share in the shop, so I want to see my share.'

He darted across the hallway into the bedroom and slid under the bed, his belly leaving a clean path as he mopped a strip of dust on his way in.

He grabbed the suitcase by the handle and yanked hard, but it wouldn't budge.

'Give us a hand. It's stuck.'

My heart was pounding and my knees shook. I wasn't at all sure about this. With a deep breath, I dived across through the door, a gap that seemed as big as the lounge room. With less skillful ease, I skidded over and grabbed the handle.

'You pull, I'll push,' he said.

He kicked with thumps of gusto from behind, while I pulled with all my might on the handle. We were making a dreadful racket and there was dust everywhere. Bits of fluff drifted around and landed on us and the bed, as our wriggling bodies stirred up weeks of neglected under-bed cleaning. We puffed and panted inhaling the fine powder with each breath. I sneezed.

'Holy cow, Bonnie. We're trying to be quiet.'

'Doesn't she ever clean under the bed?'

'Who cares. Keep pulling.'

Each push and pull eased the case until at last, with one final shove, it came free.

It was like discovering lost treasure and being on an adventure in the caves on the Cornwall coast. We couldn't think of anything other than the booty inside. Ross raised the lid and a mingle of sweet aromas hit us. We ogled the neat stacks of coloured boxes – every variety of lolly imaginable. Ross reached in, grabbed a box each of Musk Sticks, Juicy

Fruit and PK Chewing Gum, slammed the lid shut and we began to force the suitcase back under the bed. A corner covered with our blurred fingerprints remained sticking out as we dashed back through the doorway into our bedroom.

Ross tore the cellophane covering from the PK gum and it revealed two rows of tiny packets, each filled with little pillows of delicious, sugar-coated gum. He handed me a box of Musk Sticks. I unwrapped the cellophane and a wave of musk hit my senses. I picked one up, slid it through my moist lips and chewed. Ross squeezed one full packet of gum into his mouth; then another and another, until there were six packets in there. His mouth was so full, rivers of dribble flowed down his chin as he tried to control the giant chewy mass.

Then the doorway darkened. Betty. Her face was an ugly mask of anger.

'What do you think you are doing?' she asked.

Lolly wrappers and cellophane were strewn across the floor. I froze, clutching the box against my chest with a musk stick paused on the way to my mouth. Ross tried desperately to conceal his bulging cheeks. Betty wiggled her fingers for us to hand over the remaining uneaten lollies. When Dad came home from work, we were called into the kitchen where the opened packets sat in the middle of the table. He gave both of us six on the backside from the strap and we were sent to bed without any tea.

The following morning, after a chilly breakfast, Ross and I were ready to leave for school when Betty called us into the kitchen. On the table was a cardboard carton, a roll of string and a pair of scissors. She ripped two flaps from the carton, picked up the scissors and rammed them into the ends making jagged holes, through which she threaded and tied the string to make a loop.

'We're going to be late for school,' Ross said.

'If you're late, you're late,' she said. 'You will wait until I have finished.'

'Can we help?' I was wondering why we were watching her making door signs.

She slammed the cardboard flat on the kitchen table, grabbed the pen stuck between her specs and her ear then scratched large letters with wild strokes while Ross and I stood at attention, glancing at each other, wondering what she was doing.

She's cranky, mouthed Ross. *Very,* I mouthed back.

Betty picked up the signs, thrusting one at each of us and said, 'Put those on. You will wear them to school today. All day.'

We turned the signs around, stunned by what was written on each.

I am a thief.

'We have to wear these to school?' I said.

'We're not going to,' said Ross. 'You can't make us.'

'I can't wear this to school. I just can't.'

'Oh yes, you can,' Betty said. 'This is what happens when you steal.'

'But we got the strap from Dad last night for that,' I said.

'Well, that was his punishment now this is mine. Now go.'

'I don't like you,' said Ross.

'I don't like you either,' I said, in agreement. 'You're horrible and mean. I'm going to tell Dad.'

'Good luck. You do that. It won't make any difference.'

School was going to be ruined because we pinched a few lollies. Walking down the hill to school wearing horrible signs I wanted to jump into one of the holes on the slag dump and stay there.

'I can't go to school like this.' I said.

'Let's take them off,' said Ross. 'She won't know. We'll put them back on when we come up the hill.'

'Where'll we hide them?'

'The big pepper tree on the dump. We'll pick them up after school.'

We removed the signs and stuck them under the pepper tree before heading down the hill to school. On the way home, we put them back around our necks. Betty was standing at the back door when we arrived home.

'You wore the signs all day?' she asked.

'Yes,' we said.

'All day?' Hands on hips and thin lips stretched wide, she leaned in and spat at us with cigarette breath through clenched teeth, head wobbling from side to side. Around her forehead, rows of bobby pins held bits of brown hair in tight curls. I noticed one strand of hair wobbling and beginning to unwind.

'Ye...e...s.'

'I spoke to Mr Burwell. He didn't see you wearing any signs.'

'Well, we didn't wear them in class, just to school,' said Ross. I nodded in agreement.

'Didn't I say all day? You didn't wear them all day, so now you will wear them all week. Give them to me.'

She snatched the signs, whipped the pen out from her hair, scribbled on each and shoved them back at us, holding them in front of our noses.

'You will wear them for the rest of the week and I will make sure by taking you to school myself. I will take you to the gate and watch you walk into class so everyone can see what disgraceful children you are.' She shoved the signs at us.

We stared at the writing, horrified. I was sick with fright. A warm trickle ran down my leg and formed a puddle around my feet.

I didn't want to go to school anymore.

The sign now read - *I am a thief <u>and</u> a liar*.

* * *

'I can't go in there,' I said, pulling my coat across my chest to cover the sign.

'Let's get this over with,' said Ross. 'We're already late.'

'I hate being late.'

'We'll just walk in and pretend everything's okay.'

'I can't do this.'

I rubbed the back of my neck where the string scratched. The cardboard was so thick and hard I couldn't bend it so my chest looked like a signpost. Chairs scraped across the wooden floor from inside the schoolhouse and I heard Mr Burwell's strong voice begin to sing *God Save the Queen*. Hesitant voices joined him in a shaky blend of out-of-tune singing.

'Here goes,' said Ross, grabbing my hand, stepping up to the verandah and pulling me through the doorway.

We entered the classroom together. The singing dribbled to an uncomfortable silence as Ross and I stood in front of the gawking students.

'Good morning Bonnie, Ross. Hang up your coats and go to your desks,' said Mr Burwell.

'I'd rather leave mine on, if you don't mind,' Ross said.

'Me too,' I said arms across my chest.

'You can't work with them on. Sit down children.' Mr Burwell waved his hand to the others, walked to his desk and sat down. 'Open your writing books please, and begin.'

Ross and I slunk over to the coat rack and removed our coats to the rustle of books and clatter of desk lids opening and closing. I felt as if I'd been stripped bare.

'Come along you two. Sit down,' said Mr Burwell. 'We've a lot to get through today.'

'Deep breath, Sis,' Ross whispered.

There wasn't a hole big enough to swallow me. *Run, run,* my head screamed. We turned. With my chin down looking at the monstrosity around my neck, I heard the joint gasps, short squeals from the girls, followed by a stillness that soaked into my humiliation and glued my feet to the floor. Even with my head down I could see the awkward shuffling of embarrassed feet from beneath the desks. The room expanded to a thousand eyes staring with fingers pointing and voices chanting at my disgrace. *Don't wet your pants. Don't wet your pants,* I repeated it inside my head. Ross gave me a shove and I dragged myself over to the desk, sat down, lifted the lid and shoved my head inside.

'What did you do?' whispered Chris, sitting on the other half of the twin desk.

'Pinched a musk stick.'

'Jings,' he said. 'Is that all. Ross too?'

'He pinched chewing gum.'

'Okay, okay,' said Mr Burwell as the small group muttered to each other over the desks. 'Let's have a bit of quiet. You two can't work with those things on. Put them in your desks and get started in your workbook.'

'But,' I said, unwilling to go against Betty's instructions in case of further punishment.

'Betty said ...'

'It's all right, Bonnie,' said Mr Burwell. 'I'm in charge here.'

I wanted to hug him because I was on the brink of crying. I glanced at Ross who'd removed his sign and was dipping his pen into the inkwell and as I lifted the sign over my head and closed the lid on the desk, I put some of my worry in with it. Mr Burwell gave me a reassuring nod, picked up the chalk and began to write on the blackboard. It wasn't the big deal it felt like on the way to school and during the break when we went outside to the playground, the sting of Betty's punishment lessened as everyone had something to add about being disciplined by their parents.

'How can you be so cheerful?' I asked Ross as we walked back home that afternoon with the signs around our necks.

'Because everyone knows about it now and they don't care.'

'But we've got to do this for the rest of the week. Who knows what she'll think of next.'

'We have to call into the shop on our way home.'

'She's checking up on us, Ross.'

We delayed arriving at the shop by climbing on the rails of the pig pen to see if we could walk all the way around without falling into the muck on the inside and chucking stones at a drum in the middle of the paddock behind the shop. We were perched on the corner posts when Mr Burwell drove past and pulled in front of the shop.

'We'd better go,' said Ross.

As we approached the shop we heard Betty and Mr Burwell having a disagreement, Betty's voice severe and heated against that of Mr Burwell who was quiet and forceful.

'Do you think we should go in?' I asked Ross.

'Doesn't matter,' he said. 'Let's get this over with.'

He straightened his back and I followed. We stood just inside the doorway. An awkward silence replaced the lively quarrel as they both turned and stared at us. Mr Burwell stood with his hands in his pockets and Betty had one hand on the meat slicer and the other poised mid-air, pointing at Mr Burwell's chest.

'Hello Ross, Bonnie,' said Mr Burwell. 'Betty and I were just discussing your situation.'

Betty lowered her hand and added a disapproving pout to her mouth.

'I need a headache powder,' she said.

Mr Burwell reached over and removed the cardboard from around our necks.

'These can go,' he said. 'Can't they, Betty?' He gazed at her with one eyebrow raised as he tore them into small pieces and placed them on the counter.

Ross and I looked at each other, eyes wide, mouths open.

'I think you've learned your lesson,' she said as she tossed her chin in the air and reached into her apron pocket for the cigarette packet.

'So, there will be no more wearing of signs in the future, will there?' said Mr Burwell. Both eyebrows went up.

'Gee, thanks Mr Burwell,' said Ross.

'Yeah, thanks,' I said resisting the temptation to dance with joy.

'Hmmph,' Betty nodded. She reached into her pocket, placed a cigarette into the corner of her mouth and lit it.

THE TARZAN TREE

Dad employed Mr Mitchell as a storeman to help Betty in the shop. After two years on the hill, we moved to the house next door to the shop and Mr and Mrs Mitchell and their two children, Wendy and Steve, moved into the Nissen hut. We had a real house, with a pitched roof, windows on every side and walls without curves where the wardrobes could sit flat. It had four bedrooms and a screened verandah that wrapped around one side to the laundry, bathroom and one of the back doors. At the end of the hallway on a brass hook, dangled the leather strap; it's buckle rattled each time the door opened, an audible reminder of its use. Sitting in the middle of the yard was the outhouse where spiders lurked in gauze tunnels attached to knot holes and corners of the wood. On a nail, torn strips of newspaper were ready for use.

Oleander, gum and pepper trees lined the fence while plum, apricot and nectarine trees grew against the back wall of the house. Like so many other things, we were forbidden to pluck the fruit. Beyond the front fence, two more pepper trees towered above the house, providing partial shade for the patchy front lawn.

We no longer had a tree house but Dad re-built the chook pen and it sat against the fence near the wood pile. The sloping block meant we could walk underneath the tank stand and then a little way under the house where Lassie found her own crawl space to escape from humans.

The Harrisons' cows grazed in the paddock out the back.

'Damn dog'll get itself killed one day,' said Dad as Lassie burst through the gate and chased them across the paddock. 'You'd think she'd have more sense than to run between their legs.'

When we moved in, Lassie protected the house with enthusiastic delight. She stood at the gate and barked at anyone and everyone who stopped there.

'Cut out that racket, Lassie,' Dad would shout from the shed. 'For crying out loud. A bloke can't work with all that barking.'

After a few weeks, Lassie adjusted to the routine and sorted out her barking and by the variety and intensity of her bark, we would know who was approaching the house, whether friends, strangers, cows or other critters.

'Can we have a room each, Dad?' Ross and I asked as he assembled our beds in the room adjacent to his.

'Nope,' said Dad. 'You two are in here.'

'Oh, gee Dad. Zilla and Tippy are living in WA and there's loads of rooms,' said Ross

'Nope.'

'We'll be tidy,' I said.

'Nope.'

'At least it's big,' I said after Dad had left. 'Loads of room for both of us.'

'Well this is my half and that's your half.' Ross took a piece of chalk and drew a line from the middle of the doorway, across the floor to the window, dividing the room in two.

'That's not fair,' I said. 'It goes across the middle of the doorway.'

'Too bad,' he said.

I couldn't be bothered arguing but when the line faded, Ross didn't bother with the boundaries except when either of us got the strap and we wanted solitude.

The fence around the house had round, orange, metal top rails in between the wooden fence posts. We decided this was another challenge to conquer. With arms outstretched for balance, we'd grip the rails with our bare feet and run from post to post. With persistent practice, we learned to walk the entire perimeter without dismounting.

It was however, the impressive pepper tree in the back corner that interested us most.

The lush canopy of leafy branches spilled over the fence and hid the trunk from view. Deeds fit for explorers lurked inside and called to our imaginations.

'It'll take at least two minutes to climb to the top,' I said as we stood back, judging the distance, necks stretched, backs arched.

'Let's go,' said Ross as he parted the drooping, spear-shaped leaves loaded with spicy pink clusters of tiny pepper grapes and stepped inside. Peppercorns, twigs and leaves crushed beneath our feet. Branches scratched as we ducked and weaved between the tangled limbs until we were inside. The space was roomy enough for both of us to stand and walk upright. The thick leaves blocked the view of the yard but we could see light filtering through from above. We patted the bumpy, dark brown trunk as if a friend. The main branch split halfway up, one half going to the right the other to the left.

'Pretty good, eh?' said Ross. 'Look at all those big branches. I can swing from those. Come on.'

The view from up there was exciting. It was different from the hill. We perched as close as we could to the top, looking through the branches at the town scattered below us. We saw five pigs at the back of the pub scrounging around their muddy pen snorting and grunting and scrambling for kitchen scraps tossed by the publican. We counted eleven rusty car bodies abandoned around a house in the distance. Behind us, our shop was hidden by the house roof. The sound of a revving engine signalled that Dad was in the workshop, repairing a motor.

'What do you reckon?' Ross said.

"Bout what?'

'I'm gonna make it into a Tarzan tree.'

'Tarzan tree?'

'Yeah. With ropes 'n platforms 'n stuff?'

'Sounds hard.'

Tarzan was one of our favourite radio serials. At six o'clock, when Tarzan's yodel rang down the hallway, we jostled for a place in front of the radio to listen to 45 minutes of radio serials that transported us into the thrills and perils of *Tarzan*, *Biggles* and *Superman*. Their adventures gave us enough material to fill days with imagined conquests and triumphs. We longed to swing through the trees like Tarzan and fly high into the stratosphere like Superman and believed it was possible.

The pepper tree became the focus for Ross's dream of a Tarzan tree. He listened to the nightly serial with paper and pencil, sketching. Squatting on a box under the tree, he scribbled designs. He carried a pencil and paper in his back pocket just in case inspiration struck. It became a secret mission.

On his last visit, Keith had given him a chest expander and each morning Ross grappled with the tight springs in preparation for being Tarzan. Red welts and bruises appeared where it had pinched his skin. His empty billy cart disappeared down the driveway and return loaded with bits and pieces from the back of Dad's shed and the dry tip. Planks of wood, bits of rope, old boxes. Dad gave Ross a hammer because he was fed up with his going missing.

'Can I see?' I asked.

'You can't come in 'til it's finished,' he said. 'I've got a warning system rigged so I'll know.'

He pointed to a sign propped against a drum that read KEEP OUT *or else*.

'I don't want to come in anyway.' Arguing with my brother was a waste of effort. He always won.

I could understand his need for a private sanctuary though. The previous morning, Betty had caught us in the kitchen eating Milo out of the tin. Our mouths were coated and sticky and scattered around our feet were chocolate crumbs that had escaped from our jousting spoons.

'That costs money,' she said. 'Wait 'til I tell your father.'

She was stingy with the food she gave us, but that didn't mean we were allowed to serve ourselves. We forgot about it. Ross was busy with the Tarzan Tree and I was writing adventure stories. When Dad came home from work he called us into the hallway, removed the strap from the back door and said, 'You know what this is for, don't you?' He slid the leather through his hand, waiting for our reply.

Ross and I scanned each other's faces, mentally rewinding the day for wrongdoing. With Betty it was tricky keeping check on our ever-growing list of misdemeanors.

'No, Dad.'

'Well, this should jog your memory.' He opened the back door and indicated with the strap. 'Bonnie, you first.'

Even before the first thump, I was crying. First, because I didn't remember the reason and secondly, I anticipated how much it was going to hurt. When Ross went outside for his turn, I leaned against the hallway wall rubbing my backside, and listened to the swish of the strap the strokes slapped hard against his shorts. Unlike me, he didn't cry. All I could hear was the outward rush of his breath.

Through weepy eyes I watched Betty in the kitchen. She was at the sink peeling potatoes and every swipe of the knife against the skin matched the rhythm of the blows coming from outside. That night we curled up, each on our beds, facing the wall in silent hate, a little against Dad, but more against Betty for being a dobber. The price of Milo was too high. I closed my eyes and imagined Mum's arms enclosing me in a tight hug, drawing out the pain.

The next morning I was invited into Ross's tree zone. He insisted I wear a blindfold so his entrance would remain a secret. When he removed the blindfold I was impressed. Gone were the cluttered branches and tangled twigs. He had transformed the interior into a series of levels, with platforms, ropes and pipes.

'What do you think of my Tarzan Tree?'

In the corner supported by the fence and branches, sheltered from the wind and rain was a large crate, big enough for both of us to sit in. He had lined the floor with cardboard and newspaper. On top of a smaller crate was an old biscuit tin where he kept his slingshot, marbles, *Tarzan* and *Phantom* comics, *Phantom* ring, paper and pencils.

'Let me show you,' he said, crushing a handful of peppercorns and rubbing them on his palms. 'Sticky. Helps me grip the rope.'

He jumped and grabbed the nearest dangling rope, then swung back lifting his feet to reach the first platform. As he began his demonstration, it became obvious he had worked out the right position for each rope and platform. I was in complete admiration of his gymnastic abilities as he grabbed a rope with one hand, reached for another with the other hand, then landed on a platform before immediately launching himself at another dangling rope and swung up to the next platform, moving higher and higher into the tree. He repeated the moves until he returned to land on the ground beside me with a smile as wide as a slice of watermelon.

'That was amazing. You should be in the circus,' I said. 'Maybe on the trapeze, or high wire.'

'Wanna have a go?'

'I dunno. Looks hard.'

'Nothing to it really. Look. Grab this rope and swing a bit. I'll give you a lift up.'

When I climbed a tree, I pulled myself up. There wasn't much swinging involved. But this was exactly like the drawings in the *Tarzan* comics. I clutched the rope with both hands and he pushed.

'Let go,' he said. 'Let go and grab the other rope.'

I flapped my legs and clung to the rope but my body felt heavy. My swing dribbled to a struggle to hang on so I tried reaching with my legs.

'You look like a fly caught in a spider web,' he laughed.

'It's too hard,' I gasped. 'I can't hang on.'

After several attempts my hands were beginning to burn, so I gave up and decided I would listen to Tarzan and leave leaping through the trees to Ross. He showed me his hands, calloused and red from swinging and as I touched each mark, I felt his torment, sensed the hurt and knew this was his way of escaping the blows from the belt hanging on the brass hook behind the back door.

***

Now that we'd moved to a bigger house, Dad decided we should have some visitors. In mid-December 1954, his sisters arrived in a dust covered VW beetle bringing Zilla and Tippy with them. Aunty Dell was five feet tall and every time we saw her it was with a new 'Uncle'. But she was between boyfriends that Christmas and able to leave her married daughter in Perth so she could keep Aunty Ethel company on the 2,500 mile trek across the Nullabor. Her hugs were a quick shoulder grasp and a peck on the cheek.

On the backseat, squashed in between bedding and baggage, were Zilla and Tippy. They spilled from the doors as Dad, Ross and I surrounded them. When Aunty Ethel crushed us into her bosom I caught a whiff of the lavender perfume from the hanky poking out of the top of her dress.

Zilla and I compared freckles – mine splotched, hers, spots. She moved as if she'd been to modelling school even after being jammed in the car for so long. Her mannerisms were unhurried, she carried a handbag over her arm and had more dresses in her suitcase than shorts. I'd looked forward to having my sister here, but we seemed to have moved in different directions. I was a tom-boy, she was a princess.

'I don't climb trees,' she said when I took her out the back and showed her Ross's Tarzan tree. 'Aunty makes all our clothes.'

'I climb trees all the time and Betty buys our clothes from a catalogue.'

After a couple of days, it didn't matter how different we were. It was us against the adults.

Both Aunties were in their fifties. Aunty Dell had two speeds: full bore or stop. She rushed back and forth from the car, unloading the gear and issuing instructions to anyone who stood nearby. Aunty Ethel didn't smile much and only moved with haste when she was annoyed – usually with Aunty Dell. She stayed out of the kitchen until Betty left for the shop, then pulled the mixmaster from the back of the cupboard and began a baking frenzy. For the first time in this house, the kitchen smelt homey, the sound of cooking and chatter filled the house and the table was bursting with fresh cakes and biscuits.

Tippy hadn't grown much taller, but he ran everywhere and had a fondness for hiding behind doors and jumping out to scare anyone who walked by. He followed Ross everywhere, mimicked his gestures and talked non-stop. This amused Ross at first, then he became irritated, sent Tippy on errands then ducked away.

Keith was dropped off by a family on their way to Griffith and after a quick hello, threw his duffle bag over his shoulder and headed out the back to the spare room. He was fifteen, tall and skinny with a patchy stubble of red hair on his chin. We hadn't seen him for two years and it was like having someone important come to visit. He chucked his stuff on the floor and flopped down on the bed without removing his shoes, while the four of us crowded around the doorway, curious about this lanky brother.

'Buzz off,' he said. 'I'll be out later.'

Travelling from Bankstown on the train, was Betty's younger sister, Barbara Negus. Her husband was working back in Sydney so it was her and her sons, Graham and Warren, who came to visit. Bob, our likeable mailman, met them at Matakana Siding to bring them back with the mail and goods for the shop. Barbara was the complete opposite of Betty. Her hair was soft and bouncy, her eyes sparkled with mischief and she had a smile that reached inside and filled me with delight. She sat with us, asked questions and seemed interested in our exploits. She intervened when

Betty got cranky and played peacemaker on behalf of us kids. We liked her immediately.

Warren was the same age as Ross and Graham was a year older. Both were chubby and moody and we found their whining annoying.

'This place is so boring,' said Graham. 'There's nothing to do.'

'You don't have any neighbours,' said Warren.

Betty treated them differently to us. They complained about the heat, dust, being hungry and got away with it. We couldn't believe how gullible Betty was when it came to her nephews as they avoided chores and wheedled snacks between meals from her.

'How come Graham and Warren don't have to do the washing up?' I asked Betty.

'They are on holidays,' she said.

'So are we,' said Ross. 'It's not fair.'

'Too bad,' she said. 'You can speak to your father, if you want.'

We decided that would cause a bigger problem.

Lassie had given birth to pups a few weeks earlier in a tiny space underneath the front verandah so we poked chop bones through the floorboards for her.

'For goodness sake,' Dad said, finding us clustered around the front step trying to reach through the gap between the boards to pat the squealing pups.

'Leave the bloomin' pups alone. Damn dog's a perfect nuisance.'

Each of us had a go at crawling under the house, but couldn't reach. After four weeks, the pups grew bigger and wandered out into the yard, while Lassie stayed guard, belly hanging with full teats. One by one the pups found homes and Lassie resumed her cow chasing with renewed enthusiasm.

The adults had the bedrooms, so we kids were in the sleepout. Six metal beds with sagging springs and lumpy kapok mattresses lined the inner wall and stretched head to toe around the corner. There was no such thing as privacy. Being half naked in front of each other held no embarrassment for anyone except Zilla, who had not only perfected the art of dressing and undressing under the sheets but stepped out fully dressed, smoothed the few remaining wrinkles on her tightly made bed, then trotted down the line of beds and out the back, tutting along the way at our failed attempts at bedmaking.

Stored in a box underneath each bed, mingled with shoes and clothing, were slingshots, marbles, bows, arrows and other treasures used on a daily basis. We knew not to touch each others' things, and when Ross caught Graham whittling a stick with his penknife he exploded.

'What are you doing with that?' Ross said and snatched the knife from Graham.

'Just wanted to have a look at it,' Graham mumbled.

'Nobody touches my stuff,' Ross said.

'Could've told you that,' I said. 'Sometimes just looking at him gets him upset. No chance of you getting a look at the Tarzan Tree now.'

Ross punched Graham on the nose. Keith heard his howling and decided to investigate, while the rest of us stood around waiting for the fight.

'You know how Dad feels about fighting,' he said, standing between them. 'Now, what's going on.'

'He hit me,' Graham said.

'He pinched my pen knife,' said Ross.

'I just borrowed it.'

'Listen mate,' said Keith. 'We don't touch other people's stuff.'

'You touch my stuff again and ...' said Ross, rubbing his knuckles.

'Nobody's gonna touch your stuff, are they?' Keith stared at Graham and Warren. 'Nobody's gonna touch anyone else's stuff.'

'I'm gonna tell Aunty Betty,' said Graham, as he stomped away holding his nose. Warren followed.

'I'm not sure that's a good idea,' said Keith.

Before dinner, Dad called us all into the back yard. He stood with his arms behind his back shaking his head.

'It seems we had a bit of a disagreement here today,' he said, holding up his hand as both Ross and Graham tried to speak. 'I've heard all about it.'

Obviously, Graham had snitched.

'Family doesn't fight each other,' he said. 'But if you are so keen on it, we're going to do it properly.'

He produced two pairs of boxing gloves from behind his back.

'Keith has agreed to let you use his boxing gloves, so you can have a proper fight. Queensbury rules.'

'Okay with me,' said Ross.

'What's the Queen got to do with it?' I asked.

'I'm not putting those things on,' said Graham.

'You've been obnoxious lately,' said Barbara. 'Time something was done about it.'

I'd expected Dad to produce the strap and for Ross to get a walloping.

'Don't think you can punch someone when you feel like it,' Dad said to Ross. 'Especially family.'

'They're not ...' Dad's stare halted my words.

'Especially family,' he continued, 'but what you do not do is help yourself to someone else's things. I don't care who you are.'

'But, I wasn't ...' said Graham.

'No buts. Don't do it again.'

'Yes, Uncle Ben.'

'No more trouble. Now skedaddle.'

I looked at Betty. Her raised eyebrows and prune lips suggested she was unhappy Ross hadn't got the strap.

A truce was declared between the kids and we kept our disagreements away from the house. All we had to do was survive Christmas, then they'd be gone.

Jumping on our beds became our favourite evening activity. No-one had a problem with it except Zilla. She liked to keep hers flat and smooth. We solved that situation by giving her the bed on the end and the rest we used as trampolines, jumping from one to the other, with the dip becoming more pronounced each time. Tripping over the metal bedheads caused bruised shins, stubbed toes and colliding bodies. Betty tried to outlaw it.

'Let them have a bit of fun,' Dad said. 'It's Christmas.'

'If the bed breaks, what then?' she said.

'I'll fix it,' he said. 'Leave them alone.'

'I need a headache powder,' said Betty.

At five o'clock each day, the shop closed, Dad finished work and the kitchen filled with clinking glasses as the adults sat around the table having pre-dinner drinks. As the evening progressed, the whisky and beer flowed and the volume increased. The locals would pop in and out to say hello, get petrol or pay a shop bill and sometimes joined in. Betty's laughter became louder as she flirted with the men, talking in a high squeaky voice like a little girl. She sat on their knees, cigarette in one hand, whisky in the other, with her arm around their shoulders. It didn't seem to bother Dad, but it bothered us because we knew that in the morning she would be back to her cold, heartless self.

We were shunted outside with a guaranteed supply of Orbells soft drinks. Ross appointed himself the sheriff of soft drink pouring. He lined the glasses up on the front step and filled them so each measured exactly the same. If the level was too high, he'd sip the offending glass until it was correct. A chorus of disapproval erupted over his method and if not for our desire to not waste any, we would've come to blows.

A Christmas tree was dumped in a bucket of sand in the corner opposite the piano, its pine needles shedding over the lounge room floor. We decorated it with handmade streamers cut in uneven strips and thrown over the branches. Another stood at the bottom of the stage in the Mount Hope Hall and on the Saturday before Christmas, Santa Claus arrived in a trailer pulled by a tractor. He climbed down with two red sacks bulging with presents and *Ho, ho, ho'ed* his way into the hall.

'I can see the kids from school,' I said to Ross as we stood in the line that stretched in a curve around the hall, waiting to get to Santa. 'But where did all these other kids come from?'

'Out of town, I suppose,' he said.

There must have been at least thirty kids. I wondered if Santa had enough presents for us all.

'Nice tree,' he said when it was my turn.

'We helped Dad cut it down,' I said, chest out, chin high.

'Have you been a good girl,' said Santa. 'Your Dad tells me you can get into mischief.'

'I've been good.' I was terrified I'd be turned away and the only one not to receive a gift.

'Well, alright then,' he said and, fishing into his bag, handed me a wrapped present, then gave me a big hug.

On Christmas Eve nothing was put under the tree until we were asleep. In the morning we clambered around the tree and waited for Dad to hand out the presents and for the signal to begin unwrapping. Our beds became a jumble of wrapping paper, beach towels, water pistols, cap guns, books, boiled lollies and Christmas stockings. I envied Zilla with her two beach towels while I got a jar of ginger. The only thing interesting about the ginger was the colourful jar. No amount of persuasion could tempt her to exchange one of her beach towels for the ginger.

HOLIDAY HITCH

On Boxing Day, the Neguses went back to Sydney, Keith was picked up by the same family who'd dropped him off and when the two Aunties left the day after, Zilla and Tippy stayed with us. In January, Dad wheeled the caravan out of the shed, we loaded it up with supplies then headed off for a week to Kiama and our first ever visit to the beach.

We left Mount Hope at dawn so we could arrive in Kiama while it was still daylight and wouldn't have to unpack in the dark. Betty and Dad were in the front and we four kids in the back. By the time we arrived in Katoomba Dad's good humour had been strained by our boredom. Disagreements ranged from Ross's ear flicking, whose turn it was to sit by the window, or being irritated by a sibling falling asleep and leaning too far over. Dad threatened to dump us on the side of the road if we didn't cut it out. At Bulli Pass, he put Ross and me in the caravan.

'Right,' he said. 'You two in the van, but no running about inside or I'll tie you on the roof rack next time you misbehave.'

Being alone in the van was exciting as we had a bed to stretch out on, room to stand and a choice of windows to view the road without having to share. We saw patchy blue ocean through breaks in the trees as we sat on the double bed at the back and viewed the side of the mountain while the car negotiated the hair-pin bends. The corners were so tight, cars descending waited for those ascending because there was not enough room to pass. The back of the caravan would hang over the edge on each turn. This thrilling adventure became dangerous when on a turn, one wheel on the caravan dangled over the edge of the mountain and we came to a standstill. The car engine stopped and Ross and I wondered why.

'Are you kids okay in there?' Dad tapped on the back window.

'Yes, Dad.' When we looked out the front of the caravan, three strangers were standing on the tow bar.

'Walk to the door, kids. Take it gently.'

'What's happening?' Ross asked.

'Stand back,' he said. 'I'm going to open the door.'

We heard the twist of a key and when the door opened, half the road was missing. Tree tops and boulders clung to the steep hillside. Dad clipped the door open and I saw a man behind him with Dad's shirt clenched in his hands, leaning back with his boots jammed against a tree stump.

'When I reach in come into the doorway,' Dad said extending his arms towards Ross. 'Hold out your arms. Now, look at me.'

He grabbed Ross under the arms and swung him in an arc over to another man standing beside him, who grabbed Ross. 'You okay, mate?' he asked.

'Whoa,' said Ross. 'That was fun.'

'Bonnie, I want you to do exactly the same,' said Dad, stretching toward me. 'Hold out your arms.'

'It's a long way down,' I said, stepping back.

'Look at my face,' Dad stretched forward and I saw his forehead wet with perspiration, tightened muscles on his jaw.

I looked at Dad and he smiled, 'Come on lass,' he said. 'Give me your arms.'

With a huge swing I was whisked from the caravan into Dad's arms for a big hug to cheers and applause from the strangers in the array of cars and caravans that lined the road. Zilla and Tippy were clapping their hands and jumping up and down beside Betty on the opposite side of the road. Even Betty was smiling.

'Looks like you hit a bit of loose gravel,' said someone as a group of men gathered behind the caravan.

'We'll have you on your way in no time,' said another.

'You go and stand over with the others,' Dad said to Ross and me.

I looked at the van. Ross and I had been sitting in the part suspended over the edge of the cliff. One wheel dangled in space, the other perched on a ledge just below the rim. I thought of falling over the edge and tumbling down the trees and rocks into the hidden depths below and my stomach flipped.

Four men grabbed the back of the caravan as Dad grasped the wheel, stuck his head out the window and crept forward. The van shuddered as the remaining wheel loosened a rock underneath and slipped below the rim. A gasp rippled through the crowd. Boots scraped on the gravel and muscles tightened as the men seized the van with fresh determination.

'Heave men,' said the bloke. 'Give it a bit more throttle, mate.'

A cloud of smoke erupted from the exhaust, the smell of oil and petrol drifted across the road as the engine revved and the wheels churned the gravel. The crowd retreated to avoid the flying stones, despite being out of range. In my mind, our van transformed into the stagecoach I'd seen plummeting over the side of a cliff in the serial at the Cobar Cinema a few weeks before. It had splintered into a million pieces and I reckoned our holiday to the beach would be cut short if our van dropped over the side.

A few more revs and the car edged forward.

'That's it mate,' one of the men shouted as the wheel eased over the edge and gripped the firm ground. With the van out of danger, Dad switched off the engine and stepped out of the car. We all cheered and clapped, relieved the ordeal was over. The men slapped each other on the back and shook hands with Dad. I ran over and gave his legs a hug and felt them trembling beneath my hold.

'Thanks, gents,' said Dad. 'Much obliged. If there was a pub, I'd shout you a beer.'

'Glad to help,' said one. 'A few years ago, there was free beer hereabouts. A truck had a bit of a mishap and his load of beer barrels rolled down the pass.'

'Yeah,' said another. 'We were heading in the opposite direction when they came to rest in the passing bay in front of us. Never seen a crowd gather so fast. Word got around and there was a few hours of free beer. Poor truckie was a bit upset.'

'Well, we'd best be on our way,' said Dad. 'Thanks again, fellas.'

The crowd scattered, horns tooted and hands waved as one by one the line of cars drove off. We were the last to leave.

'I think riding in the van is not such a good idea anymore,' said Dad.

'Wow,' said Ross. 'Look how far down it is.'

'Well, I'm glad we're in here and not down there,' I said.

'Me too,' said Dad. 'Now let's get this holiday started.'

By the time we arrived at the caravan park it was late afternoon and we kids were itching to get down to the beach and wade into the ocean. We rumbled along a dirt road craning our necks out of the windows. All we saw were trees, bushes and different sized caravans dotted around, some with annexes and some without. Seagulls squawked and hopped, pecking at discarded chips, venturing close to folk sitting outside on deck chairs. Dad parked the car in an open grassed area beside a gum tree.

We were already spilling from the doors when he said, 'Everyone out.'

'I can hear the sea.' said Zilla. 'Listen.'

I heard a rumble from beyond the trees. It hissed, thrashed and thumped.

'It smells different,' said Ross.

'That's the salt,' said Dad.

'It's over there,' I said. 'Can we go and have a look Dad?'

We jumped up and down, impatient and excited. I stared at the cloudless sky, hearing the waves as they crashed and faded, breathing in the air and imagining the water to be clear and clean and stretch for at least a mile.

'Before you wander off,' said Betty, 'we need to get the van unhooked and the annex up.'

'But we want to see the ocean and have a swim.' Ross said.

'Hold your horses,' said Dad. 'I know you're on holiday, but we need to establish a few rules.'

'Rules?' I said. 'Please, Dad.'

Our chorused voices drowned out the seagulls.

'Oh, what the heck, shoes off, rules can wait,' said Dad. 'Let's go see the ocean.'

'I think I need a headache powder,' said Betty.

We must've been on the outer edge of the caravan park, because it took a fair bit of walking between vans, bushes and tents and along pathways before we came to a grassy bank with tracks zigzagging over it.

As we approached, the sound of the ocean grew louder and mixed with the squeal of children's voices.

Ross ran up to the top and we followed. A soft, salty breeze hit my face. A white road of sand spread in a curve across the bay. Waves splashed and foamed, reaching towards us, only to withdraw and dissolve, leaving patches of froth on the shore. The dark, gleaming ocean stretched to meet the sky beyond and I imagined a gigantic waterfall beyond the horizon falling into a mysterious land. It was so bright it hurt my eyes. Heads bobbed beyond the waves and children scattered along the beach, filled buckets with sand and built castles.

'It's so big,' said Ross.

'Where are the caves?' I asked Dad. 'I thought there'd be caves.'

'You've been reading too many Enid Blyton stories,' said Dad. 'Off you go. Have a closer look.'

The four of us shrieked our way down to the shore across the soft, spongy, sand squeaking beneath our feet until we reached the tightly packed edge where the cold water tickled and our feet sank into the wet sand. We ran back and forth, dancing to the movement of the water as if it were alive. Tippy plonked down on the foamy, wet sand, digging troughs and watching them disappear each time the sea streamed around him. Ross and Zilla ran in and out, kicking and splashing each other. I turned and waved at Dad and Betty, standing on the bank watching us. Betty had her arms folded and Dad had a big grin on his face.

'Dad, come down,' I shouted. 'It's beaut.'

He shook his head. 'Tomorrow. Come on you lot. We've work to do.'

The sun was setting when Dad finished attaching the annexe to the caravan. Four camp beds were squashed into the small space on one side of the entrance, and a table and two chairs sat on the other. Dad bought hot, battered fish with chips for tea from the shop at the edge of the caravan park. We sat on the tarpaulin floor and ate from the newspaper. My glasses fogged up from the heat and we jiggled the hot chips in our fingers not wanting to miss a mouthful of the crunchy batter and crispy chips. We showered under a tap in the park after dinner and crawled into our beds, willing the night to fly so in the morning we could swim in the sea and play on the beach.

Tippy woke me in the morning by jumping on my bed.

'The beach,' he said. 'We're going swimming. I'm gonna make a big sandcastle and you can help me. There's buckets and everything. Get up, Bonnie.'

'Can we have our bathers?' I shouted into the caravan.

I could hear soft mumbling from inside as Dad plonked his feet on the floor from the bed and the van rocked from side to side with each slap of his bare feet as he walked towards the door.

'Hold your horses, Bonnie,' he said as he shoved his arms into his dressing gown sleeves. 'Breakfast first.'

After breakfast Betty handed us our bathers. The same ghastly ones we wore for swimming in the dam at home.

'Do we have to wear these?' I said. 'I thought we'd have new ones for the beach.'

'This is it,' she said. 'Those or don't go swimming.'

'What's wrong with them?' said Dad. 'They look perfectly good to me. Money doesn't grow on trees, you know.'

I was embarrassed to go to the beach because all of our bathers were made from the same dreadful material.

'But we'll be laughed at. It's alright for the boys.'

'Up to you,' said Betty. 'You can sit on your bed all day.'

The only difference between the boys' and girls' bathers were the straps. The material was heavy and when wet, sagged with the weight of the water. We hated them, but didn't care at Mount Hope because at the dam we got covered in mud. Here at the beach all the bathers I'd seen on girls were light and colourful, covering both top and bottom. These ones appeared to be made out of army uniforms. The thought of wearing them was horrifying because I would be unable to cover my nipples. We envied the kids trotting down to the beach with modern bathers and colourful fringed towels hanging from their shoulders. We despaired at the thin bath towels Betty gave each of us. We tried positioning the straps across our nipples, but they were too thin so Zilla and I decided we would wear our towels to cover ourselves. We paddled on the edge while the boys went swimming.

On the second day, with zinc cream on our noses we discarded the towels and went swimming, despite the sniggers from other children. On the third day, after a lecture from Dad about the cost of a holiday at the beach, we abandoned our towels and built sandcastles, learned to body surf and put up with the sagging bathers when they filled with water and sand. We ate fish and chips every night and made friends with the other kids our age who were staying in the caravan park. I thought if my freckles all joined together I'd have tanned skin but instead they turned green from sunburn and our bodies were tight and pink from calamine lotion.

On the fourth day we were too sunburnt to care that we couldn't go swimming. Movement of our tender, hot bodies was torture. Our camp beds were as scratchy as our bathers. Ross had climbed over the rocks and cut his foot and Tippy had jumped on a jellyfish and stung his feet. Zilla had scraped her knee racing up the road on a borrowed bike and Dad spent most of the time under the bonnet of the car, fixing a rattle in the engine that started on Bulli Pass and hadn't stopped. We had more mishaps here than at home. I went to bed eating chewing gum that ended up stuck to the back of my hair.

Betty tried to remove the tangled mass and each brush stroke hit my sunburnt shoulders. She gave a final tug and slammed the brush down on the table.

'It's no use. I'm getting the scissors.' She rummaged in a top cupboard and brought out the nail kit extracting a tiny, curved pair.

'I don't know about this.' Even though the scissors were small, I imagined a large patch at the back ending up as bald as my father.

'Well, you can wander around with it stuck in your hair or I can cut it out. What shall it be?'

'Okay then. Cut it out.'

She snipped around the offending obstacle and dumped a hairy, misshapen blob into my hand. I decided never to eat chewing gum again. I thought about going outside to join the others when the first drops of rain splattered on the roof of the caravan. The canvas buckled as a large pool gathered on the roof of the annexe from the heavy downpour. We congregated around the opening and watched as trickles turned into flowing rivers outside. The floor of the annexe flooded and our clothes were damp and smelly. We were stuck inside and fought with each other over the boredom of board games and colouring books.

For three days it rained. The temperature cooled, sunburn faded and injuries healed, but the crowded caravan tested Dad and Betty's patience so we packed our soggy things into the repaired car and our holiday at the beach was over.

'Well,' said Dad as we drove out of the caravan park, 'that was a precipitative interlude of multifarious proportions. Let's try the northern beaches next year.'

STAGE DRAMA

For the end of the school year, Mr Burwell organised us all to perform for the parents in the Mount Hope hall. It was an evening of plays, readings and recitals, including an Aboriginal dance which both Zilla and I were in. During the week, Betty had permed her hair and it always put her in a good mood. The bobby pins were discarded and she put on face powder and lipstick each morning. We both wanted her to like us. Mum had been absent for three years and although the memory was fading, we missed having a mother. If we had permed hair like Betty, perhaps she would be kinder towards us. To our surprise, she agreed to perm our hair for the concert.

Our hair was secured with bits of paper into tiny rollers that stretched our foreheads and pinched our scalps. The foul-smelling chemicals were poured over our heads, then we were splashed, rinsed and rinsed again. By the time the rollers were removed, the process had taken several hours of torture. I wondered if the snazzy hair-do was worth it.

When Betty showed us the results in the mirror, Zilla, with her abundance of thick red hair, had a mass of springy curls that spilled over her shoulders and danced as she shook her head. Mine was a frizzy shambles.

'I hate it,' I said to Betty. 'It looks horrible.'

'What?' said Betty. 'I've spent the afternoon ... not to mention the expense of solution.'

'It looks okay,' said Zilla.

'I look ugly,' I said, as I pulled the hair, hoping to stretch the curls out.

'Well that was a waste of time and money. I'll rub Vaseline through your hair,' said Betty, 'Maybe some of the curls will come out. Is that what you want?'

'Yes,' I said. 'I'm sorry.'

Betty dug into the Vaseline jar and seized a large wad which she squelched all through my hair. It made no difference. I was stuck with greasy, frizzy hair.

'There's nothing I can do,' said Betty. 'You will have to let it grow out. For now, it's time for tea then you'll need be at the hall to get ready for tonight.'

When we arrived at the hall, Mrs Thomas, one of the mothers in charge of getting us in order and sorting costumes backstage, grabbed me by the arm.

'What have you done to your hair,' she said.

'It's just a perm,' I said. I didn't know this woman and she was angry with me.

'Aborigines don't have frizzy hair. Wait here.'

I looked at Zilla. She had permed hair but nothing had been said.

Mrs Thomas returned with a bucket of water.

'Right,' she said, pushing my head down into the icy water. 'You will ruin the dance.'

Zilla decided to escape into the dressing room while I had my head dunked several times. A towel was thrown over my head and Mrs Thomas began to rub hard and fast.

'My clothes are all wet,' I said, shivering.

'That's unfortunate. Time for you to get ready for the first dance.'

'What happened to your hair?' said Mr Burwell when I walked towards the dressing room.

'Mrs Thomas said Aborigines don't have frizzy hair, so she stuck my head in a bucket of water.'

'I've seen lots with frizzy-hair,' he said. 'Ah, well, can't worry about that now. Best go get ready.'

The hall filled with all the folk from the district. Chairs scraped, the lights dimmed along with the chattering and Mr Burwell stepped in front of the curtain announcing the start of the concert. Our Aboriginal item flowed without mishap as Zilla and I danced in and around the trees one of which was Tippy. He found it difficult to stand still and halfway through, began to dance along with the rest of the painted bodies. There were several poems, a short Shakespeare recital, then intermission before the main performance for everyone bar those required to change their costumes.

When the hall lights dimmed for the second half, I realized I had a problem.

'I need to go to the toilet,' I said to Betty.

The small room where we sat, had benches on either side and our knees didn't leave much space to move about as we waited for the play to begin. It was cramped and hot, so we'd been encouraged to drink water to keep our fluids up.

'No. You cannot go to the toilet. You've left it too late,' said Betty.

'But I'm really busting.'

'Too bad. You should have thought of that earlier.'

'But I didn't want to go earlier. Besides, it hasn't started yet.'

'The matter is closed.'

A short distance from the back door of the tiny dressing rooms were the outside toilets. One for boys, one for girls.

'Please. I'll be quick. I really, really, really need to go.'

I jiggled in my seat and tried not to think about my full bladder, without success.

I didn't recognise some of the children sitting in the dressing room across from me as I hadn't seen them at rehearsals because they had not been attending school. During morning roll call absences were rarely from illness. '... He's helping his dad with the dipping,' or '... they've gone to the dentist in Dubbo,' or, '... was up all night lambing.'

Everyone had a part in the play. Ross played the father. It was the story of two children who had been sent to bed early by their parents as punishment. The children made a wish to change places with them. Chris and I played magic pixies who sprinkled fairy dust on the parents and children to make it happen. We had a simple dance routine that required a considerable amount of jumping across the stage in bare feet. I was wearing a skirt made from strips of streamer paper that scratched my legs. While dancing in front of the beds on stage, we sang a short song and scattered magic dust. It had worked perfectly during rehearsal.

I tried to take my mind off the situation by staring at the back of the curtain, a large sheet of canvas attached to a wire running the width of the stage. It had splotches of paint the same colour as our kitchen and laundry, with intermittent blobs of grease that added an interesting contrast. I thought I saw the shape of India somewhere in the middle and wondered if it was the same sheet that draped over the caravan in the garage. The piano had been pushed to the back of the stage and I recognised our beds from the verandah.

'Ladies and gentlemen. For our main presentation tonight we ...' Mr Burwell was speaking to the audience from the front of the stage with another introduction.

My legs were crossed and I was beginning to jiggle on the seat.

'Betty, I have to go to the toilet, please.'

'For the last time, no.'

The other kids stared. Those who played in the opening scene were already on stage while the rest of us waited for our cues. The curtain had opened and the play had started. I was in trouble when I stood and was terrified. When our music started playing I couldn't move for fear of disaster.

Chris was standing in the wings, arms above his head ready to go on. He was signalling me but I knew as soon as my legs moved, I'd be in trouble, so I stepped on the top step and squeezed as tight as I could.

'Get moving. You are supposed to be out there.'

Betty gave me a shove and I exploded through the opening and instead of waving my hands above my head wanted to clutch myself. The trickling began. The more I tried to hold tight as I bounced and pranced, the more I leaked. Red and green streaks from my streamer skirt became soaked and the soggy bits dropped. It became a flood as I persisted with my jerky dance, seeing the faces of the audience staring at me as my shame intensified. The stage was becoming a sloppy mess as the rest of the cast filled either side, pointing and sneering. Laughter from the audience and the dressing rooms drowned my shaking knees and thumping chest.

Ross, who was supposed to be asleep, was sitting up, hands over his mouth, eyes boring into mine. I winced as he watched me splashing across the stage. I abandoned the dance and released the remaining contents of my bladder. Chris leaped on to one of the beds and jumped back and forth singing in an effort to keep continuity but he dribbled to silence with everyone else. I ran off stage crying, ashamed and embarrassed, into the dressing room filled with staring faces. Mr Burwell closed the curtain, found cloths to mop the floor and the play recommenced without me.

'How embarrassing,' said Betty as she grabbed my hand and dragged me out the back through the dressing room and over to the house.

'I couldn't help it.' I didn't want to show my face at school again.

'The entire district sitting out there and you have to wet your pants in front of them. If ever I needed a headache powder ...'

'You should've let me go to the toilet.'

Even Dad found an excuse to avoid me the next day. I heard the ute door slam, Ross climbed in the passenger side and they drove up to the mine. Tippy was sitting in the back yard making dirt roads for his toy cars, both Zilla and I were on our beds reading. Betty was hanging out the washing when we heard Tippy howl.

'For goodness sake, you stupid boy.' Betty was cross.

We all arrived at the kitchen door as Betty yanked Tippy up the back steps.

'As if ... It's bad enough ... I've just about had enough of this!' Betty was furious.

She hauled Tippy up the back steps, yanked him by the arms and dumped him in the laundry tub.

'What's wrong Tip?' I asked.

'Don't you speak to him,' shrieked Betty as she forcefully removed his clothing and gave him three hard smacks on his backside.

'Hey,' said Zilla, 'don't you treat my brother like that.'

'That'll teach you to wet your pants,' said Betty as she turned on the tap and splashed water all over Tippy.

'It was an accident,' I said thinking of last night's event. 'He can't help it,' I added in sympathy for Tippy's situation.

'You're being mean,' said Zilla, 'leave him alone.'

'You watch your mouth, young lady,' said Betty still slopping water

'He's shivering, you horrible person. Stop it.' Zilla lunged at Betty and thumped her on the back.

'I'll wash your mouth out with soap, if you don't stop this instant.'

Tippy was crying and shivering, Zilla was pounding Betty and I didn't know what to do.

Betty let go of Tippy, turned, grabbed Zilla and the cake of Sunlight soap sitting in the wire basket dangling from the tap.

'You nasty, horrid, dreadful, terrible, unpleasant ...' Zilla rattled off as many words as she could think of as Betty grabbed her by the hair and shoved the soap in her mouth. Zilla grabbed Betty's arms in a desperate attempt to dislodge the soap, but Betty had such a tight hold Zilla was beginning to have difficulty breathing.

'You leave my sister alone!' I screamed and sprang at Betty. 'Get off her!'

I launched myself at Betty and with both fists, punched her in the stomach as hard as I could. At that moment, Tippy rose from the tub like a monster from the deep, grabbed a jug from the other tub, filled it and poured it over Betty's head. She released her grip and the soap dropped to the floor.

No-one moved. Tippy gently placed the jug back in the tub, the colour in Zilla's face began returning and I stopped shaking. I walked past Betty, lifted Tippy from the tub, took Zilla's hand, walked into the bathroom, and left Betty dripping by the laundry tub.

NOT AN ADVENTURE

'Time to get up.' The voice was hazy, distant. My limbs felt heavy as I struggled to leave my dream. Before I opened my eyes, a soggy cloth was slapped on my face and I couldn't breathe. Drips ran down my neck as I wrestled in panic.

'What the blazes are you doing, Ross?' I heard my father's voice as he strode into our bedroom.

'Just waking up Bonnie.' Ross pulled the cloth from my face and I gasped for breath. 'She wouldn't wake up. I called lots, honest.'

I wiped the drips off my face with the sheet but neither of them took any notice.

'This is how you do it? You're lucky we have a long trip ahead, or you'd be in trouble. Apologise to your sister.'

'Sorry, Bon.' He grinned.

'That's better. Now get a wriggle on, both of you. Breakfast will be ready in a minute.'

'I'm okay thanks Dad.' I glared at Ross and poked my tongue out as Dad left the room. 'I hate you. I'm glad we're going to separate schools. You're mean.'

'What do you think it'll be like?' said Ross, as he pulled the blanket over crumpled sheets and stuffed his pyjamas under the pillow. It was cool inside and dark outside.

'Dunno. I don't want to go.' I was trying to smooth the lumps in my bed without success.

'Come on, you two. Breakfast,' Dad called from the kitchen.

'Where's Betty? Ross asked.

'Three o'clock in the morning is too early for her. She's got to open the store at nine. We're setting off straight after breakfast.'

'How long will it take to get there, Dad?' I asked. 'Where's Moss Vale? Is it near the beach? Will I have my own room? Is it a big school? What's my teacher like?' I leant over the bowl, elbows on the table, spooning corn flakes into my mouth between questions.

'We won't be going anywhere if you don't get a wriggle on and stop asking questions.'

We left at four o'clock. Ross and I both fell asleep before we reached Euabalong West, forty-eight miles east on a dirt road. At Lithgow we stopped to eat vegemite sandwiches and have a toilet break before heading off again.

After seven hours of driving, we arrived in Moss Vale. Dad took us to a cafe for a milkshake with delicious cold, fresh milk with two scoops of ice-cream. The strawberry flavouring on mine dribbled over the side and Ross had chocolate all around his mouth.

'Time to get changed,' Dad said when we finished our drinks.

He drove to the local park and we changed in the toilets. I heard their mumbling in the adjoining men's toilets as I changed into my new school uniform - a baggy, checked dress that was three inches above my knees. My shoes were big, with growing room for my toes. The white hat that sat on my head had a strap that went under the chin and there was no mirror for me to see what I looked like.

Ross was waiting for me when I came out. He wore baggy shorts held up with a belt tied tightly around his waist and a shirt tail hanging out the back of his pants. I felt self-conscious in my outfit.

'Your socks are falling down already.' I pointed to his ankles. He laughed.

'Hat looks funny.'

'Yeah, well, I feel stupid.'

'Okay you two. Let's take a photo. Over by the Oleander bush.'

Dad lifted the box brownie from his bag, instructed us where to stand and fiddled with the camera, checking the film, shielding the viewfinder with his hand, before taking the photos. He was terrible at taking photos and didn't take them often. First Dad and me, then Dad and Ross. When a stranger walked through the park, Dad asked if he would take one with the three of us. We would have to wait until the first school holidays to see them. We squinted into the sun with Dad's shadow in the centre, ears sticking out. Ross and I had been wearing spectacles for about a year and I was still adjusting to the discomfort of the wire around my ears.

It was decided to drop my brother off at Tudor House first. The journey from the park to the school was short.

When we pulled up outside the school, I realized this was the first time I would be separated from my brother. He got out of the car and Dad lifted his suitcase out of the back. We gave each other a clumsy hug, I was afraid I was going to cry.

'Bye, Ross,' I said and hopped back in the car with my face pressed against the window.

'Bye, Bonnie.'

He walked with Dad up the huge steps of the school with his knobbly knees and baggy school shorts. One rebellious sock had already moved down his leg to the shoe. He turned and raised his arm and waved to me before disappearing through a large archway into a dark corridor beyond. I wished to be back climbing trees and playing Cowboys and Indians with him in Mount Hope.

Dad climbed back in and we drove to my new school. We went through gates with *S.C.E.G.G.S. Moss Vale* on the ironwork and up a long tree-lined driveway. A massive two-storey building loomed in front of us. Girls spilled from cars and spread over the gravel, filling the open spaces with checked dresses and straw hats. There seemed to be so many who knew each other. Some hugged and greeted friends, jumping and dancing up and down, all talking at the same time. Others stood beside their parents looking as scared as I was. I stayed close to my father as he grabbed my suitcase and walked with me toward the big building. In Mount Hope there was a total of twelve students and only four girls. How would I cope with so many girls?

A large-bosomed woman with a welcoming smile greeted us in the carpark.

'You must be Bronwyn,' she said. 'I'm Miss Graham. We can take it from here, Mr McLernon. We'll look after her.'

She was wearing a green skirt and jacket with a white blouse underneath. Her hair was short and her face had lines around her eyes when she smiled.

I didn't want to leave the safe and familiar clutch of my father's hand, but he slipped it from mine, gave me a hug then a gentle push towards this strange woman. I looked up into his eyes and, for the first time, I saw tears as he turned and walked away.

'Dad, don't go.' I said, turning to follow him. 'I want to go home.'

He kept walking to the car. I didn't see him drive away because Miss Graham brought her face down to mine.

'It's all right, Bronwyn. I know you are afraid and you don't know anyone yet, but I will keep an eye out for you.' She gave me a hug and it was strange because only my Dad and my Aunties hugged me. I hadn't seen Mum since I was five and she didn't hug me when she left. Betty didn't hug at all.

'Elizabeth,' Miss Graham signaled to a tall girl standing near. 'Take Bronwyn into the sunken garden and stay with her. We will be gathering in the dining room at two o'clock.'

'Come on.' Elizabeth took my hand and led me through to the rose garden. I looked back to find my father but he was gone. I tried not to cry as we stepped down three steps into the sunken garden. Girls gathered around the small flowering bushes in the centre chatting and laughing together. Elizabeth waved to a girl coming down the step then turned to me.

'You'll be okay for a bit, won't you?' she said.

She left me standing beside a red-flowering bush and raced to her friend. She was the only person I had met so far but the two of them walked away together. I was forgotten. No one approached me. No one talked to me. One by one the girls walked up the steps into the main building. The footsteps and chatter faded until I was alone in the silence. I didn't know what to do. I didn't know where to go. My chest was tight, my eyes filled with tears. I crawled under the bush, curled up into a tight ball and wished for a sprinkle of Pixie Dust so I could fly home.

As I sat with my head on my knees. I could hear a bell ringing. Was I still in Mount Hope daydreaming at my desk?

'Bronwyn?'

Polished shoes stood beyond the bush and when a hand parted the branches it released a scent of green leaves and sweet perfume. Elizabeth poked her face in.

'Gosh,' she said, 'I'm so sorry. I was supposed to look after you.'

The realisation I was not at home brought on a fresh stream of tears.

'I want to go home.'

'It's not so bad. Come on.' Elizabeth swept the branches aside and extended her hand to me. 'Didn't you hear the bell? Now I'll have to take you to the dorm myself. You're in Hammond House.'

I took a deep breath and clutched her hand. We walked out of the sunken garden, past the rose bushes and across the circular, gravel driveway towards a towering red brick building. Windows stretched from one end to the other. Elizabeth released my hand and danced up the steps through the darkened doorway before noticing I had remained on the gravel. I was afraid to enter this huge place.

She flicked her fingers, 'Come on, it'll be dinner time soon.' I took a deep breath and climbed the steps and entered a foyer that seemed bigger than our house. I could smell the polished wooden floors that stretched beyond a staircase climbing higher than Jack's beanstalk. It split into opposite directions half-way up. The smooth banister caught my attention and sliding down it would be fun, but the curve at the end could be a problem.

'Sliding down the bannister is forbidden,' said Elizabeth, reading my mind.

As we climbed the creaky stairs, I was distracted by the activity beyond the glass doors below.

'That's the dining room,' said Elizabeth.

A small group of girls quietly weaved in and out between the tables and chairs that filled the entire space, placing knives, forks and white serviettes on all the tables.

We made our way to the landing and turned left onto another set of stairs.

'Hurry up,' she said. 'The others in your year are already unpacking.'

When we reached the top stair, I heard voices drifting down the corridor. We approached a door on the left in the centre, and the woman standing there had a bosom that collided with her waist, reminding me of Aunty Ethel. She squinted at me over spectacles perched on the end of her large nose. A pen stuck out of the bun on the top of her hair and the hands clasped at her belly gave me the feeling I was in trouble.

'This is Bronwyn, Miss Barker,' said Elizabeth. I moved to hide behind her. I'd met so many people, I didn't want to meet any more.

'Ah, yes. Bronwyn. Your suitcase is under your bed. Third from the end on the left. Follow me.' She swivelled on her heel and clomped through the doorway.

'You may go Elizabeth.'

Elizabeth winked at me. 'You'll be fine.' I felt as if my only friend was deserting me.

Animated girls chattered, exchanging photos and examining items of clothing.

Miss Barker clapped her hands. 'This is Bronwyn, everyone. Say hello.'

'Hello, Bronwyn,' sang the room.

Nobody I knew called me Bronwyn. It was weird and unfamiliar as if I had invaded someone else's body. I wanted to be Bonnie back in Mount Hope, climbing trees, following Ross around and causing Betty grief. My face was splotchy with nerves. I ignored the whispers and stares and followed Miss Barker along rows of beds with identical tight covers and a small chest of drawers tucked between. I focussed instead on Miss Barker's ample backside rippling in time with her footsteps. She stopped abruptly and I crashed into her. The laughter in the room was stilled by her raised hand.

'This is your bed,' she pointed to my suitcase on the floor underneath. 'You can unpack and by then it will be time for dinner.' She glanced at her watch and walked away.

'Hello,' said the girl in the bed opposite. 'I'm Sue. This is my first day too. Where are you from?'

'Mount Hope.'

'Never heard of it,' she said, opening a drawer and shoving a pile of underwear inside.

I soon discovered nobody had heard of Mount Hope and almost all of the girls were from Sydney or the south coast.

At the bottom of my case, wrapped in a calico bag was a pearl-handled brush, mirror and comb set. I'd never had one before. It was beautiful. I placed it in a neat line on the top of my cabinet. A folded note fell from the bottom of the bag.

Dear Bonnie,

I thought you would like a new set for your new school.

Betty.

Seeing her handwriting made me homesick again, but I was determined not to cry in front of everyone.

I'd just finished unpacking when the bell rang. The rumble of footsteps hit the stairs as waves of girls swarmed from every opening above and below. They clambered into the dining room; each stood behind a chair, seeming to know where she should sit.

'What are you doing standing there?' The voice came from behind. A tall thin, woman in a pleated skirt looked down.

'I don't know where to sit.'

'Didn't you check the list?'

'List?'

'Goodness me girl, haven't you been shown …' she trailed off with an exasperated sigh and led me to a wall with several sheets of paper stuck on it.

'What's your name?'

'Bon, er Bronwyn McLernon.'

'You're on table one. First on the left.'

The idea of entering another room with so many staring eyes terrified me. A different teacher met me at the door then led me to the vacant seat at table one. She sat down at the head of the table.

Potato pie, peas and gravy was served to each by an older girl.

I picked up my fork with my right hand and glanced around the table.

I soon discovered my eating habits were unsatisfactory.

'Knife *and* fork, please Bronwyn …'

The pie was delicious. Mince in gravy topped with creamy mashed potato, fresh peas and carrots.

'Bronwyn, keep your elbows down …'

I tucked my elbows into my side, turned the fork over and loaded it with peas.

'We do not turn our fork over to eat peas …'

The kitchen doors opened and closed, plates rattled and splashing water added to the hum of conversation around me. I took a slice of bread from the centre of the table and scraped a dollop of butter onto my knife from the butter dish.

'That is not how we butter our bread …'

'You must eat everything on your plate, Bronwyn.'

By the end of the meal I was exhausted from endless instructions.

We were led back to the dormitory to get into our pyjamas, clean our teeth and be in bed ready for lights out at seven o'clock. Girls crowded in the bathroom, jostling for positions around the washbasins in the centre of the room. I stood with my loaded toothbrush and towel wondering if I should plunge in, when Miss Barker walked past the opening.

'Lights out in ten minutes,' she said. 'I suggest you get a move on, Bronwyn.'

Bare feet slapped on wooden boards and echoed around the tiled walls then streamed out the door. I was alone; a relief.

I returned to my bed and climbed in to whispers and giggles from the beds at the far end. The lights went out and the room was silent. I straightened my legs and slid down into the bedclothes. Halfway down I felt a sticky, wet patch. I screamed and the giggles returned.

'What's the matter?' said Sue.

'There's something in my bed.' I sat on the pillow wiping my feet on the top sheet.

A torch light zigzagged down the corridor and Miss Barker pointed it in my face.

'What's going on here?'

'There's something in my bed.' I squinted into the light.

'Good grief, girl. No need to carry on.'

She whipped back the bedclothes and shone the torch onto a stinking mass of squashed snails and chopped grass. The top sheet had been folded in half, preventing my legs from stretching to the end of the bed.

'Oh, that's unpleasant.' She shone the torch down the line of beds. 'Who short-sheeted Bronwyn's bed?'

Silence.

'I want to go home.'

'We will change your sheets and then I expect EVERYONE to be quiet and go to sleep.'

With fresh sheets and further warnings from Miss Barker about misbehaviour, I snuggled into the blankets and tried to go to sleep. The whispering faded and as everyone's breathing steadied, I could not contain my sobbing.

'Shuddup, Bronwyn,' came a voice from the dark.

'We can't go to sleep.'

I tried to stop, but the tears flowed.

'For goodness sake, shut up.' The whispers were angry.

'What's going on with you girls?' Miss Barker and her torch appeared.

'Bronwyn's keeping us all awake with her crying.'

'Well, I'm sure she's a bit upset about her bed,' said Miss Barker.

I jammed the pillow over my head and kept crying.

'Bronwyn, stop that crying this instant.' Miss Barker removed the pillow and once again shone the torch in my face. 'Stop crying.'

'I can't.'

'If you don't stop crying, I will have to punish you.'

I took a breath, but unable to control it, the weeping continued.

'Oh no,' I heard someone mutter.

'All right then,' she said with a sigh. 'Step out of bed.'

Miss Barker picked up my new, pearl-handled hairbrush.

'This will do just fine.' She slapped it a couple of times against the palm of her hand.

'Not my new brush, please?'

'Bend over.'

When I bent over, she wacked me three times on the backside and on the fourth, the head of the brush snapped. She stood holding the handle.

'My brush,' I sobbed.

She picked the brush head from the floor and gave it a quick look.

'That will teach you a lesson, Bronwyn,' she said as she returned it to the dresser and trotted away. 'Now, get back into bed. I'll have no more nonsense tonight, everyone – go to sleep.'

I slid down under the covers, stuffed the sheet in my mouth and cried myself to sleep hating my new school, Miss Barker and crowded rooms. I was eight years old and I couldn't have known this would be my home for the next six years.

BATTLE LINES

The tin door scraped closed, reducing the outside light to a sliver. I stood in the darkness and heard the metal bolt screech into place. With a final click, the lock was secured. Betty's footsteps faded, along with the pungent smell of cigarette smoke. I thumped the door but my reply was a shower of dust. It filled my nostrils, as did the stink of oil, turpentine and paint. I kicked the door in the hope of someone hearing but I knew it was hopeless.

After twelve weeks at school, Ross and I were both glad to be home and away from the rules of boarding school. Dad was away for a few days on business and Betty in charge. It didn't take long for us to get on her nerves.

The shed was the size of our bathroom and sat in a part of the backyard where we didn't play. It was Dad's junk room, the domain of creatures of the dark: real and imagined, big and small. We called it *The Spider Shed* and locking us in was Betty's favourite punishment. When Dad was away for a few days on business, her methods of discipline were harsh. We had learned over the years it was useless to complain. Adults were right and kids were naughty.

'Stop banging on the door, you'll scare the spiders.'

I spun around and squinted.

'Ross? You're in here too? I thought you were under the house. Cripes, something's crawling up my leg.'

'Probably a centipede. Don't stamp your foot. Crikey Bon, now I can't breathe with all that dust you've made. For goodness sake, stand still. I saw a snakeskin when I came in. Looked fresh. Could be hiding in the back. They can get pretty cranky.'

'Don't say that. I hate it here. I hate her. She's horrible. How long do you think she'll leave us this time?'

'Dunno. Don't panic. You'll get used to the dark soon, then you can sit down. There's a chaff bag next to me.'

I fought my fear in the gloom and caught a whiff of pongy socks and brown vinegar amongst the odour of mice and damp wood.

'You farted, Ross.'

'Yeah, sorry. It was the cabbage last night.'

'She's a terrible cook.'

'She can't cook cauliflower and makes awful cakes.'

'Burns sausages.'

'... and can only chop tomatoes and slice Devon.'

'... and drink whisky by the gallon.'

We laughed together and it eased my fear. Daddy Long Legs, Huntsman and Red Backs inhabited the walls, lived behind boxes, in shovel handles, under paint tins and between the stacks of wood. My stomach tightened and I shivered at the thought of a giant spider with spooky eyes staring at me, its hairy legs spinning me into a silky tomb.

I took a deep breath, curbed my imagination and shuffled towards Ross. On the way, I walked into a spider's web and panicked when the sticky lacework clung to my face and hair. The reality of a spider hanging in the middle filled me with dread. I leaped about, clawing at my head, screaming.

'They're crawling all over my face. They're in my hair. Ross? Do something!'

'You're fine. There's nothing there.' He was unruffled by my hysteria.

'How can you say that? The horrible stuff is everywhere and there's got to be a spider. There's always a spider. I can feel it. Ross?'

'Come and sit down. Stop being a sissy.'

I was trembling. I knew he was right. I collapsed on a scratchy chaff bag to the sound of crumpling cellophane as mice scattered from beneath. They were not freaky like spiders. I pulled my legs up to a ridge on the side of the bag and hugged my knees, miserable and helpless. I sucked at my bottom lip and clenched my teeth to stem tears. The stink of the mice mixed with the aroma of fart, grease and fuel was just like Dad's workshop. It took a few minutes for my breathing and mood to calm.

Ross was sitting on the mower. His skinny legs were the same as mine, all knees and feet. His hair was dark brown, mine blond. At nine years, I was one year and ten months younger but we were the same height and often mistaken for twins. Ross hated it, but I liked it. We both wore tortoise-shell framed spectacles, our mannerisms were similar and I felt the same age. We scrapped, teased and fought, but love bonds in moments like these.

'What did you do?' I asked.

'She caught me smoking under the tank stand. I think she counts her cigarettes. What did you do?'

'The new jumper she got me for school was too small so I cut the sleeves off.'

'I hate her. She's not our mother. I've always hated her,' said Ross. 'She only puts us in here when Dad's away.

'This is the third time we've been in here.'

'Yeah, I know.'

'Ross, do you think she does it because she hates us?'

'Who knows.'

'But it's no use saying anything. Dad likes her.'

'Well, I don't,' said Ross. 'I want to push her into the toilet pit and watch her drown in poop.'

'Well, it's a long drop down, but not deep enough to drown.'

Ross fiddled with the starter rope, winding it around his fingers pulling, twisting, punishing his hands. Often tucked in his pockets were bits of string, rubber bands or a piece of rope. He'd pull one out and fidget with it when he was concentrating. He stared ahead, his mind searching, thinking. I waited.

'I'll find a way,' he said.

'It'll have to be soon. We go back to boarding school next week.'

'I know. I hate boarding school. I get the cane more than here. You can't climb trees. The teachers are crabby and strict – and old,' said Ross.

'I've had my bed short-sheeted every night and the house mistress broke my new brush hitting me on the backside. The teachers call me Dolly Daydream.'

'They throw blackboard dusters and chalk.'

'Yeah. At least the food's okay and we don't have to wash up or any of that stuff.'

'School was better here with Mr Burwell. I liked him.'

'Yeah I did too.'

'You know one night I heard Dad and Betty talking about the mine and the shop.' Ross lowered his voice and leaned in as if someone could overhear, but I figured the throb of the generator at the back of the shop would take care of that.

'When was this?'

'Yonks ago.'

Our bedroom wall was next to theirs and when they talked we heard their muffled conversation but not words. On a radio play one Sunday night, a character used a glass to listen to conversation on the other side of the wall and we decided to give it a try. Their conversation was louder but still muffled. Ross took time moving the glass, listening, checking and testing places on the wall. I got bored and watched the sky deepen and change as the summer evening flicked moonlight off the glass when it moved. My fingers couldn't catch the stream and I daydreamed of getting a painting kit, a desk and not sharing a room with my brother.

Betty coughed. The bed creaked. Dad mumbled. I was jolted from my fantasy, Ross was motionless. When all our attempts failed at hearing their conversation clearly, we decided sneaking up to the door to eavesdrop was a better way. It was fortunate their bed creaked when one of them turned over or decided to get up, giving us time to scarper back to our bedroom.

'Bonnie, do you want to hear this?'

'Oh yes. Sorry.' We were back in the Spider Shed.

'They were talking about school. About sending us to live with Aunty Ethel in W.A. with Zilla and Tippy.'

'I don't know if I'd want to live over there.'

'Well, it doesn't matter because Dad told her that Aunty was too old to look after any more kids. They decided we should go to boarding school instead, so they could concentrate on the mine and the shop.'

'Dad said it was for a better education. Do you think she likes us?'

'No, I don't. She's weird,' said Ross. 'I'm going to kill her,'

'I try to like her, but she's mean and cruel.'

'She's horrible. I hate her.'

We heard the rasp of nylon stockings as Betty approached, then the release of the padlock and familiar scraping as the bolt was freed. I imagined Betty's death by stench from all the terrible smells in here when she opened the door. As it ground across the metal strip, a wave of cigarette smoke floated into the shed followed by Betty.

'Right you two. Have you learned your lesson?' Betty said, blocking the exit. 'Well?'

'Yes, Betty,' we said,

'Yes, Betty what? Bonnie?

'I won't cut up my clothes,' I said.

'Ross?'

'And I won't pinch your cigarettes,' said Ross.

'Why are you both so naughty when your father's away?' Betty sighed, then turned and strode up the path. 'Your lunch is on the table.'

'Bonnie, you in?' Ross whispered, winding the starter rope between his hands and pulling it tight.

I looked into his eyes and knew we both wished for better things.

'Yeah. I'm in.'

We'd been in the shed for an hour and it had felt like a lifetime.

GYMKHANA

In the middle weekend of the September holidays the Mount Hope Gymkhana was held. The week before, utes and trucks sped back and forth from the racecourse as the job of repairing and painting the fences, cleaning the toilets and grading the racetrack was carried out. Sheds had been repaired and roofed, railings painted white, fly screens replaced and the signs on the toilets were so big, they could be read from the air.

Ross and I dashed about in front of the loader clearing broken branches, pointing out root growth and any hazards we felt would benefit from a good scrape, while we took turns on Dad's lap assisting with the steering. When we got bored, we walked around the rails of the bull pen and climbed the trees nearby.

To cater for the expected crowd, the publican ordered extra kegs for the beer stand, a 10'x4' shed with a wooden counter. The back storeroom at the shop bulged with boxes of extra supplies. Betty had ordered ice-cream for sale on the day. It was packed in dry ice and came in a large canvas bag. When it arrived on Saturday morning, the ice had melted and most of the ice-cream blocks were soft.

'I can't sell these,' said Betty. 'You two are going to have to eat them.'

'Really?' said Ross.

'I'm not throwing money down the drain,' she said, handing us the canvas bag. 'Take this out to the back yard and eat them all.'

Having ice-cream was rare. A treat reserved for a visit to Cobar or to compensate for the loneliness of boarding school. Our fridge didn't have enough room in the tiny freezer to store it. Still we were stunned by this show of generosity by Betty. It was hard to contain our excitement, an entire bag to ourselves! Inside were foil wrapped blocks the size of a black board duster. Some were mushy and oozed from the seams, but others were firm and cold. We grabbed one each. All this ice cream was a dream. We tucked in.

After the fifth one, my stomach was tightening and they seemed a lot sweeter when soft.

'Eating all these is harder than I thought,' I said. 'I'm getting full.' My hands and arms dripped with the sticky liquid and there were still plenty left in the bag. 'How many have you had?'

'I've lost count. But I think I can eat a few more.'

His arms were in the same mess as mine and we each had a patch on the ground in front of us where ice cream had dripped down our chin and mixed with the dirt. I managed to eat three more.

'I'm gonna be sick. If I eat any more I'll explode.'

'Well, I'm not leaving any,' said Ross, as he discarded the thirteenth foil wrap. 'There's only two left. The rest are mush. Come on Sis, one each.'

At the thought of having to eat one more, I groaned and remembered the thrill of that first mouthful, then sighed and unwrapped the foil as if I was about to eat castor oil.

When Betty came to collect the bag both Ross and I were propped against the office wall surrounded by empty foil wraps. Our bellies were stretched and we looked as if we'd dived into a bucket of milk.

'Oh good,' she said. 'You've eaten them all.'

Ross tilted the bag, too full to speak.

'You two need a good scrub. We're leaving in the car in fifteen minutes to go to the gymkhana. You can come with us or walk.'

'I don't think I can get up,' I said.

'Suit yourself. Maybe you'd like to stay home?' she said, walking back into the house. 'At least you won't be hungry.'

'Stay home?' we both said.

Missing the gymkhana, a once a year event was unthinkable. Fifteen minutes later we were clean, dressed and waiting by the car.

The racecourse was crowded. Loudspeakers blasted out horse races from all over the country as the bookie scribbled on bits of paper and shouted out betting odds. Ink-stained fingers grasped the notes from the flapping hands and jammed them deep into his scratched and weather-worn leather bag. The beer stand was crowded. The publican filled beer glasses with brisk efficiency to shouts of *schooner* and *middy, please mate.*

In the food shed, the babble of conversation and the scrape of knives filtered through the screened walls as ladies from the CWA prepared sandwiches, cut cakes, and plated biscuits ready for lunch. As far as I knew, all the ladies in the district belonged to the CWA and were wonderful cooks. Betty was the exception to this rule.

'Here you are kids.' Into each of our hands, Dad placed a shiny, silver two bob coin. 'There's some money for you to spend. Now off you go. Betty and I have things to do.'

'See ya, Sis,' said Ross, flipping his coin in the air. 'I'm gonna have a look around. Don't follow me.'

I stood watching strangers walk back and forth from the beer stand, the food shed and the toilets until I spied the Chocolate Wheel behind the bookies stand. Torn tickets were scattered around a short, fat man holding a small cardboard box.

'Win a prize on a spin of the wheel,' he shouted, in competition with the bookie's loud speaker. Stacked on a table beside him were prizes wrapped in cellophane and numbered to correspond with the wheel. The big, brown teddy bear with the number eight pinned to its chest, stared at me and I wanted to take him home and sit him on my bed.

'Can I buy a ticket?' I asked the man.

'Certainly can, little lass,' he said. 'That'll be threepence for three.'

I handed him two bob and caught a whiff of his sweet, pungent breath as he put a threepence, sixpence and a shilling change into my hand. He held out a box filled with small cards and I picked three.

'Right-o. Spin the wheel.'

I grabbed the side of the wheel as high up as I could reach and pulled as hard as I could. It spun once and landed on number 15.

'No prize little lass,' he said as I glanced at the teddy bear. 'You've still got two more spins.'

I spun hard with both hands and watched the numbers flash by the rubber flap and slow to stop on number 23.

'You're not having much luck, are you, little lass? Here, let me help you this time, might bring you luck.'

He covered my hand with his, then gave the wheel a whopping yank. I could still feel his cold and greasy touch as the wheel spun and while the flap ticked, I wiped my hand on my pants.

Please, please, please. I willed it to stop at number 8. It stopped on number 5.

'You've won a prize this time, little lass.' He rummaged on the table.

'Can I have the teddy?'

'Look. You've won a three-tiered cake and biscuit container.' He held it out to me. 'It's got gold labels on the front and each one is a different colour.'

'I wanted to win the teddy.'

'Sorry, little lass. Not this time.'

Betty was delighted when I showed it to her later. 'It can sit on the kitchen bench and we will fill it with biscuits.'

After wasting threepence on the Chocolate Wheel and not winning the teddy, I decided to hang on to the rest of my money. I was still full from the ice-cream binge before lunch and spent some of the afternoon wandering around trying to find someone to play with. Being at boarding school had distanced me from the kids at the Mount Hope school. They were not unkind, just distant. Chris had moved to Griffith with his family and Paddo was busy with his horse. I felt insecure and shy.

I spent the afternoon at the rails, watching the horse races. There were five races and since Paddo was a keen horse rider, he'd entered a few of them. He flew past the finish line whacking the horse's rump with the whip and making the same weird hissing sound through his teeth he did when he was racing in his billycart. The last race of the day was the Mount Hope Cup and I was leaning against the rails watching the horses jostling together over the other side of the racetrack.

'That's Dad on number seven,' said Ross as he joined me as the starting pistol fired.

Five horses galloped around the bend and entered the straight for the first run past and I stared at Dad as he flashed by on number seven. He was leaning forward, hugging the horse's mane, cap jammed on his head and backside bumping up and down. One arm whipped the flank and the other held the reins as clods of dirt and dust danced around the pounding hooves. He was wearing a black and yellow striped, silk cap. The hissing from the spectators around me got louder. It fascinated me. Why do they do that? I wondered.

'Gosh. I didn't know Dad could ride a horse? He looks like a bumble bee in goggles,' I said. 'Where'd the horse come from?'

'Dunno, 'cause we don't own one,' said Ross. 'Do we?'

'Don't think so.' The horses had reached the turn for the final run down the straight. 'Look, he's coming first.'

A cloud of dust followed the riders as they approached the finish line. I noticed Paddo, his face contorted as he edged his sizeable horse alongside Dad's. The oldest and the youngest riders. We joined in the collective roar of encouragement with the crowd as the two riders became level, horses straining, heads stretched and noses snorting. Tearing down the outside, another rider joined Dad and Paddo and as the flag dropped the crowd became a muffled hum as they debated who was the winner. The competitors trotted off into the scrub, to slow and cool the horses then returned to the finishing post as the officials huddled to discuss the results. Dad waved to us and I was still too shocked to respond. He didn't look like my Dad, sitting on a horse.

The loudspeaker crackled. 'First place ...' the crowd stared at the loudspeaker and waited. The name mentioned was neither Dad nor Paddo. Cheers exploded in agreement. Paddo was second and Dad, third.

'Some ring-in from Hillston,' said the bloke standing behind me.

Dad went off to the beer tent with the winner to slaps on the back. Someone handed him a beer and he became lost in a sea of men while Ross and I hovered on the edge watching them congratulate him on his ride. When Dad had had a few beers, the loudspeaker declared the final event of the day; bull riding.

The bull pen was a patch of ground in the middle of the racetrack ring. The crowd walked under the wooden rails and crossed the track, jostling for the best position to view the bull riding. Inside a small barrier, snorting and pawing the ground was the bull. When the gate flew open, out he shot, man on top, kicking in a crazed attempt to dislodge his unwanted cargo. Coins flew from the pockets of the bull's passengers and were buried in the dust by thrashing hooves. Ross stood high on the fence, shouting encouragement to the bull while I preferred to remain with a bigger gap between myself and the action. So far, it had succeeded in removing all but one rider before the one-minute whistle sounded.

'Look at all the money flying out of the pockets,' said Ross as another rider made an ungainly dismount. 'We'll come down in the morning and collect what's left.'

'We won't get into trouble, will we?' I was concerned with the fallout from Betty.

'Nah, they're all drunk,' he said. 'Hey look, there's Dad.'

I peeked between the rails. Dad had one hand clinging to a rope tied around the bull and one arm chopping the air above his head. Oh no. I could handle the horse riding, but this was an embarrassment. He was too old. With weird fascination I watched as the sweat sprayed from beneath his hat and he swayed and jerked, thumping and banging against the bull's back. I waited for disaster, holding my breath in fear. When the whistle blew, the crowd roared, the horse rider grabbed Dad, pulled him off while the bull was distracted by two other men, and put him on the fence. He grabbed the top rail with shaking arms and jumped over, slapping his hat against his dusty trousers. He'd made it through to the two-minute whistle and despite my unease, I was proud of him.

'Boy, wasn't that something?' said Ross. 'Dad bull riding.'

'Not really,' I said. 'I hope he doesn't do that again, it's too scary.'

The bull was loaded on the truck and it wasn't long before the grounds emptied and the gymkhana was over.

'I didn't like it when you rode the bull, Dad,' I said as we hopped into the ute to go home.

'Keeps a man young,' said Dad. 'Does shake the bones around, though.'

'I didn't know you could ride a horse, Dad,' said Ross. 'When did you learn to do that?'

'When I was a boy ...' he began.

I wanted to listen this time.

***

The wind howls through the cavern as they descend the rocky path. The lamp flickers, then dies ...

Ross wrenched the covers back and I threw the book and torch into the air in fright.'

'Come on,' he said, 'it's time to go.'

'Don't do that. Crikey, I thought you were a ghost.' He knew how to scare me, choosing moments when I was under the covers, lost in a book.

'We're meeting Paddo at the racecourse tonight, remember?' He thrust my sandshoes at me and I held out a shaking arm.

'Dad? Betty?'

'Asleep, snoring their heads off. It's nearly eleven o'clock. Hurry up.'

'Moon's up,' I said seeing beams of light filling the room.

'Yeah, so we won't need the torch,' he said.

We climbed out the window, taking care we were as quiet as possible. On the way through, my nightie caught on the latch and I heard it rip as I jumped down. In the quiet evening, the sound was magnified.

'Oh no. Look at this. It's torn right through to the hem. Boy, am I going to get it if Betty finds out,' I whispered.

'You worry too much. We'll think of something. Let's go.'

He jumped onto the fence and walked along the top rail to the gate post then jumped over. I followed, and we jogged down the dirt track to the racecourse. It was as though a spotlight had been turned on. The full moon highlighted every building and tree in town. The night was warm and quiet. A slight breeze rippled the hairs on my arm as the torn flaps of my nightie hit the back of my legs, reminding me I'd need to find the sewing box when we got back. The bushes rustled as invisible creatures were disturbed by the sound of our soft chatter and footsteps. Above us, we heard flapping and saw the silhouette of an owl gliding across the face of the moon. I shivered and rubbed my arms.

'Do you think it's safe?' I said.

'No, 'course not. This is going to be fun.'

'I'm not sure about this. It only happened last week.'

'Don't be a wuss. It'll be fine.'

When we got to the racecourse, Paddo wasn't there. He lived with his mum, dad and brother down the road from the pub in a house that Dad said would blow over in a willy-willy. He could drive a tractor and ride a horse but when we met at the racecourse he wouldn't walk. He'd ride his bike because it was too far, often cutting through the bush rather than take the road.

'Maybe he's not coming,' I said.

'He'll be here.'

We sat on the wooden table beside the pepper tree that had been struck by lightning and split into a deformed shape. The boughs drooped either side of the blackened trunk like hunch-back twins.

'This is where it happened,' said Ross. 'You're sitting right on the spot where he died.'

'Holy smoke.' I leapt off the table and backed away but something blocked me from behind. It took hold of my arms, then reached across my chest and squeezed. Warm breath engulfed my face, words exhaled on stale cigarette smoke. They whispered in my ear.

'You ... are ... going ... to ... die ...'

I couldn't breathe. Ross stared at me, mouth open.

'Please don't hurt her. She's only ten.'

'Course not,' said the voice, dropping me to the ground.

Ross slapped the table and laughed. 'You should see the look on your face, Bonnie. So, you made it then, Paddo.'

Paddo strutted over to the table and hoisted himself up, his coal-black hair and deep brown skin a silhouette against Ross's pale skin. For a moment they were cardboard cut-outs sitting side-by-side on the picnic table.

'Geez your breath stinks. You're such a jerk, Paddo,' My nightie was both torn and dirty now and I fought to control tears of anger. 'That was not funny.'

'Couldn't get away,' said Paddo.

'Where's your bike?' said Ross.

'Left it back there near the fence. So, this is where Charlie died.'

'Yeah. He was eating his dinner,' said Ross.

'I heard someone in the shop say he was eating fish and chips,' I said.

'Fish 'n chips? His wife must've cooked them,' said Paddo. 'You can't buy them here.'

'His head was bashed in and his brains spilled all over the table,' said Ross, 'and as the rock crushed his head, lightning struck the tree and it split in two right when he died. Thunder covered his screams as the murderer hit him over and over.'

'How would you know? You're making that up.'

'Even the copper was sick when he saw it.'

'You're both gross,' I said. 'Anyway, I thought he was shot.'

'The killer could've got angry and bashed his head afterwards,' said Ross.

'Dad took the body to Euabalong West and Mum had to clean up the mess,' said Paddo.

'I didn't know that, Paddo.' I said. 'Must've been horrible.'

'Yeah. She was pretty upset. Dad told me Charlie still comes here and wanders around in the full moon because he doesn't know why he was killed.'

'Yeah. And wanders around looking for the fellow who did it.' Ross was standing on the top of the table acting like a zombie.

'You two don't know what you're talking about,' I said.

'I thought his son did it?' said Paddo. 'They put him in the lock-up in Euabalong.'

'Didn't they let him out, 'cause they couldn't find the gun?' said Ross.

The tree beside us sighed and the wood creaked as wind whispered through the leaves. We were silent as the branches rose and fell in a slow-motion waltz. Silver pools reflected on the surface of the leaves, transforming them into winking eyes. With the quiet came a chill that turned our breath visible. Ross grabbed the edge of the table and sat back down. Paddo was motionless. I was transfixed by the shifting display. The breeze lifted a branch. It moved forward in slow motion, shedding leaves with each step. It raised an arm. I saw a gun pointing at me.

'RUN.' I screamed, 'RUN.'

Paddo hurtled into the bush and for a moment I wondered if he was going in the right direction for his bike. Ross charged past me, vaulted over the fence, and was already halfway up the road before he turned to see if I was behind him. I wasn't. I had tried to copy his leap. The take-off had been perfect, but my nightie had caught a wire on the top rail as I sailed over, causing the minor tear to become a major disaster. No amount of sewing could repair it. Once again I was lying face down in the dirt. My concern over the pursuing ghost faded and was replaced by the terror of facing Betty with my dirty, shredded nightie.

SHORT DELAY

In 1957, winter term at boarding school loomed. After two years, I still hadn't adjusted to the number of girls, their personalities and the cramped dormitories. It was a chilly midnight start in soft drizzle when we left Mount Hope for the journey to Moss Vale. Ross and I soon fell asleep on the back seat of the Oldsmobile to the warmth of the heater, throbbing motor and swish of the tyres on the wet, dirt road.

When the car stopped, we woke to the lowering revs and increased racket on the roof. Rain blew sideways against the windscreen, pushed upwards by the blustering wind, preventing a clear view of the road. The wipers struggled against the flow, the blades thumped across the glass with the pulse of a damaged metronome. Sandy Creek was no longer dry. The concrete tracks, a guide to preventing car wheels sinking into the sandy bed, were buried beneath a surging river. Through the deluge we watched as the banks of the creek crumbled against the fast-flowing torrent, carrying debris caught in the rush. A branch sailed past, its leaves reflected in our headlights.

Dad grabbed a spare army blanket from the boot and stuffed it into the grill at the front to prevent water seeping into the engine.

'Brace yourselves kids,' said Dad. 'This could get rough.'

Despite the trust I had in Dad's ability to conquer any difficulty, I was filled with dread at the thought of driving into the murky stream. My fingers squeezed the leather on the front seat, my heart knocked against my rib cage. Dad put the car into first gear and gripped the steering wheel. Boarding school had introduced me to a daily dose of the bible and the comfort of belief. I prayed for Moses to appear and part the water.

I glanced at Ross. His hands matched mine. As we edged forward into the current, the car stalled. The headlights dimmed and all I heard was our breathing inside and the lapping water outside, pushing against the car.

'Bugger,' said Dad, 'looks like we're stuck.'

'We'll get washed away,' said Ross. 'The car will float all the way to Dubbo.'

'Stop that, Ross. You'll scare your sister.'

'Dad? There's water coming through the door,' I said as the frigid liquid began oozing through the bottom of the door against our warm feet.

'Wind your window down. I'll have to carry you to the other side.'

With the window down, we heard the rush of the water coming from upstream. The warmth inside the car was replaced with biting night air as Dad reached in, lifted me through the opening and carried me over to the dryness of the other side. He waded back through knee-high water and returned to the bank with Ross.

'We have to walk,' he said. 'I know a bloke who owns a farm a couple of miles up the road. We can stay the night.'

'What about the car, Dad?' I looked at the Oldsmobile, stranded and alone in the middle of Sandy Creek. 'Are we going to be late for school?'

'The car's not going anywhere. We'll sort it in the morning.'

We walked in the middle of the road, Ross and I on either side, holding Dad's hand. The rain became a drizzle then stopped. At the end of a long, straight stretch of road, the moon hovered, spreading a shaft of light in front of us.

'God will look after us,' I said, feeling an overwhelming desire to offer comfort and reassure Dad I was absorbing some of the lessons from school with chapel twice a day and scripture a couple of times a week. God was a force I tried to embrace despite the lack of interest from my family.

'Hummph,' said Dad.

There were no open fields or blinking lights as we journeyed along an avenue of swishing trees. Dad answered our questions on space travel, super-heroes and volcanoes with brevity, while Ross and I clashed over small details of opinion, interrupted only by the occasional movement of a creature in the bush. I felt as if we were alone, explorers in another land, yet the comfort of Dad and Ross's presence scattered my fear. I wanted it to be like that all the time. Just us. Together. Family.

We turned on to a side road that curved and zig-zagged around the scrub, dodging puddles and broken branches. The protection of light from the moon dimmed as the growth above us formed a domed roof across the road.

'The farmhouse is just up ahead,' said Dad.

The sound of a barking dog indicated we were close. A few moments later, a light quivered, its beam flickered back and forth forming a circle around a shadow of a man. We walked across a clearing and stopped at the steps leading to a front verandah.

'Ben? What the blazes are you doing out here?'

A man in dressing gown and rubber boots, holding a tilly lamp, gazed down at us.

'Bit of a problem at Sandy Creek.'

'Not surprised with all the rain we've had. Been a few years since that flooded. Come on in. It won't take long to get the fire going, then we can get you a hot drink.'

We walked through the screen door past the living room with three rocking chairs and the wall mural of a bullfighter.

'Son's an artist. Haven't the heart to paint over it.'

'I like it,' I said as we walked down a long hallway and entered the kitchen, one of the biggest I'd seen. Pots of every size and shape dangled on hooks from a rack above the enormous wooden table in the centre of the room, one that could sit at least twenty people. Around the walls, cupboards stretched to the ceiling.

'Wow.' Ross and I exclaimed together.

'We feed the shearers in here,' said the man. 'Sit down. It's a bit of a trek from Sandy Creek. You kids must be tired.'

'A bit,' said Ross.

'Then let's get you a warm drink and a bit of a feed, then your Dad and I will go and sort out your car.'

'Thanks mister,' I said, laying my head on my arms. I fell asleep to the hum of conversation and the clank of a kettle being placed on the stove.

A beam of warmth spread across my face and I opened my eyes to sunshine seeping through a gap in the curtains. I was wearing a white cotton nightie and lying in a small brass bed covered in a colourful patchwork quilt with three teddy bears propped against the end staring at me. A cosy, friendly room. The matching bed opposite was empty, but unmade, so I climbed out, opened the door, and followed the sound of chattering voices.

The door at the end of the corridor opened and Dad stepped through.

'Oh good, you're awake,' he said. 'Everyone's having breakfast.'

I followed him into the kitchen where almost every place at the table was occupied. Plates were filled with lamb chops, bacon, eggs, and toast. In the centre were a jug of fresh milk, a bowl of jam and two racks of toast. Everyone said *Morning Bonnie* as Dad showed me to the empty chair beside him. A short, chubby woman in a dark blue apron placed a plate full of food in front of me.

'Tuck in, love,' she said. 'There's plenty.'

A glass of milk and the butter dish appeared. I looked up to see Ross sitting opposite, eating with gusto. Breakfast at home was cornflakes with lumpy powdered milk, burnt toast and, on occasion, boiled eggs, so this was a feast. I counted twenty people seated at the table - seven children and thirteen adults, chatting and laughing as salt, pepper, sugar and butter travelled back and forth across the table from one hand to another against a background of jingling cutlery and scraping chairs.

'The car,' I said to Dad. 'Is it still stuck in the creek?'

'It's loaded and ready to go,' said Dad. 'Harry pulled it out this morning.'

'Not before getting the truck bogged too,' said Harry, the man who met us last night.

'Yeah,' said one of the lads sitting at the table. 'Dad had to come back and get the tractor to pull out both the truck and the Ols.'

'Sandy Creek looked like a traffic jam,' said Harry. 'But we got her cleaned up and she's ready for you to finish your journey.'

'We'll set off after breakfast,' said Dad.

'I'm going to be late for school,' I said. 'I'll have to catch up.'

'Can't we stay here?' said Ross.

'What do you reckon, love?' said Harry to the woman in the dark blue apron.

'Charlie, you got room in the shearers' quarters for a couple of kids?' she said to the giant at the end of the table, sucking the marrow from a chop bone.

He licked his fingers, 'Yeah, we can fit 'em in,' he said, 'but they'll have to sleep standin' up.'

The room became still and silent. I looked at Ross, then Dad. I tugged his sleeve.

'Dad?' I said.

'Can you drive a tractor?' asked the giant.

'Ride a horse?' asked another.

'Crutch? …'

'Plough? …'

'Shear? …'

'Weld? …'

The questions came from everywhere.

'Ah ...' Ross looked dazed.

'It's tempting,' said Dad. 'Maybe in a couple of years.'

'That's a shame,' said Harry. 'Always lookin' for good workers.'

One by one, the men said goodbye and left, the children cleared the table, stacked the dirty crockery and cutlery and began to tackle the washing up while Ross and I changed into our clothes, collected our things and walked out to the car.

'Come and visit again sometime,' said Harry. 'When the creek is empty and we're not in the middle of shearing.'

He and Dad shook hands. We thanked him and recommenced our trip in a clean car with the lingering smell of wet leather inside.

'They were nice,' Ross said.

'Yeah. They were,' I said. 'But we have to go to school. I can't miss my piano lesson.'

I'd been studying piano for two years now and I loved it. Dad bought a used Beale Player piano in 1955 so we could all practice during the holidays. It was my escape from the terrors of home and the loneliness I felt at boarding school.

Despite the flooded creek, these times with Ross and Dad going between school and home, was when I felt happiest.

EASY ON THE BRAKE

Another term at school was over and then we were back home to the routine of house chores and shop work. It was Saturday. The shop was closed and Ross was fiddling with his bike.

'Bonnie, put on your boots and come with me. You can drive.'

Dad's bald head filled my bedroom window and I pricked my finger, startled by his voice. I was sitting on the floor poking pin holes around the pictures on old Christmas cards. I had made the mistake of saying I was bored and this was Betty's solution for curing it.

'Pardon?' I said, ' Did you say, drive?'

'The back fence-line needs spraying.' He disappeared and I heard his boots crunching up the gravel driveway. 'Get a wriggle on, girlie.'

The pile of cards scattered as I darted out the back, shoved on my boots and dashed over to the ute. Had he said something about me driving? My driving experience consisted of kangaroo hops up the driveway in the automatic and I found it difficult seeing beyond the bonnet because of the upward slope. On another occasion both Ross and I had a turn at the wheel on a trip to Cobar. I lost control in the corrugations, ran off the road, almost hit a tree and did a one-eighty spin that got applause from my brother.

Dad was leaning against the door, arms folded and legs crossed, when I charged up bursting with excitement. I looked upwards from his patched overalls into glasses streaked and splashed with splotches of oil.

'Ready, Dad.' The fact that I was ten didn't bother either of us.

He opened the driver's door and I jumped in.

'The windscreen's dirty.'

'Never mind about that.'

Dad reached under the seat and the bench shot forward so fast I slid off, hit the steering wheel and landed on the floor.

'Tight springs,' he said. 'Up you get. We'll be here all day at this rate.'

He closed the door and I found I was able to reach the steering wheel and accelerator if I sat on the edge.

Dad climbed into the passenger seat, with his legs pressing hard against the glove box because the seat was so far forward.

'Windscreen's dirty,' he said, unfolding from the seat and getting out.

He sloshed water from a bucket kept on the shop verandah and rivers of red dirt ran down the glass and over the bonnet. I decided this would be a great time for revision and glanced over the controls trying to remember what everything did. Brake, Gas Pedal, Gear stick, Park, Reverse, Drive, Low. I thought back to the driveway stint when he'd showed me the basics. I wanted to impress him with my brilliant recall, but was distracted by the remaining dribbles weaving down the glass and distorting the road. They spilled over a grasshopper crushed against the windscreen wiper and dripped into the grill below. Dad hopped back in, put his left arm out the window and tapped the roof.

'Let's go.'

I stared at him, emptying my mind of watery patterns, panic filled my brain. He must have cleaned his specs because I saw the grey in his eyes.

'Now?'

'Yes, now Bonnie. The key, turn it.'

I turned the key and when the engine started I grabbed the steering wheel with both hands, pushed the lever over to the 'D' and stamped on the accelerator, gripping the wheel with all my might. We didn't move and the high engine revs almost drowned out Dad's words.

'Hand brake,' he shouted.

Dad didn't see the need to fill the instructions with unnecessary words and I was too busy concentrating to talk. I stretched to the hand brake under the dashboard near the driver's door and wrestled with both hands trying to release it. I twisted, pulled and wrenched, my energy and confidence draining. I felt the lure of poking holes in Christmas cards and wanted to give up.

'It's too tight.' I was on the verge of tears.

He reached across me and with a quick jerk put me out of my misery. The car hurtled forward because I was still pressing the accelerator.

'Brake. The brake, girl.'

I slammed my foot on the brake and Dad whipped forward, his head hitting the windscreen. There was a red mark on his forehead to add to the existing grazes and bruises from the workshop and underground. I scanned his face for signs of anger. As he reached toward me and I thought I was getting a cuff on the ear, but his arm went behind to the back rest for his hard hat.

'Sorry, Dad.' I sniffed and wiped my nose on my sleeve.

'That'll save my noggin. Go easy on the brake girl. Righto. Take us out to the fire break.'

The fire break was on the back fence-line and a five-minute drive. The only bitumen was a strip in front of the pub, everywhere else was dirt. The roads were rarely graded and wheel ruts, potholes and half-hearted rabbit burrows were common. I eased down on the gas pedal and we jerked forward, bouncing up and down in the cabin as I struggled to regulate the pressure of my foot on the pedal. We could've walked faster.

'The weeds need sprayin' today' said Dad, 'so give it a bit more gas.'

'My leg's straight out and I can only just see over the top of the steering wheel.'

'Well, look through the wheel. Keep your eye on the road. Watch out!'

A red tail disappeared under the car.

'Bert will be cranky if you kill one of his dogs.'

I was crawling along, so the dog could weave in and around the wheels without the risk of being killed. I felt the ridge of vinyl sticking into me as I gripped the seat with my bum. My hands held the steering wheel in a vice-like grasp. The limited view of the road dictated the speed.

'Can I stop for a minute, Dad? My backside's gone numb.'

'Strike me pink, girl. When I was your age I was roping horses, rounding up bullocks and branding cows. There was no time to be wasting because of a numb backside.'

'Sorry I mentioned it.' I wriggled on the seat and tried to ignore the numbness. After driving three times up and down the fire break, I was doing it without the jerks and revs.

'Time to go to work.' Dad hopped out and shook his legs to get the circulation back. He banged and thumped around in the back as he moved drums and set up the equipment for spraying. If I got out I'd have to wrestle with the handbrake again so with the engine running, I sat and waited.

'I'll be standing on the back.' Dad appeared at the driver's window.

'Two taps on the roof to start.'

He demonstrated.

'One to stop.'

Another demonstration.

'Put it in low gear and drive at five miles an hour and for goodness sake, easy on the brake.'

'Yes, Dad.' It sounded simple enough. One – stop; two – go; five miles an hour. I repeated it out loud just to make sure. I missed the first two taps.

'Get moving, girlie,' Dad shouted from the back.

The trial run seemed easier. Now that Dad was in the back, I noticed potholes and broken branches in my path as I peered through the wheel from the road to the speed gauge. I was so busy concentrating on these that when I heard Dad's one bang on the roof, I jolted in fright, slammed my foot on the brake and came to an abrupt halt. Dad became airborne and, with the hose clutched in his right hand, went sailing over the side of the ute past the driver's window in a magnificent arc, landing face down in the dirt.

I thought about the various ways Ross and I had researched learning to fly and wondered if this would be a method worth further investigation. It also reminded me of the various riders who had been ejected by the bull at the gymkhana.

'Dad, Dad, are you all right?' Should I get out? I took the cowardly route and stayed where I was with the safety of the door between us.

He groaned and rolled over. Thank goodness he was alive. He'd landed beside the front wheel, was spitting dust and trying to breathe, clutching the hose in his left hand. I would be banned from driving forever. He shifted his legs and I could see they were working. *Move your arms, please Dad.* He used both arms to prop himself up and for a short time sat on the ground catching his breath. I was silent. Good. His arms worked. I felt uneasy now, because he was okay and a bollocking would be next.

Dad looked at me. His specs were lying somewhere and his face was covered in dirt. All that was visible were his eyes and the pink inside his mouth. He scrambled around in the soft soil searching for his specs. He blew on the lenses in an unsuccessful attempt to remove the dust. I braced myself for the worst of his wrath.

'Dad?'

'Easy on the brake, girl.'

* * *

The ute raced down from the mine and came to an abrupt halt at the front of the store scattering stones across the concrete. Dad sprang out and charged through the doorway accompanied by a wash of fine powdery dust that obscured the front posts and followed him into the store.

'Gee Dad, I just swept ...'

'Get on the blower, Betty. Tell Pansy to get the fire brigade to the pub. All hands on deck. We've got a blaze happening the other side of Violet Cignet's place. Saw the smoke from the hill.'

Betty was standing behind the counter, beside the phone on the wall. She reached over, lifted the ear-piece from the phone and wound the handle on the side to connect with the exchange down the road. Pansy was the Post Mistress and we shared our line with three others on a party line. Each had a special ring. One long ring connected to the exchange. The mouthpiece was a good height for Betty, but not low enough for me to reach without standing on a box. But then I wasn't allowed to use the phone.

'Pansy said George put the word out his end. They're on their way,' said Betty as she hung up.

'The fire truck's out the back,' said Dad as he lifted the counter flap and stopped to unscrew a jar containing musk sticks. He removed two, popped them into his mouth and the horror of wearing a cardboard sign around my neck for stealing flashed through my mind. I tried not to look at Betty.

'How bad's the fire, Dad?' I followed him out to the workshop.

'If it gets to Violet's house we'll be in trouble.'

'Bonnie, where do you think you're going?' said Betty.

'I was just ...'

'Back to work, miss. I think your father can manage without you.'

Dad arrived out the front with the truck loaded with the water tank.

'Fill 'er up, Bonnie.'

While I was doing this, more trucks arrived and lined up waiting to be filled with petrol.

'Where's Ross?' I asked Dad.

'He's on the hill loading the equipment with the others,' he said, as he climbed up the steps of the truck.

'Ya got the kids on the job, Ben,' said the publican as he came alongside ready to fill.

Betty rushed out the door to Dad. 'Ben, Pansy says the train's stuck at Roto. Fire's close to the railway line. There's a team heading from Euabalong to help. Some from Condobolin and Lake Cargelligo are out there fighting from the other side.'

'Struth,' said Dad. 'Must be a big one. Is everyone at the pub, Merv?'

'Yep. I'm the last to fill.'

'Let's get cracking. Time's wasting.'

The publican sprang into his truck and they both drove up to the pub. Truck doors slammed, engines revved and horns tooted as the team headed out to Violet's house.

In the distance, smoke stretched across the horizon. The hills were covered in a grey haze as intermittent orange flames leapt above the tree line.

'He'll be all right, won't he?' I asked Betty.

'Right Missie, back to work.' Betty shoved a scrap of paper at me. 'These are the potato and onion orders for deliveries.'

'Yes, but will Dad be okay?'

'I'm sure he'll be fine. Now we work.'

Betty didn't waste paper. New sheets were for business orders and correspondence and everything else was recycled. Customer orders were written on the backs of discarded letters and Betty wrote everything down in shorthand. None of us kids could understand the loops and curls. I expressed an interest in learning but after a month of lessons with Betty, I had failed to grasp the basics. She thrust another order at me written in shorthand.

'You'll find all these out the back,' she said. 'Bob's waiting for the extra order.'

Hieroglyphics meant nothing to me.

'Oh, that's right. You can't read it, can you?'

She wrote the message in English and I trooped out the back. After a morning of filling orders, I was returning to the front of the shop when Dad pulled up. He entered through the front door and removed his spectacles. Rings of soot surrounded his eyes. There were streaks of black ash across his cheeks. His hat had left a white circle around his forehead and he smelt as if he'd been standing beside the incinerator.

'Nearly lost Violet's house,' he said, rubbing his eyes, smudging more soot. 'She wouldn't leave. Damn fire was burning the back fence and she still wouldn't leave.'

'Is she okay?' asked Betty.

'Yeah.' He flopped down on a chair near the front door. 'Grab us a soft drink out of the fridge, Bonnie.'

'Do you want Creaming Soda, Orange, Lime, Lemonade or Pineapple?' I said, rattling off the list of flavours.

'Crikey, Bonnie,' he said. 'Something cold will do.'

Betty reached over my shoulder, pulled out a Lemonade, flipped the cap off with the bottle opener and handed it to Dad. I hated it when she did that.

'What happened?' I asked, deciding to remain included in some way. Dad glugged from the bottle.

'Ah, that's good. Took a lot of persuading. She grabbed hold of the door frame and wouldn't let go. You can't shove an old lady about. Might get hurt. The fire breached the fence and started on the bushes in the back yard. It was getting hairy.'

'What did you do?' Betty asked.

'Well we couldn't leave her and we couldn't leave the fire, so we tackled the fire. It wasn't as crotchety as Violet.'

'Gosh, Dad. Is the fire out?'

'Yes, little lady, it is. Some of the blokes used chaff bags trying to put out the flames. Fire almost made it to the back door. Burnt a lotta trees and no doubt we've lost a lot of animals, but the town is safe. We can stand down now. Good job we worked on the fire break the other day eh, girlie?'

Dad's compliments were rare. He put his hand on my shoulder and gave it a squeeze. I puffed out my chest and smiled feeling a moment of importance.

'Okay little lady, how about you come over to the house and put the kettle on?'

PIXIE DUST

Ross stroked the top of the small, hinged, wooden box he'd received for his twelfth birthday. Inside, among rows of test tubes was a splendid lineup of jars, labelled and filled with powdered chemicals. A *Fun with Chemistry* booklet sat inside the lid. I was jealous. Boys got the best presents. Fun things like sling-shots, cap pistols and chemistry sets. Maybe I'd get something exciting next year for my birthday instead of a jar of ginger, hairbrush or piece of tight clothing.

'This is great Dad, thanks.'

'Now you've got your own chemistry set to play around with you can stop pestering me at the Assay office,' Dad said as he walked out the door.

'Can I have a look?'

'Sure Sis. Look at all those jars. Just imagine what I can do with this. It'll be fun.'

'Do you think you'll be able to make a potion of some kind? Maybe, you know to ... '

'You mean? ...'

'Yeah.'

'I think I'll have a go at invisibility first. I reckon if you can make invisible ink, you can make an invisibility potion,' said Ross. 'Just think of it – invisible.'

'You can't do it in the house, she wouldn't like it. I think she can read minds.'

'Don't be an idiot. She's just sneaky and mean.'

'I wish we had an attic or a basement.'

'She'd still go there. A cave would be better, like the Phantom.'

'Or the Famous Five.'

'She doesn't go under the house. She's too tall.'

'There are wasps in the tank stand.'

'Perfect,' said Ross.

For the next few days, we grabbed empty crates from behind the shop and wood off-cuts from the grain shed. We dragged them under the house. Lassie sniffed, snorted and kept a protective eye on her spot even further under the house. As we stirred up dust, scratching and scraping to create a flat surface for the shelving, Lassie plonked herself down with her head on her paws and watched, eyes and eyebrows moving together in a rhythmic wave. When her farts become overpowering, a product of Betty's scrap food, she was shunted off in disgrace.

By the time we'd finished, wobbly shelves, held together with an abundance of nails, sat precariously on broken bricks and bits of wood. Cut chaff bags dangled from the floor joists providing some protection against the wind. Since the wood heap was beside the tank stand, it was easy to drag in large chunks of wood for our seats. An empty four-gallon drum sat in the middle as the table.

Ross had scribbled K*EEP OUT OR ELSE, NO ENTRY,* and *DEATH TO TRESPARSES* on cardboard flaps and nailed them to posts on the tank stand. Tin cans and bottle tops hung on tripwires twisted around rickety sticks as a warning to those who dared ignore the signs.

Our activity had stirred up the wasps and they were starting to be a nuisance.

'You can die from a wasp sting,' said Ross. 'A boy from school was really sick and nearly died once.'

'Remember when you got bit on the lip last year,' I said. 'You had to go to school with a fat lip.'

'Yeah, I remember.'

'They hurt when they sting,' I said, recalling a recent bite on the back of the neck. It was swollen for days and I couldn't move my head.

'Let's get Betty to get rid of the nests for us. There's got to be at least a hundred wasps.'

'Do you think that'll be enough to ... you know?'

'Yeah.'

During dinner we mentioned our wasp problem and asked Betty if she would get rid of them for us.

'Your father can do that,' she said. 'I'm allergic to wasp stings.'

'Oh, really?' said Ross. 'What about bees?'

'Yes, bees too.'

'I'll do it in the morning when I start the generator,' Dad said. 'What are you doing under the tank stand?'

'We're building a laboratory,' said Ross. 'I'm going to be a scientist.'

'And I'm helping,' I said.

'That's good,' said Dad returning to his newspaper. 'No working after dark, Mr Scientist.'

'Yes, Dad.'

The following morning, the nests were gone.

'Told you she's sneaky,' said Ross. 'We'll have to try something else.'

'We should've let some loose in their bedroom during the night.'

'Don't be dumb. We don't want to kill Dad.'

Now the lab was finished, I was bored with extracting black powder from firecrackers, crushing chalk and keeping watch. Since the tripwires and dog did a better job, I left Ross to his experiments and sat on the top bar of the swing practicing acrobatics. Boarding school had a set of monkey bars and I was teaching myself how to swing and dismount without falling headfirst into the dirt.

Our swings hung on ropes from a metal bar jammed between two pepper trees outside the front fence. When Dad finished putting them up, there were two swings side by side, so Ross and I rushed forward excitedly, keen to test them out.

Fifteen year-old Keith home for the holidays, strode forward and said, 'I'm the oldest, I'll go first.'

He'd sat on the wooden seat and pushed back as far as his long, skinny legs would go. When he swung his legs from underneath he shot forward and the bar groaned and bent. His toes scraped along the gravelly dirt and the seat dropped to just above the ground.

'Look what you've done to our brand, new swing.' I shouted at him.

'Was an accident. I didn't know the pole would bend,' he said, hobbling into the house with his bleeding toes.

'That's yours,' said Ross. 'I'll have this one.' He pointed to the swing that had suffered a less dramatic fall.

'Dad, it's not fair.'

'Too bad, Bonnie. I'm not fixing it,' said Dad as he turned and walked back to the workshop. He came back later and shortened the ropes on the swing, but the pole stayed bent.

'This is boring,' said Ross. 'I'm going under the house.'

'It's all yours, Bonnie,' said Dad.

I was pleased to have the swings to myself without it becoming a competition between my brothers. An hour later, I was rocking back and forth on the swing examining the blisters on my hand from my latest efforts of swinging on the overhead bar, when Ross yelled, 'FIRE IN THE HOLE,' I vaulted over the fence, raced down the side of the house and heard a faint bang. A tiny puff of smoke erupted from behind the toilet and Ross emerged from underneath the pepper tree, hard hat on his head.

'Expecting a bigger bang?' I said. 'I thought you were working on an invisibility potion?'

'Experimenting. Wondering if I could blow her up instead.'

In the Christmas holidays Ross renewed his commitment to crack the invisibility code because now that Zilla and Tippy were over for the holidays, he had new subjects for his experiments. I was relieved. Since his birthday, I had consumed a dozen of his disgusting concoctions, each time with the assurance that this was *it*. This time he had the recipe right. He was undeterred by the stomach aches that followed each time I drank one. If he swallowed it himself, I was unaware of it, but he was persistent and I believed with certainty Ross would unlock the mystery of invisibility one day, so I continued to drink his horrid potions. If it worked, perhaps we could run away or use it to escape punishment. Our idea was vague.

The flavour of his mixtures were disguised with a large dollop of Colgate toothpaste. The increased use of toothpaste for teeth cleaning did not go unnoticed by Betty.

'How many times did you clean your teeth today?' she confronted us, as we crowded around the basin in the bathroom after dinner squeezing toothpaste into a small jar for chemistry purposes. Ross shoved it down his pants.

'Twice,' I said.

'The rest of you?' said Betty.

'I forgot yesterday,' said Tippy. Betty raised her eyebrows.

'You seem to be using rather a lot,' she said.

'We like to do a good job,' said Zilla.

'Hmm,' said Betty. 'We still seem to be using rather a lot.'

'Well, there are more of us using it,' said Zilla.

'Don't be cheeky,' said Betty.

'We'll be more careful in future,' said Ross as he nudged Zilla on the hip.

Ross decided to wait a couple of days, then he presented Zilla with a pale, milky liquid in a tin mug.

'I've got it this time,' he said. 'It's a new potion.'

'I'm not drinking that,' said Zilla screwing up her nose.' It stinks. You drink it.'

'But you have to,' said Ross. 'I know it's going to work this time.'

'How?' I said. 'You've said that before.'

'I'll drink it,' said Tippy.

'It has to be Zilla,' said Ross.

'Why should it make any difference who drinks it?' Zilla said.

'It just does,' he said. 'Do you want to get rid of Betty or not?'

'Well ...' As Zilla lifted the mug, I wondered, what if it does work?

'That was ghastly,' she said. 'Worst thing I've ever tasted. What did you put in it?'

'It's a secret,' said Ross. 'And you can't tell.'

We all stared at Zilla, turning her hands over, looking at her feet, checking to see if any part of her became invisible.

'It doesn't work,' I said.

'We'll have to wait 'til tomorrow,' said Ross.

I'd heard that before, but maybe, just maybe ...

At dinner, Zilla pushed her food around her plate, mixing corn beef, cabbage and mashed potato together.

'You're looking a bit pale,' said Dad. 'You feeling all right, Zil.'

'Not really, Dad,' she said.

'Off to bed with you then,' he said. 'I'll check on you later.'

During the night, Zilla complained of terrible stomach pains.

'Feels like you've got a bit of a temperature,' said Dad, so he wrapped her in a blanket and took her up to the bush nurse.

Ross twirled his curl and picked his nails. When Dad came back, he asked if she'd be okay.

'She'll stay overnight,' he said. 'Sister Cousins will keep an eye on her.'

In the morning Dad and us kids walked up to the hospital to see Zilla and wondered if she'd be invisible.

'I'm puzzled as to what caused this,' said Sister Cousins. 'She said she hadn't taken anything different from usual. She had a nasty turn during the night and I was quite concerned, but she's feeling much better now.'

'Can we see her?' we asked.

Sister Cousins took us through from the verandah into a room with four beds. Zilla was propped up in the far corner, still pale but quite visible. Sister Cousins and Dad went into the office and Tippy climbed up beside Zilla and put his arm around her shoulder. Ross lifted the blankets and checked her feet.

'Didn't work,' I said. 'Gosh Zilla, I'm glad you're okay.'

'I'm not taking any more of your silly potions,' said Zilla. 'You're gonna have to find another way.'

'I'm sorry,' said Ross. 'I was so sure it would work.'

'What did you put in it?' Zilla asked. 'I was really, really, really sick.'

'I peed in it,' he said.

'What?' I said.

'That's disgusting,' said Zilla.

'Oh, yuk,' said Tippy.

'But it couldn't have been that,' said Ross rubbing his chin. 'Must've been the white shoe polish.'

Ross was alarmed by Zilla's shocking reaction to his potion, but encouraged by her recovery. It was time to change direction, so he scrapped developing invisibility and decided to think bigger.

'We are going to invent Pixie Dust,' he announced as we sat on the fence beside the empty chook pen.

'How are you going to do that?' said Zilla. 'Because I'm not going to drink anymore of your stupid stuff.'

'You won't have to drink anything,' he said. 'Can't be that hard. I've just got to work out a few things.'

'You mean we'll be able to fly?' I asked. Every night I dreamed I was flying. Soaring above the house, over the trees swooping and dipping with the air stream. 'Won't that be wonderful.'

I wanted to fly up into the air and keep going and if Ross said he could do it, I believed him.

'You're mad,' said Zilla. 'Nobody can fly.'

'Course you can,' said Tippy. 'Peter Pan can.'

'That's a fairy tale you ning,' said Zilla.

'Well I'm going to give it a try,' said Ross.

Ross decided we needed to find a suitable place where we could jump, catch the air current and fly. It seemed easy. Climbing trees took us to heights that were unsuitable and the branches got in the way, so we started with what was familiar; the fence. Ross, Tippy and I became enthusiastic in finding the best places to use as a launch pad. We left few places untested. Arms outstretched, we experimented holding towels, umbrellas, pieces of tin, wood and bits of clothing.

'We're not high enough to get proper air flow for flight.' Ross clamped the lid on the jar, shoved a stack of messy notes under his arm and jumped off the tank stand.

'You said that last time at the pig pen.' I rubbed the grit off my knees and slapped the dust from my shorts.

'Sloping roof and hot tin was the problem there.'

'Yeah. Ten feet up and a slippery roof. Tippy landed in the middle of the pigs when he jumped.'

'The chook pen's too wobbly.'

'I've still got a splinter in my foot.'

'They were test runs. We need to go high, Bonnie. I haven't got the mix right yet.'

'I'm not climbing up the drainpipe again. My bum's still sore from Dad's walloping,' I said.

'Gosh Sis, that was fun. Pity Dad caught us,' he said giving his bum a tap.

'We should try the slag dump,' I said.

'Could be a bit rough with all the hard rock.'

The slag dump was huge. The top was flat and it was where I practised tennis with a ball on an elastic string. The tall trees were perfect for climbing contests. The dump was gradated into the side of the hill towards the mine, but the highest edge was along the main road. The spot we chose for the test site was higher than the top bar on the monkey bars at school.

'Perfect,' said Ross as we leaned over the side and looked at the sharp pieces of black rock sticking out all the way down. 'The higher the better.'

'Gosh, I dunno.'

Ross licked his finger and poked it in the air. 'Wind's good. Let's give it a try.'

'Can't someone else have a go?'

'Who? Zilla and Tippy are not here.'

'Why is it always me?'

'You're my sister, that's why.'

Ridiculous reason, but this was a mission for siblings.

'Take a good run up and I'll sprinkle you with Pixie Dust just as you get to the edge,' he said, unscrewing the jar containing a black powdered mixture.

'I thought it was supposed to be a gold colour.'

'The colour is not important. It's the ingredients.'

I was too gullible, I trusted Ross and his ability to find a solution. He was the inventor– I was the assistant.

Moving back to the middle of the dump, I ran towards the edge in my best sprint. As I got close, Ross threw the black dust over me and shouted 'ABRACADABRA'. I skidded to a stop, panting.

'What did you stop for?'

'It's too high.'

'That was my last batch. I'll have to make some more now.'

Rain, the cold and school hampered our efforts to resume the experiment and it wasn't until Zilla and Tippy returned at Christmas that we all climbed up to the slag dump to continue. Zilla thought we were crazy in persisting with the ridiculous notion of flying. She was amused at the enthusiasm and seriousness with which Ross and I approached this task. Although doubtful of results, she took on the role of timekeeper and recorded details in a notebook containing additional hard-to-read squiggles and scratchings by Ross. She was also responsible for first aid and carried a bunch of band-aids for the increasing flying-related wounds of the test pilots – Tippy and me.

We cleared the sharp rocks from the slope and slid down on cardboard to check for any nasty surprises. It quickly became a distraction as we skiied until the cardboard shredded. My initial apprehension at launching myself from a great height was diminished by Tippy's eagerness. His method was to run full bore towards the edge, stop, then swing his arms like a windmill and spring over. But the skid down the rough slag dump was more painful than a belting or a belly flop onto the dam. Our clothing was unsuitable for the harsh treatment it was getting, and it didn't occur to us that it might help if we padded our bodies. I decided to run, arms stretched, as fast as I could and jump but we only succeeded in becoming exhausted from the bounce down the side. We'd drag our bruised and scraped bodies up to the top of the slag dump as our failures repeated. Zilla's clerical duties were overtaken by nursing our increasing injuries. When the supply of band-aids ran out in the house, we were forced to spend our pocket money to replace them.

'I can't run anymore,' said Tippy.

'Me either,' I said.

The patience Ross showed on our initial attempts turned to bursts of frustration and anger. He wasn't concerned about our wounds or our exhaustion.

'You're not doing it right! Arms like THIS, straight out,' he demonstrated.

Either the incantation had the wrong emphasis, the wind was blowing in the wrong direction, wasn't strong enough, or we weren't trying hard enough. He stomped back under the house to his lab muttering, 'I must've forgotten an ingredient.'

We persisted in the belief he would get it right and one day we would be able to fly. With a new batch of Pixie Dust, healed wounds and restored energy, we trooped back to the slag dump to resume our testing. Following a repeat of our previous attempts and despite Ross's confidence in our success this time, neither Tippy nor I could fly.

'I'll have to do it myself,' said Ross, thrusting the jar at me. 'I'll show you how it's done.'

'Good luck,' said Zilla, pencil poised.

'Don't forget, AB-RA-CA-DAB-RA as you sprinkle the dust.'

'Yes, I know what to do,' I said.

Ross licked his finger and tested the wind direction before heading to the cricket pitch length run-up site. He adopted the pose of a track sprinter and with arms outstretched and the speed of an Olympic runner, he leapt off the edge at a distance the envy of any long jump champion as I sprinkled and incanted. Zilla and I held our breath as we witnessed the miracle of flight: for a millisecond. His billowing shirt disappeared out of sight and we saw a minor avalanche in his wake as he skidded down the rough slope on his backside and stopped at the base of the hill. We all rushed forward and leaned over to see Ross on his back, arms still straight out, a dribble of stones coming to rest at his feet. We waited for signs of life. As the dust settled, Ross leaped into the air, his pants and shirt were torn, his shins and elbows bloody and he was covered in black dust from head to toe.

'Did you see that. I WAS FLYING!'

We were convinced we were on the right track. His short flight boosted our resolve and our quest continued for years.

BUSH PICNIC

Ross and I had been on our way to the slag dump to investigate an empty mine shaft when Dad called us back.

'Freddy Funk's sweet on the bush nurse, Sister Cousins,' Dad said. 'He's taking her on a picnic for lunch.' Picnics were unheard of around here. There was nothing but bare ground, ant's nests, prickles and flies. 'You two can go and keep Alexander company.'

'Please, Dad, do we have to?' said Ross.

'He's not allowed to do *anything.'* I said.

Sister Cousins' eleven year-old son, Alexander was afraid of climbing trees, jumping off fence posts and using a bow and arrow. He always had a sniffle, always whined about the flies, heat and dust, and wasn't allowed to get dirty.

'That's not very neighbourly,' said Dad, 'now off you go. He's waiting for you at the shop.'

Ross and I thought Freddy, with his pointy head, big nose and the weird smacking noises he made with his lips, was strange and scary. He always wore khaki overalls and checked shirt but didn't live in Mount Hope and stayed at the pub while he worked on the railway near Matakana as a fetler.

We climbed into the back of Freddy's ute and sat on the tool box. Alexander, in white shirt, cream shorts and with perfectly combed hair, and Sister Cousins, looking strange out of her nurse's uniform in a pink dress and white sunhat sat upright on the front seat with Freddy.

He drove off in a skid, spraying gravel across the front of the shop. Three miles down the main road, he turned off. We went through a gate and into the scrub for a couple of miles before Freddy pulled off the road, weaving through the pine trees until he reached a small clearing.

'Great place for a picnic,' he said. 'All out.'

We climbed down and inspected the area. Bare ground, ant's nests and prickles.

'Here?' asked Sister Cousins.

'Spread the rug,' said Freddy, heaving the toolbox and a shovel from the back. He dumped them on the ground.

'Build the fire, Bonnie. Come on Ross, let's get lunch.'

As they drove off, Sister Cousins said, 'Come on Alexander, we're going home.'

'You can't go home,' I said. 'It's too far. You can't leave me here.'

'We'll wait on the main road for a motor vehicle to come.'

'It's Sunday,' I said. 'Nobody will drive past.'

'This is dreadful,' she said.

'Let's see what's in the box,' I said. 'Look at this.'

Inside was a box of matches, an army blanket, tin mugs, plates, knives, forks and five round tins, each containing cakes, salad and sandwiches.

'Good heavens,' said Sister Cousins. 'I've never seen so much food. He's thought of everything.' She reached in and pulled out a bottle of whisky. 'It seems – everything.'

'We should build the fire,' I said. 'Come on Alexander, let's collect wood.'

'I'll set the table,' said Sister Cousins.

Two rifle shots echoed through the trees.

'Good heavens,' said Sister Cousins.

'Looks like Freddy has found lunch,' I said. 'Best we have a fire ready when they come back.'

Alexander and I collected wood of all sizes, I dug a pit and we'd just finished setting the fire, when Ross and Freddy arrived back with two sizeable emu drumsticks.

'You surely don't expect us to eat that, do you?' Sister Cousins said.

'This is a treat. Who gets to eat emu meat on a picnic?' said Freddy. 'Great job with the fire, kids.'

We had an empty emu egg in the cabinet in the lounge room at home and had eaten kangaroo meat, but not emu. With the fire lit and the drumsticks sizzling in the middle on a metal rack Freddy had in the ute, the flies arrived. Pine branches became fans as we swished them back and forth across the flames while dodging the smoke. After half an hour, during which we climbed trees, fought, played with fire, kicked dirt and watched Freddy take frequent sips from his whisky flask, he declared the meat cooked.

Freddy pulled a drumstick from the fire and brushed off the ashes still clinging to the charred underside with his fingers. He put it on a metal plate and took another swig from his whisky flask. He whipped the penknife out from his back pocket and flicked it open gunslinger style, but it flew out of his hand and landed in the fire.

'Damn,' he said, scratching through the ash. 'Me dad gave me that.' He dragged it out and wiped it on his pants. 'All bug free now, eh Sister?'

His smile revealed crooked bottom teeth and gapped top teeth. It was weird and fascinating. He dug a big chunk of meat off the drumstick with the blackened penknife.

'Here,' he said, extending it to Sister Cousins. 'Get that into ya. Good bush tucker.'

She held the piece between two fingers, sniffed then screwed up her nose. 'You said it's like steak, well, it doesn't smell like steak. It smells off.'

'Can't be off,' said Freddy. 'This is as fresh as it gets.'

'Maybe that's the problem,' said Sister Cousins. 'Too fresh.'

He sliced meat from the drumstick and handed each of us a piece, popping chunks into his mouth then washing it down with whisky. He chewed in large circular movements, making the same noise our dog did when he ate. I tried not to look.

'It tastes awful,' said Alexander spitting it out.

'It's like chewing a paper bag filled with string', said Ross.

'I feel sick,' I said jumping up and racing over to the trees to vomit.

Then Alexander vomited on the dirt beside Ross.

'Oh you poor boy,' said Sister Cousins.

'Oh yuk. Couldn't you have at least got up?' said Ross. 'It stinks. Now I feel sick.'

'I think we should take a drive,' said Freddy, taking another swig. 'It'll clear the air.'

'I think we should go home,' said Sister Cousins. 'Alexander is not well.'

'What a sook,' said Ross. 'He'll be okay in a minute.'

'I would prefer to go home, thank you,' said Sister Cousins, 'and I'd like to go now.'

'Okay you lot, let's clean up.' Freddy grabbed the shovel and began to heap dirt on the fire, swaying with each scoop of the shovel. He missed with the first shovel full of dirt then most of the rest went where it was supposed to. Sister Cousins stood up, straightened her dress and held out her hand.

'Come on Alexander,' she said. 'The children can pack up.'

'We all help out here, lady,' said Freddy.

'Alexander is not well.' She took his hand, walked over to the ute and sat down.

We packed up, making certain the fire was covered and out, then Ross and I hopped in the back. Alexander was arguing with his mother so she decided to let him ride in the back with us. Freddy drove us down a narrow track and suddenly swerved off the road into the trees. The branches were low, so we needed to duck while he weaved in and out over the bumpy ground. We were enjoying the ride, sliding and bouncing about, keeping upright until Freddy missed the turn at the fence and hit the brakes hard. Ross and I were used to hanging on, but Alexander's face hit the top of the cab; blood dripped down his white shirt.

'My nose,' cried Alexander. 'My nose is broken. You've broken my nose.'

'Now look what you've done,' Sister Cousins screamed at Freddy. 'You could've killed him, you stupid man.'

She dragged Alexander over the tailgate and searched around for something to put over his nose to stop the bleeding. The blanket was caked in prickles and no-one had a handkerchief. All the rags in the back were covered in grease and dirt.

'Take off your sock,' she said to Ross.

'No,' he said. 'What's wrong with Alexander's sock?'

'Give me your sock,' she said again.

'I'm not giving you my sock.'

Alexander was crying. He had both hands over his nose and blood was oozing between his fingers.

'Give him your sock,' slurred Freddy, 'or we'll never get out of here.'

Ross took off his shoe, removed his sock and thrust it at Sister Cousins.

She held it over Alexander's nose and shoved him into the cabin.

'Mr Funk I would like to go home.'

'No doubt Betty will have something to say about me only having one sock,' said Ross as we sat down in the back of the ute.

Freddy managed to get us back onto the track and sped back towards the gate. He was weaving from one side of the road to the other and driving at such a speed that when we hit the bend he ran into the corner gate post, knocking it over. In the back we banged against the metal sides trying to keep hold and avoid being thrown out. The wheels were jammed either side of the post, now on its side, and the ute was wedged on the axle. Freddy pushed and shoved at the door, but it was jammed so tight he had to climb out the window to check the damage.

'We're a bit stuck,' he said. 'I think you'd all better climb down and let's see if I can shift it off the post.'

'This wouldn't have happened if you were sober, you stupid drunk. How the hell ...'

Sister Cousins followed Freddy as he leaned over and inspected the front wheels.

'... are we going to get back to Mount Hope ...'

he continued around to the front bumper and looked underneath.

'... now we are stuck on this damn gate? As if ...'

Sister Cousins stood in front of Freddy and was poking him in the chest when he jumped on the bonnet and started bouncing up and down.

'... causing Alexander to get a bloody nose wasn't enough. As if eating horrible emu wasn't enough.'

Freddy hunched down, grabbed the bumper and tried to lift the ute. His face was red and his veins bulged as he grunted and heaved. The ute wouldn't budge.

Ross and I sat on a log with Alexander as his mother continued shouting at Freddy.

'Mr Funk. Are you listening to me?'

'She's stuck, all right,' he said. 'I'll go for help.'

He jumped over the distorted gate, tripped over and landed on his back in the dirt. Leaping up, he jogged off towards Mount Hope weaving all over the road, leaving Sister Cousins standing with her hands on her hips.

'This is fun,' said Alexander. 'I've never heard her shout like that.'

'Betty does it all the time,' I said.

Alexander's nose had stopped bleeding. Its tip was red and his eyes were bloodshot. Dark blue patches were appearing around his eyes.

'You're going to have a couple of great shiners,' said Ross.

'A real beauty. It'll be black and blue tomorrow,' I said, looking closely at his face.

'Really? Mum's going to fuss and carry on.'

While we waited for Freddy, Ross pulled out a bag of marbles from his pocket. He drew a circle with a stick and we played ringer while Sister Cousins sat on a log, silent and sullen. Since all the marbles belonged to

Ross, any won during the game were returned to him. We discovered that Alexander was a keen marble player and Ross had to fight to stop this serious challenge to his championship status. We were all arguing over a possible breach of the rules, when our ute pulled up on the other side of the fence and Dad climbed out.

'Where's Freddy?' asked Ross.

'He had things to do,' said Dad.

'He's been drinking whisky all day,' said Ross.

'He is a raging drunk,' said Sister Cousins. 'He is responsible for Alexander's injuries. It's possible, thanks to him, he has a broken nose and concussion.'

'Aw, Mom, it's not that bad,' said Alexander.

'He's a menace on the road. My association with him is over, Mr McLernon. I want nothing more to do with him.'

'Let's get you all home,' said Dad. 'Everyone into the ute and we'll sort this out later.'

Alexander didn't wear his white shirts when he played with us after that. He became quite good at climbing trees and turned out to be good fun. After the picnic, Freddy wasn't seen in Mount Hope for quite a while and we were relieved to know there was no danger of being served emu drumsticks.

FRESH MILK AND BUSH TUCKER

While having breakfast we heard a truck engine revving in our back paddock. We raced outside and watched it reversing into a newly built pen in the corner of the paddock near Ross's Tarzan tree. Half the pen was roofed, half was open, it had been built with materials taken from the pile of discarded wood and tin stacked behind the grain shed.

The rusty roof was concealed by the drooping pepper tree branches and the wooden posts and rails looked out of place beside our orange-railed fence. The feed and water trough were halves of a forty-four gallon drum with another for the milking stool, something we had in abundance. Fresh straw covered the entire pen where once a variety of weeds had afforded Lassie her personal back scratching patch.

Dad was leaning on the fence talking to Archie and Tom, our neighbours. Both men were over six feet tall, wide shouldered, with solid arms and legs. Ross and I raced over and climbed on the fence. Dust and straw escaped through gaps in the sides. Inside the truck, snorting and grunting accompanied the pounding hoofbeats that hammered and thrashed against the wood.

'What's in the truck, Dad,' Ross asked.

'How would you like fresh milk every day, kids?'

'That'd be great,' I said.

'Yeah,' said Ross.

It didn't matter if we had cereal or porridge, eating it with lumpy, watery powdered milk was unpleasant, so fresh milk would be a treat. I would however, have preferred a horse since I'd been asking for one every Christmas since I was five.

'Can we call it Daisy, Dad?' I asked.

'We'll see. Best you two keep out of the way though, we're about to unload the cow,' said Dad. 'She just needs to settle down a bit after the trip.'

It was evident the passenger was tiring as her barrage on the side of the truck became less intense. Snorting subsided to heavy breathing and nostrils sought fresh air through the crevices between the boards. Archie climbed on the roof to release the tailgate while Dad and Tom stood either side. As it lowered, the cow began bellowing, head thrust forward, nose in the air, mucus dribbling from it. I jumped off the fence, sprinted to the corner and shimmied up the pepper tree. Ross raced past me, leaped up to the first branch, swung over and clambered skyward. We resumed our view from the safety of distance.

'She's a bit jumpy,' said Dad, hand on chin, as if re-thinking the venture.

'The trip got her het up a bit, she'll settle once she's out and in the pen,' said Archie as he moved in to release the ropes.

Grabbing the rope, Archie held the head and began to pull it forward but this enraged the cow and prompted another shot at escape. I moved further up the tree, clutching the branch, wanting to be as far as possible from the kicking hooves. The ground shook, the branches rustled and the birds had long gone. Even the pigs at the pub were quiet.

'Tommy, get side, get side.'

'Bloody stupid cow.'

'Ben, hold firm, she's getting ready to kick.'

'Gwarn. Move. Git out!'

'Hold that side, Tom. Flamin' stupid cow.'

I climbed a branch higher watching as three men gasped and panted, wrestling with this big, frightened animal.

'Pull hard. Don't you step on my foot, you fool of a cow. Je-sus. Stop pushin' me.'

'Turn the head, TURN THE HEAD.'

'Hell, she's strong.'

'This is one crazy cow, Archie.'

This is not how I expected a cow to behave. Aunty Ethel had a cow called *Blossom* and Zilla told me she trotted up to you when she wanted a nose rub. She'd stand quietly while Aunty milked, chewing on a straw and flicking the flies with her tail. Daisy was supposed to be like that – docile and friendly. Watching this cow, it seemed like fresh milk was a dangerous business. Somehow the men managed to evade being trampled by the hooves. With every stomp, bellow and snort they bounced, sweated and shoved the animal into the pen. At last, she was inside.

'Mongrel cow,' said Dad.

'She'll be right in an hour or two,' said Archie.

'Come on kids,' said Dad. 'You can come down now.'

'Do you think she'll be okay?' I asked. 'Will we have fresh milk in the morning?'

'Quite possibly,' said Dad. 'But right now us blokes are off to the pub.'

Despite her magnificent accommodation, we heard Daisy bellowing as we set the table for dinner and she was still in full voice when we finished the washing up. When the generators in town stopped their throbbing, Daisy could be heard punctuating the quiet evening with her racket, and she continued as we settled into bed. I fell asleep wondering if cows got sore throats.

The following morning, we found Dad in the pen dressed in overalls looking like a farmer and not a miner. He was sitting on the drum washing the teats getting ready to milk. The cow had a leg rope and her head was buried in the feed bag.

'Wow Dad, she looks much happier.' I said, stepping up to the rails as he squeezed the teats and squirted white, frothy milk into the bucket. I could almost taste it on my cereal.

'Yep. She stopped her complaining at about two o'clock this morning and settled down with a good feed.'

It was exciting to see the level in the bucket climbing as each squirt bubbled and splashed. The cow raised her head from the bag and looked directly at me. Did I see a twinkle? Without warning she kicked the bucket. The precious liquid cascaded across the floor, mingling with dirt and straw as the bucket became airborne and landed in front of us. With equal swiftness, Dad moved into the back corner and swore.

'Bloody stupid cow. Archie's sold me a crazy cow.'

Pandemonium erupted as the cow broke the halter and she began kicking and thrashing in an effort to free the leg rope. We stood in stunned amazement, terrified. Dad's beaut new pen was being demolished by this demented beast. As she continued her rampage, the side gate splintered and Dad launched himself in the opposite direction to avoid being pummelled. This action caused the leg rope to loop around his right leg the instant the cow blasted through the smashed gate.

The tall scotch thistles were no deterrent to the cow as it blazed an unswerving pathway over the hill despite Dad's ineffectual attempts to free the tether and remain upright. We watched in horror as he was dragged through the thistles and prickles, voicing expletives unknown to us. When they both disappeared from sight and the sound abated, we stood in silent distress. A moment later Bert Lloyd's jeep hurtled past, dashing in the direction of the two runaways. We hoped he was rescuing Dad from this mad cow, otherwise we'd be left with Betty.

An hour later, he arrived back and my brother and I didn't quite know what to do, but we knew it was not a time to be asking questions. A few days later when Dad's limp was less visible and the bruises were starting to change colour, we noticed the empty pen and asked about the cow.

'She's gone,' was his reply. 'We won't be getting fresh milk after all.'

The cow calamity didn't dampen Dad's commitment to introduce Ross and me to the abundant produce surrounding our small town, however.

'Come on kids,' he said the following weekend, 'the Aborigines knew how to find food and they didn't have cows.'

'Dad?' I asked. 'Where are we going?'

'You'll soon find out. Hop in. We're going bush.'

* * *

'Take the humble witchetty grub.'

Dad was holding a large, fat, fleshy grub between his forefinger and thumb, its legs rippled and twisted.

'Now, there's no point in screwing up your nose, Bonnie,' he said, pushing his specs up with the back of his hand. 'It's first-rate tucker and one day, when you're lost in the bush and hungry, it'll mean the difference between living and dying. A bloke can survive out here for days, if he knows what to eat. You've gotta be careful 'cause there's lots of poisonous things too. Berries especially, but we'll explore that another day.'

We were trapped beside a large Acacia tree listening as he talked about surviving in the bush. Every so often he asked questions so we tried to stay focused. I found it difficult. I looked up through the branches. The sun had not yet reached mid-day and I wondered if Dad was planning a picnic lunch. Freddy and the emu drumstick had made me apprehensive about picnic lunches. A kookaburra perched on a branch sat motionless, its eyes riveted on the twitching white shape Dad held out. Ross reached for the slingshot in his back pocket.

'Anyway - now pay attention, you two.'

The slingshot was pushed back down and I ignored the kookaburra to listen to Dad.

'Today I'm gonna teach you all about this little fella. Not only are they good grub, ah, so to speak, they're pretty good medicine. One time when we were musterin' for Healeys outside Wiluna, this bloke burnt his arm on the branding iron mucking around being a silly b... ah, twit. Rouseabout was an Aborigine from Meekathara. He'd dug up some witchetties for tucker. Quick as a flash, he grabbed a couple, squashed 'em with his hands and dumped it on Joe's arm. Healed in a couple of days.'

While he talked, the grub spurted a jet of brown liquid from its backside. It missed Ross and landed on Dad's pants leg.

'You'd best be prepared for that. They do it in self defence. Not good if it gets on the skin, it can sting.'

'Oh yuk, we're not really going have to eat it, are we Dad?' I said.

All I saw, were brown legs and face, yellow body squirming, and imagined it filled with horrid brown gunk. I was never getting lost in the bush.

'Too right we are, Bonnie. Just remember little miss, this is for your benefit. Here Ross, you hold this one while I dig out a couple more.'

Dad grabbed his screwdriver and poked it around between the roots of the gum.

'Good time of day. Catch 'em when they're snoozing,' he said, pushing his hand into the soft dirt and pulling out another one.

'Get that thing out of my face,' I yelled as Ross shoved his grub in front of my nose. Its coffee coloured head squirmed, while it jaws moved from side to side and the hundred legs sticking out of its plump, ugly body wiggled back and forth.

'You're not going to last long in the bush if you behave like that,' said Dad, handing me a witchetty covered in dirt.

'I'll die before I'll eat one of those.'

'You're gon-na die-e, you're gon-na die-e,' sang Ross.

'Oh shuddup.'

'That's enough of that, you two. Here, take this one, Bonnie.'

I took the creature between my fingers and held it out as far as my arm would stretch. The soft, mushy body was trying to escape my hold when it ejected brown fluid that missed me and hit Ross's shirt.

'You did that on purpose,' said Ross.

'Now cut it out, you two. Listen. Hold it just below the head.'

I had both hands clamped on my charge, holding it as far from my face as possible, in the hope the distance would ease my disgust.

Dad leant against the tree as he talked about the benefits of the witchetty his hand holding the grub moved up and down to emphasise his points. Biology was never this interactive at school.

'You can jam them on a stick and cook 'em in the campfire, or even sizzle a few in the pan. They taste a bit like chicken.'

'Chicken?' The comparison didn't make it to my taste buds.

'Today, we're going to eat them raw.'

'Raw?' Ross looked at Dad, then me and down to the live creature still searching for escape.

'Eat it? Couldn't I have a vegemite sandwich instead?' My stomach turned over at the same pace as the moving feet on the grub. I tried to visualise chicken. It didn't work.

'Right,' said Dad. 'It's important to do this part quickly. Watch.'

He held the grub below the head, folded the body into his palm and covered it with his remaining fingers. With one swift move, he bit off the head with his teeth, spat it on the ground, then popped the witchety into his mouth and chewed as if it was a piece of cheese.

'Good bush tucker,' he said, swallowing. 'Long time since I've had one of those. Tastes just like almonds.' He licked his lips, wiped his mouth with his hanky, shoved his hands into his pockets and leaned back against the tree.

'Okay. Your turn, kids.'

This was worse than the time I found a grub in the mashed potato at boarding school. My teacher had insisted it was an unmashed lump and that we must eat everything, lumps and all. As she pointed to the lump, it began to crawl towards the edge. She grabbed the plate and ran into the kitchen, screaming. Watching Ross, I had a strong desire to scream and run.

Ross held the grub up to his face. He opened and shut his mouth several times looking like a suffocating goldfish. I could tell he didn't want to disappoint Dad but he was fighting to control his revulsion. He looked at me shaking my head from side to side, my lips pressed so tight they were numb.

'Come on, lad, don't take all day. Best do it quick.'

I stood, rigid. Ross made several false starts. My mouth mimicked his. It was like watching the mechanical arm on one of the clowns at the Royal Easter Show as it popped ping pong balls down its permanently open mouth.

In an abrupt move, he squeezed his eyes tight, bit into the flesh, spat out the head and shoved the grub between his lips. I caught a glimpse of movement from the white blob before he clamped his teeth together and swallowed. His mouth squeezed and twisted, with his shoulders raised to his ears, he stood, head shaking, hands around his throat.

'Good lad,' said Dad.

'Ross? You okay?' My jaw ached from the stress of what I'd seen and the expectation I must follow. I examined my brother's face.

He opened his eyes and looked at me. The frown deepened, black polka-dot freckles stood out against the changing colour of his skin from pink to white. His hand smacked against his mouth as he hurled himself into a wattle bush and unloaded the witchetty grub and breakfast.

I stared at Dad, torn between my duty of obedience, sympathy for my brother and an intense desire to dodge this lesson. Maybe, if I fainted or pretended I was being attacked by bull ants or, maybe if the kookaburra swooped and flew away with my witchetty, I'd avoid it. Ross leaned against the ute, pale and still. I swallowed and realised my arms were cramped from the fierce hold I had on my grub. With resignation comparable to standing in front of a firing squad, I accepted my fate and that of the grub. I slowly lifted it to my mouth.

'Well,' Dad drawled as he moseyed over to the ute, shoulders shaking in silent laughter, 'I think we can let you off the hook, Bonnie.' He turned, and with a serious nod, pointed the screwdriver at me and added, 'Next time we'll cook goanna and it'll be your turn first.'

FIRE AND GOATS

'It's the annual visit of the Padre, Sergeant and Councillor,' Dad said as he trailed the last smear of pickles across the plate and licked it off his finger.

'Then there'll be a movie in the hall tonight,' I said.

'We never get to see the movie all the way through,' said Ross. 'The kids get asked to leave.'

'I wouldn't worry,' said Betty. 'The projector usually breaks down before the last reel, so nobody gets to see anything all the way through.'

'That means there'll be church in the morning,' I said.

'I've got better things to do than go to church,' said Dad.

'Can Bonnie and I have better things to do too, Dad?' said Ross.

'Don't be cheeky, young man,' Dad said, spreading jam across his bread. 'A little bit of religion never hurt anybody.'

'But you just said ...' Ross said. Dad glared.

'Not many people go,' I said.

'Padre's just doing his job,' said Betty.

'Gathering for his flock,' I said.

'What?' they chorused.

'Heard it preached at school. Something about fishers of men. *Come all ye who …*'

'All right, all right,' said Dad. 'That's enough of that kind of talk. You'll spoil my lunch.'

'Your father's picking them up from the airstrip around three o'clock,' said Betty. 'You can find something to do away from the pub.'

'Yes Betty.'

'Waste of an afternoon,' said Dad. 'The Padre will offer advice on overindulgences, quote passages from the bible and enjoy a steady supply of schooners provided by the publican. The sergeant will sit at the end of the verandah and collect fines and hand out licences. The councillor will divide his attention between the farmers griping about neglected roads and falling sheep prices and the next shout. I've never seen him pay for a beer yet.'

'Why do you go?' said Ross.

'President of the Association,' said Dad. 'Got to put in an appearance.'

'Chris and Paddo are coming over after lunch,' said Ross. 'We were going up to the slag dump.'

'When did Chris get back?' I asked.

'He's visiting for a week,' said Ross.

'No slag dump today. Make it the back paddock,' said Dad. 'I'm sure you'll be able to amuse yourselves. See you include your sister.'

The back paddock had become the favoured place to engage in battles because of the countless hiding places there. The slag dump was an open area with trees but the Scotch thistles, cow pats, wet and dry, and long grasses in the back paddock had the advantage of camouflage for surprise attacks. It could be a jungle, forest or open plain depending on the game.

Drum rolling was a test of balance and skill, and clearing pathways often became a competition between Ross and me to see who could reach the post in the middle of the paddock first. We used empty forty-four gallon drums to create pathways in between the cow and animal tracks. By laying the drum on its side and standing on the middle rim in our bare feet, we rolled down the sloping driveway and into the paddock. Dodging thistles and fresh cow pats required clever manoeuvring and good eyesight. I was good at steering and guiding, but being short-sighted, often didn't spot the offending pat until it was too late and a leap was the only way to avoid the slippery mess.

The post in the middle of the field became the stake to which baddies were tied for the finale of any chase. In the token pow-wow to select the cast, Ross elected himself the leader. He had two cap guns, one on each hip, a bow over his shoulder and a home-made quiver with six arrows. His slingshot was tucked into his back pocket. Paddo and Chris had twin holsters, two guns and water pistols tucked in the waist band.

'I'm not being the Indian again,' I said to Chris, Ross and Paddo. 'Why can't I be a cowboy?'

'But you're a girl,' said Ross.

Yeah,' said Paddo. 'Everyone knows Indians are girls.'

'It's not fair. Why can't it be one of you for a change?'

'It's decided,' said Ross. 'Do you want to play or not?'

I was eager to be part of the battle and being the only girl, my participation was always conditional. I would be chased, caught and tied up at the post.

'Then Lassie is on my side,' I said. 'But I want a bow and arrow.'

'Here,' said Paddo. 'You can have my water pistol.'

'Indians don't have water pistols,' I said. 'They have a bow and arrow.'

'It'll have to do,' said Ross. 'We'll give you a five-minute start, Bonnie.'

I bolted into the field and doubled back towards the grain shed as the boys argued the rules of battle. It was hard to keep track as Ross shouted amendments during the game. If you were shot you had to lie still for three seconds. You could be killed three times, no more. This caused extra battles because it was a rule Ross ignored. The rest of us just sighed then carried on with the game. As soon as an arrow was loaded onto the bow, Lassie abandoned her lookout post and skedaddled under the house.

I was captured by Paddo in front of the grain shed as I attempted to run over him with a forty-four gallon drum, which was against the rules, as stated by Ross at the time of my capture. They grabbed my arms and dragged me over to the post in the centre of the paddock, which was concealed from the road by long grass and thistles due to the downpour from the previous month. Ross and I had cleared a small space around the post earlier with a token bonfire surrounding it for authenticity. I was strapped to the post with rope and my hands were tied behind my back and my feet secured to the bottom of the post.

'Make it good and tight,' said Ross, removing a box of matches from his pocket.

'Hey, what are you doing?' I struggled to free my hands.

'It's okay,' said Ross.

'Just light a bit on the edge,' said Paddo.

'No. You will not.' I said.

'It's okay, Bonnie,' said Chris. 'We're not going to let you burn.'

Overhead, the steady drone of an airplane approached. It circled the air strip behind the racecourse and descended with intermittent spluttering as the engine prepared for landing.

Ross dropped the lighted match into the sticks. It fizzed in a puff of smoke and the flame died.

'Let's go,' he said to Paddo and Chris. 'We'll be back in a minute.'

'Don't you leave me here,' I shouted to the receding backs. 'I hate you!'

This was not an unusual ploy with the boys. They would tie me up, then on the pretense of forgetting me, dash off and watch from a distance while I thrashed about on the post in an effort to untie my restraints. It was entertaining for them and terrifying for me, yet I subjected myself to this torture repeatedly. I was confident they would not leave me for long.

I caught a glimpse of the dust from the ute as Dad drove out to meet the Padre, Sergeant and Councillor and again as it returned and drove up the road to the pub. The boys had not returned. Several cars drove into town to join the gathering at the pub. The grass in front of me moved. A mouse poked its head through the blades, nose twitching. It turned and retreated into the dense growth.

Betty was walking from the house over to the shop so I yelled to attract her attention but the noise of a truck driving up to the bowser drowned out my voice.

A lizard scrambled out from behind a rock and followed the route of the mouse as a thread of grey smoke weaved a lazy trail from underneath the sticks at my feet. It evaporated but another followed, dissolving in the soft breeze before one more drifted upwards. Watching the drifts was distracting until, beneath the swirl, an orange leaf, flickering.

'ROSS,' I screamed, twisting my hands, trying to reach with my feet. 'FIRE.'

The smoke spread upwards and across the ground as the branches began to burn.

'HELP.' I tried leaning over to the side to see if the post would come out of the ground, but it remained firm and the bonds on my hands were hurting my wrists. The post poked into my shoulder blades and the leaves were beginning to catch.

I stretched my feet and tapped at the glow below the sticks, but it had the opposite effect. The flames progressed to the upper branches of the pile and edged closer to my feet. I had nowhere to move. I tried twisting around to the side, but the splinters from the post stung my arms. The smoke went from small puffs increased to clouds around my face. I was scared I would be burnt.

The three boys strolled past the front gate, laughing and jostling having forgotten about me tied to the post. Chris stopped.

'Holy smoke,' he said running into the paddock. 'She's on fire.'

The trio began stamping out the fire with their shoes, performing a weird dance around me. They scraped dirt over the offending mound until the last puff of smoke withered and died. Ross untied my hands.

'Gosh, Sis,' said Ross. 'We kinda got lost with the time.'

I glared at him as I rubbed my wrists.

'Yeah, well,' he scraped a bit more dirt on the pile. 'It was an accident. I thought the match was out.'

'Accident?' I said, with fear turned to anger. 'Accident?' I was hysterical now. 'You ever do that to me again and I'll kill you.'

'Sorry Sis,' he mumbled as I strode away. 'Was an accident. Come on. Let's have a swim in the dam.'

* * *

Four of us stood in a row, chins on arms, and leant on the top rail, towels over our shoulders, swimmers and Dunlop sandshoes on ready for a swim in the dam. Despite the leeches and yabbies, the muddy water was cool for our daily summer swim. To reach the dam we took a shortcut through the paddock and past the post office, where Chris Mutton lived. It took ten minutes less than going by the road.

Nancy and Sluggo, the Muttons' pet goats, were the terror of the shortcut.

'Where are they?' I searched the trees dotted around the fence line, feeling the strain of being a girl, trying to fit in with the boys.

'They won't hurt you, Bonnie,' said Chris. 'Run fast to the other side and you'll be fine.'

'Yeah, but they'll run faster.' My mind was filled with the memory of my previous attempt at the shortcut; Nancy and Sluggo, heads down, horns aimed at my backside. 'Last time they got too close.'

'I'll go first, draw them out, then the rest of you come afterwards,' said Chris as he vaulted over the fence and sprinted across the paddock. Nancy and Sluggo burst through the trees in the left corner and hurtled after him. Ross followed, heading straight across to the other side before the goats realised they had another quarry. Paddo was next. He zig-zagged, puffs of dust spurted from his heels as he sprinted across the open paddock and bounded over the fence to safety.

I did the exact opposite. With my towel held high like a parachute, I dithered about, changing direction while keeping my eyes on the two goats. Sluggo gazed at the three missed possibilities in safety on the other side as they shouted and waved in my direction.

'Come on Bonnie, stop prancing about,' said Ross.

'They're just being playful,' said Chris.

'Don't stand there, run.' Paddo beckoned with his hands waving.

I watched Sluggo and crept to the left.

'Run. For goodness sake, run,' they shouted from the rails.

Sluggo turned, saw me making slow motion moves into the middle of the paddock, shook his head and lowered his horns. Nancy swivelled around and launched into a gallop. Sluggo, with his nose down and eyes boring into me, bolted across the paddock at an alarming speed. I hesitated, frozen, undecided if I should go left or right.

'What are you doing?' hollered Ross. 'Move, you idiot.'

Sprinting was not an activity I found easy. Whenever I participated in running races, I tripped on my feet and stumbled headfirst into the dirt. That couldn't happen because I needed to move. Sluggo's horns were gleaming blades pointing at me.

Panic nailed my feet to the ground, embarrassment crammed my head with past blunders and I was conscious of the audience on the other side of the paddock witnessing my cowardly behaviour. While I searched for an escape route, I spotted the lone tree in the middle. Both the goats would need to go around it to get to me and although the low branches were cut to short stubs, I was a skilled tree climber. I ditched the towel and, for a split second, worried about the repercussions of that action, before realising the goats were so close I could hear them snorting.

With a burst of speed I thought impossible, I rushed towards the tree and flung myself at the first branch at the moment Sluggo arrived. He skidded to a halt and stabbed at the spot where my feet had been a moment before, as I climbed, desperate to get out of reach. When I felt I was far enough up and the branches had become too thin, I stopped to watch the goats stamping on my towel, flinging it around the dust and prickles.

'That was better than the gymkhana.' Cheers and whistles from the boys followed Chris's comment. 'I've never seen them have so much fun.'

'I'm not moving until you come and get these goats,' I yelled back.

'We'll come for you on our way back from the dam,' Ross said, throwing the towel over his shoulder while I watched from my high perch. They jogged past Chris's house and headed down the hill to the dam, their laughter fading with my courage.

'Don't you leave me here. Come back here. I HATE YOU.'

I sat in the fork of a branch, hoping they were teasing and that they'd turn around to come back for me. Nancy and Sluggo were having fun chewing on my towel. Occasionally they gazed into the tree. I was sure they were feeling smug at having trapped me here. It wasn't long before the goats became bored with the towel and wandered off and I was brave enough to climb down, hoping they wouldn't notice. Sluggo turned when I reached the bottom and trotted back as if he were a cat teasing his captive mouse.

I climbed back up the tree, cross with myself and angry with the boys when the screen door slammed and Chris's father came out to go the loo. He'd already unzipped his pants as he stepped inside the ramshackle wooden structure. Half one side was painted blue as if they'd run out of paint. The Muttons' toilet was in the front yard, perched in the middle of a circular driveway and in full view of the main road. A small pepper tree grew sideways on one corner, but its direction didn't provide shade or protection for the toilet. It was twice as big as ours with twin seats, one big and one small hole, something I had found fascinating. I'd once asked Chris why.

He said, 'A family who pees together, stays together.' I wasn't sure if he was joking.

When I saw Mr Mutton leaving the toilet, hitching up his trousers, I yelled, 'HELP', and he stopped tucking in his shirt and glanced in all directions. He shook his head and continued adjusting his clothes as he walked back to the house. Then I remembered his hearing wasn't good, so I screamed louder and kept screaming until he turned around and walked to the fence. Nancy and Sluggo trotted over to meet him.

'Bonnie?' he said, shading his eyes and peering into the tree. 'What are you doing up there?'

'Nancy and Sluggo ...' I trailed off, feeling stupid.

'Ah, chased you, did they?' He climbed over the fence with the two goats walking like docile dogs beside him.

'They won't hurt you.'

'That's what Chris said.'

'You can come down, now.'

I climbed down, but Nancy and Sluggo rushed over, so I scampered back up.

'I can't. They scare me.'

Mr Mutton laughed. 'You can ride on my shoulders, okay?'

'My towel.'

He walked over, picked up the towel, gave it a shake.

'Damn goats will eat just about anything.'

'I'm gonna cop it.'

I climbed on his shoulders and he carried me over to the fence, then put me on the other side so I could walk back home.

'I'll have a word with those boys. They shouldn't have left you behind.'

'Thanks, Mr Mutton. Can you have a word with Betty, too?'

BREAD

At the end of term two, Ross and I travelled on the train back from school and were met by Dad at Lake Cargelligo. It was dark and past our bedtime by the time we arrived at Mount Hope and into the comfort of our beds.

We woke next morning to the smell of cut wood. The sounds of buzzing, sawing and hammering mingled with the regular morning sounds. Not since the building of the shop had we heard such activity.

'What's happening at the pub,' said Ross at breakfast.

'There's going to be a bakery on the other side of the pub,' said Betty.

'They start far too early in the morning for my liking,' said Dad, turning a page of the Sunday Herald then picking up a piece of toast and jam. 'Hammering all hours of the day and night.'

'A bakery?' I asked.

'What about the bread we get from the shop at Euabalong West?' said Ross.

'Just think. Fresh bread every day,' I said. 'Yum.'

'It'll be finished in a few days,' said Betty. 'The shop won't need to sell bread if we have a bakery.'

'Bakers don't keep normal hours,' said Dad. 'They're up before dawn when the rest of us are still in bed.'

The grand opening of the bakery happened in the second week of our holidays and there were more people in town than I'd seen at the last gymkhana. For the few days before, the generator for the bakery interrupted the solitude of the bush as it cranked to full power at three o'clock each morning. The spread from the lights extended beyond the perimeter of the pub into our window and I could hear Dad through our bedroom wall tossing and muttering about his broken sleep.

A permanent floury haze hovered above the pub and bakery, and the aroma of freshly baked bread wafted down the hill and through our bedroom window. The bakery shelves were stacked with cakes, large and small, decorated with icing, hundreds and thousands and mock cream, biscuits of various shapes and soft spongy bread. Ross and I ogled at all the glorious, colourful cakes on our quick visit to the grand opening with Betty. Despite our encouragement, she bought a loaf of bread but no cakes.

For the rest of the week the regular interruption of sleep by the bakery generator caused a grumble every morning from Dad.

'A bloke needs his sleep,' he said slurping tea from his saucer. 'I think I might start the mine generator at one o'clock in the morning. See if they like that.'

The conversation in the shop ranged from the praise of delicious bread and cakes to the intrusion of the generator. The publican had a whinge one morning when he came to fill up with petrol.

'I'm not sure how I'll cope with all this racket in the middle of the night,' he said to Betty as she entered the amount into his shop account. 'I don't get to bed 'til one o'clock some mornings, then that bloody generator starts and sets off every dog in town.'

'Perhaps we'll get used to it,' she said, closing the book and placing it under the counter.

'I much prefer the bread from Euabalong West,' he said. 'I can't hear the generator there.'

Any thoughts of intruding generators were forgotten when Ross and I returned to boarding school a week after the opening. The bakery didn't last long. On our second night home for the September holidays, we woke to a commotion at the back of the pub.

'Bonnie, can you smell that?' said Ross.

'It's another bushfire,' I said as we leant out the window.

'No, it's not. The bakery's on fire.'

We jumped out of the window and ran into the back yard. Wood crackled and hissed and cinders drifted above the pub as flames swallowed the back of the bakery and rose higher than a Guy Fawkes bonfire. Smoke swirled and billowed above the trees and formed a foggy bank over the bakery as it floated in the direction of our backyard. Dad was issuing instructions to the few men heaving buckets of water on the fire. Everyone was shouting at each other over the din. I could see Dad's pyjama pants poking out the bottom of his pants when he turned and spotted us standing on the fence in the corner of the yard.

'What are you kids doing there?' he said. 'Get back in the house.'

'Gosh, Dad ...' Ross began.

'NOW. Skedaddle.'

The roof groaned then collapsed as the walls crumbled inwards. Buckets dropped as everyone ran beyond the spray of sparks and hot ash.

'Dad's too close,' I said.

Dad ran past the pig pen towards our back fence.

'There she goes,' he said. 'I thought I told you kids to go back in the house.'

'We were,' said Ross, ' but then we saw the roof go and were worried.'

'I'm fine,' he said. 'Now off you go.'

'Your father didn't get back to bed until five o'clock,' said Betty at breakfast next morning. 'So you kids be quiet.'

'Did you see the fire last night?' said Ross. 'It was big.'

'I'm sure it was,' said Betty.

'Can we go and have a look after breakfast?' I asked.

'Sure, but I'll come with you,' she said. 'I'd like to have a look as well.'

The building was in ruins. Gone were the colourful cakes and biscuits. What remained was twisted metal and ruined shelving blanketed in charred wood and ash. The smell of fresh bread was replaced with incinerated wood. The walls of the pub had been so close, they were scorched and charred from the flames.

'Do you know how it started?' I asked Betty.

'Rats chewed the matches,' she said.

'The great fire of London started in a bakery,' I said, proud of my recalled information from school. 'I wonder if the rats chewed the matches there?'

'Really?' said Ross.

'How interesting,' said Betty.

* * *

Ross and I worked in the shop stacking shelves, weighing potatoes, onions and tomatoes and packaging salt and sugar for customers with regular reminders by Dad and Betty to appreciate what we had. But we were interested in our own needs and felt the increased hours in the shop deserved a pay rise. We wanted to spend it on the new selection of lollies Betty had ordered for the store: fizzy packets, long ropes of licorice and columbines.

As the memory of the disaster faded, we presented our request for a pay rise during their pre-dinner drink session the night before. Our pleas had been turned down.

'You both need to know money doesn't grow on trees,' Dad said, taking another sip of whisky while Betty stirred the ice in her glass with her finger. 'A visit underground is the ticket. We'll go in the morning.'

Ross was excited and woke early, keen to be shown around the mine, but I'd had nightmares about being buried alive, or worse, left behind. It was all right to read about caves and caverns, finding them fascinating, but exploring them in person was scary. The one area at the mine where we were permitted entry was the office and for emergencies only. Everywhere else was forbidden. On the other side of the unfenced open cut was a turquoise acid pond where wild goats sometimes ventured too close and fell in. Dad showed us the consequences to impress upon us the importance of keeping our distance. It worked, because the sight of bloated goats disintegrating was ghastly.

Acid, petrol, grease and body odour lingered around the site. As we followed Dad past the rumbling generator inside a tin shed we had to shout to be heard above the noise. A large heap of scrap was stacked beside the vats. When forked into the rectangular concrete baths and added to the mixture, it broke down the copper into powder as the fires underneath heated the mixture. When dry, the powder was bagged and railed to Port Kembla for processing. We passed the office and the vats, where one of the men was stirring, sweat dripping, face flushed from the heat. Inside the tool shed, the smell was as familiar as Dad after a day at work. Metal shelving held hard hats and re-chargeable battery packs. On a sheet of timber on the wall, tools hung from metal hooks and above them, the word BOOMERANG was written. Several spots were empty.

'Boomerang?' I asked.

'Boomerangs come back,' said Dad. 'And so should my tools. Looks like someone has a few out.'

He removed overalls from the metal cabinet and handed us each a pair.

'Put those on over your clothes,' he said.

We looked like midgets in the baggy overalls and wellies. He then removed hard hats from the shelves and took two battery packs from the charger.

'Let's get kitted up,' he said, 'The hats will be loose and the battery a bit heavy, but you'll be fine,' said Dad as he attached the batteries and hooked them on our belts, then did the same for himself.

'Feel for the switch at the back on the battery,' he said as I fumbled about while he directed my fingers. 'I'll let you know when to turn it on.'

Ross didn't have any bother locating his switch.

'Stop flicking it on and off, Ross,' said Dad. 'You're wasting the battery. They'll last for about ten hours if you're careful.'

'Are we going to be down there for ten hours?' I asked.

'I certainly hope not,' said Dad. 'Right, come on.'

We stood outside the lift shaft while Dad opened the cage door and we stepped into a space to fit two men, but not three. The wire door clicked into place and the cage began a wobbly descent. I wasn't prepared for the light to fade so soon. Wind howled up the side of the shaft and the walls outside the cage were close enough to rip off an arm despite the slow speed of our descent. The floor quivered beneath my feet so, to keep balance, I reached for Ross in the dwindling light.

'Hey, quit that,' Ross slapped my arm.

'You're such a jerk sometimes.'

'Time to turn on your lights,' said Dad, ignoring our bickering. I grabbed his leg instead.

The lights on our hard hats had a cable on the back that ran down to the battery pack clipped onto our belts. I was still trying to locate the switch on the top of the battery when Dad reached over and flipped it on. Three narrow beams pierced the darkness. Like two fireflies flitting back and forth over the walls, Ross and I tried to control the angle and direction.

'It's not a very big light.' I looked up at Dad.

'Get that flamin' light out of my eyes girlie,' he said. 'You'll get used to it. Point it down to your feet. You need to see where you're walking.'

The cage stopped with a bump and I was glad I was clinging to Dad's leg.

'This is level four. Haberdashery, menswear and alterations,' Dad said as he pulled the wire door open.

He thought it was funny because in 1955 we'd been to David Jones in Sydney to be fitted for school uniforms. We knew Betty had lived there once, but this was another trip where it was just Dad and us. It was our first visit to the city and first ride in a lift. The lift operator sang out the department levels as we approached each floor. The tiny space became crowded with women wearing hats and gloves with matching handbags over their arms and as the lift jerked its way up, I was surrounded by high heels, swishing petticoats and rosewater perfume. When the lift finally stopped and we got out, I became lost among the clothes racks.

The cage was a lot smaller than the lift in David Jones and the mine smelt of dampness, engine oil and sulphur. My light reflected on the water dribbling down the grooved wall outside the bars tracing the paths of drill holes. As we stepped out, a rush of cold wind rumbled past, followed by a spray of fluid I hoped was water, as a small creature flew past.

'Golly, what was that?' I said, clinging to Dad's legs.

'Forgot to mention the bats,' Dad said.

'Any ghosts down here?'

'Yep, sure are son. Bloke who used to work here. Fell over the side of the open cut. Might have been him chasing the bat earlier.'

'I'm not sure about this,' I said.

'You'll be fine. It's time you both saw where I work.'

This underground venture was a result of both Ross and me asking for more pocket money.

'This is beaut,' said Ross.

'You like anything scary, Ross.'

'Yeah, and you're a scaredy-cat.'

'Am not.'

'That's enough, you two,' said Dad. 'Now let's go. Stick close. Watch for holes in the middle of the tunnel. There are bits of wood over the top but you can still fall down.'

'There's an awful lot of water,' I said stepping into puddles too big to walk around.

'We pump it down into the shafts so we can dig out the copper and send it to the vats up top. Bonnie, you're going to have to let go of my leg. We'll both end up down a hole and there's no telling where we'll land.'

'Sorry Dad, but I'm having trouble getting used to the light.'

We stood in the middle of the tunnel as Dad shone his lamp against the wall.

'See the lines along the walls,' he said.

'We saw them when we were in the cage,' said Ross.

'They're all through the tunnels and shafts. This is where we drill and set the dynamite to blast out the ore, take it up to the surface, crush it, put it in the vats and make copper powder.'

'How do you make money?' said Ross.

'It goes to Port Kembla in bags and we get paid for each bag.'

'But you make money from the shop too,' I said.

'Not enough to pay for your schooling, your clothes, your food, holidays and your pocket money.'

'Oh.' I thought mining was boring, but being underground wasn't. Scary, but not boring. I was sure I should be asking questions, but I couldn't think of any.

As Dad took us out to the end of the tunnel to where we could see the open cut, the temperature warmed and the light increased. The drop from the end into the open cut was bigger than the slag dump. A goat climbed up the side, finding rocky edges to place his hooves.

'Clever b..., animals, goats,' said Dad. 'They can stand on a sixpence. They're always getting down then having to climb out. Beats me why. There's no food in here and the water isn't fit to drink.'

The goat circled the rim, jumped an impossible distance to find a footing, then with a final leap, launched himself to the top of the hill.

'Time to leave,' said Dad as we applauded the clever goat.

As the cage ascended to the surface, Dad decided to reinforce his message about money.

'Money doesn't grow on trees, you know. You have to work hard to be able to put a roof over your head.'

'Yes, Dad.'

'So we'll have no more talk about wanting more pocket money, will we?'

'No, Dad,' we said.

THE VEGGIE PATCH

Dad plonked a bulging shoe box jammed with packets of seeds on the breakfast table between the marmalade and melting butter.

'Today,' he announced, 'we are going to dig a bed in the backyard for growing vegetables. Everyone will pitch in.'

Everyone was Ross and me. We were the only ones still seated. Betty was stuffing dirty clothes into the washing machine, humming an out-of-tune Scottish folk song.

'But it's Saturday,' said Ross, rifling through the box, nose scrunched up at turnips, swede and cabbage.

'What's wrong with tinned veggies, Dad?' Ross kicked me under the table for asking a question that would launch Dad into a lecture.

'Can't beat fresh ones, Bonnie. Planting the seeds, watching them grow then picking them straight from the garden ...'

Crikey, here we go.

'... one day, you will have a garden of your own, so today you might learn something useful ...'

'Ok, Dad.'

'When I was a lad, we grew all our own vegetables ...'

Too late.

Ross nudged me. 'It must be time to move the lav.'

Dad was always inspired to do a backyard makeover when it was time to blast a new hole and move the loo. When this happened, we had to hop over the fence and use the one at the pub during the day and the potty at night. I'd rather die. It was OK for Ross, he could jump out of the window and pee in the bushes. I avoided outside visits at night. Generations of spiders lurked in all the corners, unseen, bouncing across their netted trampolines ready to strike an exposed bottom.

Job number one was to dig out the bricks from the old path then scrape, clean and stack them, so they were ready to lay at the new spot further down the yard. To accommodate the extra length, it narrowed from a three-brick path to a two-brick one.

Next job was to prepare and blast the new hole. Ross and I hovered, fascinated, as Dad drilled, poked and prepared the dynamite. Then, when he was ready and we were safely behind the grain shed, we all shouted, 'FIRE IN THE HOLE!' at the top of our voices before he pressed the plunger.

Soil, rocks, various animal bones and the remains of buried pets shot up in the air and rained down all over the backyard. It was as exciting as the fireworks on Guy Fawkes Day. The dust cloud moved across the road and enveloped Jack Swazbrick Jnr as he sat on his front verandah, watching. In a small town, such events were spectator sports.

After lunch, it was time to fill in the old hole and clear the debris for the new one. This was Dad's favourite moment and as soon the low loader engine roared in the shed, Ross and I bolted to the Tarzan Tree, climbed up and watched. Dad negotiated the narrow driveway and burst into the backyard with the speed and deftness of a formula one racing driver. He spun, scooped and turned, hands flashing back and forth on the controls faster than a wasp in a tea cup. Up and down he revved and anything even half dead was ripped out and dumped. The pub verandah was lined with spectators holding pints of beer, offering encouragement and betting on his finish time.

Before he returned the loader to the shed, Dad did a few wheelies out front for the benefit of those watching. It was getting dark. The entertaining part of our makeover was over, so the patrons moved inside to the bar to quench the thirst raised by all the heckling. Dad wandered up to join them and find out who won the bet.

The following morning, Dad framed and poured the concrete pad. When we began laying the brick path, my artistry and Ross's precision clashed.

'It's a brick path.'

'Yes, but why not make a pattern?'

I had learned the elegance of symmetrical design in art class at boarding school and wanted to introduce my family to a tasteful, alternate method.

'It's a brick path. A line of bricks to the loo.'

'I could play hopscotch on my way up. Two bricks here, a row of stones there. It'll look nice.'

'Crikey Bon. Nice? I just want to get to the toilet.'

'Cut it out, you two,' said Dad. 'Two bricks, side by side up to the toilet. Okay?'

'Yes, Dad.'

I pushed aside my need to inject style into our backyard, so the finished path looked as it always did – raised edges, chipped sides and uneven spacing. In a couple of days, the loo was ready for action, complete with seat, pan and chopped newspaper on a string. The veggie patch was postponed to the coming weekend.

The extra run to the new loo was a challenge. A habit of last-minute dashing caused near misses and accidents. The frolicking dance of waiting for an occupant to finish was dicey for any full bladder and when Dad walked down the path with the morning paper, it was a jog to the pub loo.

On the second day of the new loo, I rushed around the tank stand to get there in time to see our clothes prop sticking out the toilet door making crazy figure eight circles in the air. Inside, Ross had the rest of it down the hole.

'What are you doing?'

He looked up and wiped his nose across his sleeve.

'You're crying.'

'Yeah, well, so what.'

'I've gotta go. I'll be back in a minute.' I ducked behind the spider shed and relieved myself and returned to find him swirling the stick back and forth, muttering to himself.

'What happened?'

'I had an accident, all right? So I threw my underpants in the loo. Betty said I had to get them out.'

'Really? That's awful,' I said. 'It's not fair. Gee, it's dark down there. You saw how deep Dad made the hole. It pongs something aweful.'

'When has anything been fair with her. I've been ages trying to get them out.'

'Can't just climb down.'

'I could tie a rope around your feet and lower you.'

'That's crazy.'

'She's crazy. Come on Sis, you know what she's like. I have to get them out.'

'I'm not going down that hole.'

'Well, think of something then, 'cause ... 'cause ...'

I didn't see my brother cry much, not like this. It wasn't fair. Just for a pair of underpants?

'How about I get Dad's big torch? We might be able to see them and we can take the seat off.'

The torch was great. Without the seat, we had a clear view of the ghastly contents. Ross moved the prop through the brown muck, picking up discarded newspaper and lumpy bits of this and that before we spotted the coated, cloth underpants.

'Look, look. That's them.' I said. 'All that stirring. It stinks in here.'

Getting them to stay on the end of the prop wasn't so easy. He twisted, wound and adjusted but just when we thought we were getting somewhere, they slid down the prop and dropped back into the sludge with frustrating frequency. We took turns. Scoop, turn, lift. The prop and torch got heavy and all the mixing caused an unpleasant reminder of the contents to drift up to us. I didn't know how long we'd been at it, but we were lucky no-one had wanted to use the loo while we'd been poking about.

'If I push it against the side, it should stay on. We'll drag it up,' said Ross.

He hooked the underpants on and jammed it against the rock wall.

Together we pulled, keeping the prop firm and steady until at last, we got to the bottom of the metal pan.

'You'll have to reach in and grab them so they don't fall off.'

'Ooooohhh, yuck, ick.' My skin crawled, it was more horrifying than being asked to eat a witchetty grub on our bush tucker excursion with Dad. I held my breath and, with two fingers I reached in, got hold of the coated, brown mass and flipped it over the end of the prop. My face was scrunched, I panted through tight lips and jerked in disgust. Ross backed out of the toilet with the dribbling blob on the end. We blasted the underpants, clothes prop and ourselves full bore with the hose then, after an extra wash in the laundry tub with Sunlight soap, hung everything on the line now supported by a sparkling, clean clothes prop.

'Just for that,' said Ross through chattering teeth, 'I'm gonna kill her twice.'

* * *

Killing Betty was delayed for a couple of months while Ross and I caught the train back to Moss Vale again for another term at boarding school.

Back home in August, a new extension had been built onto the shop, with an office and mechanic's workshop attached at the back. The telephone exchange had also been moved from Mutton's house to the far corner of the shop. Betty's sister, Barbara now lived in Mount Hope and had moved in with the mailman and she and her two boys were helping with the mail and grocery deliveries. They attended school in Cobar, staying in a hostel during the week coming back home on the weekends. It was easier because they were not living with us, but the treatment from Betty was the same as before.

When we got out of Dad's car, Lassie didn't rush out to welcome us as usual. Her presence was a permanence I counted on each time I came home. Her greetings never varied. She slobbered, danced with a whipping tail and revolving backside, and gave us her undivided attention.

'Where's Lassie? I asked Betty as she prepared breakfast for us all.

'She died.'

'She's dead? When did she die? What happened? Where is she buried?'

Betty sighed. 'She died shortly after you returned to school. Snake bite. Your Dad took her out to the bush and buried her.'

'Why didn't you write and tell me?' Lassie dead was unthinkable. She was our secret keeper, our pal, our friend and I didn't get to say goodbye to her.

'Now, what good would that have done? Your father thought it best.'

'I'd still like to have known,' I muttered. 'I don't feel like breakfast anymore.'

'Suit yourself.'

On Saturday, Dad plonked a familiar box of seeds on the breakfast table.

'Today we finish preparing the veggie patch,' he said. 'Come on you two, we've got work to do. I've had enough of your moping about.'

I'd wanted to spend time on the piano, but there was little point in grumbling so we followed him outside to where a shovel, spade, and a couple of crowbars stuck out of the wheelbarrow that stood beside the loo. The mounds of dirt left from the toilet relocation a couple of months before, had sprouted weeds among the rocks and stones. Small runners of buffalo grass poked out the sides and the whole area had become packed and hard.

'Right. First, we mark the area. No point in doing any unnecessary digging, eh kids?'

As far as I was concerned all of this was unnecessary. I'd hoped it would all have been finished when we were away.

'This is a good spot,' he said grabbing an old hose from the wheelbarrow and weaving it around the mounds stacked on one side of the toilet. From the size of the area, I figured we were embarking on a market garden, providing enough produce for the shop and the house. We'd be digging for the entire holidays.

'Okay kids,' said Dad. 'Dig in.'

Ross lifted a pick from the wheelbarrow and dragged it into the centre of the patch, lifted it above his head and let out a squeaky Tarzan call then thrust it into the ground where barely the tip got buried.

'You'll need to work on that a bit, son,' said Dad.

I wasn't certain if he meant the Tarzan call or the digging but when he looked sideways at me grinning it brightened my mood. We shoveled and levelled, filling the barrow with weeds and removing stones. Although Dad did most of the work, once the top layer was turned over, the soft soil underneath made it easier for us kids to dig. We worked all morning and I rubbed my blisters, thinking my dream of becoming a concert pianist was evaporating along with my enthusiasm. As far as I was concerned, who needed fresh vegetables? Tinned ones were just fine.

When Dad was satisfied the soil had been turned over enough, he replaced the hose with a stone border and added dolomite and chook poo. It smelt as bad as the old loo.

'Look at that,' he said, standing back with his hands on his hips, eyes roving over the freshly dug earth. 'Makes a man proud when he's got his own piece of land so he can till the soil and grow his own veggies.'

'Till the soil?' I asked.

Ross gazed skywards and let out an exasperated sigh when I realised this was an opportune moment for Dad to present another life lesson. He leant on his shovel and gazed into the distance and I wondered if he was thinking of rows of plump cabbages and tasty fresh carrots when he began.

'One day you'll appreciate that everything is not handed to you on a plate. You have to work hard in life ...'

Ross leaned on his shovel, possibly lost in the jungles of Africa with Tarzan, as Dad continued his talk about gratitude and sacrifice. I squatted on the ground and watched the ants navigate a new pathway across the fresh ground.

'... so perhaps you'll keep that in mind, next time,' said Dad.

'Yes, Dad,' we mumbled.

'Time to put the tools away,' said Dad. 'We'll plant tomorrow.'

The following day we scattered seeds. I started placing one seed at a time along the furrows, carefully setting them the correct distance apart.

'Good grief, we'll be here all day if you do it like that,' said Dad. 'Here. Scatter them like this.' He took a small handful and spread them along in random rows.

We planted carrots, radishes, watermelon, tomatoes and cucumbers each with labelled tags on a post. If we could have grown devon we would have, because it was on our plates every day. Ross and I took turns in watering the seed beds which was as boring as the preparation. We carted bath water and bucketed it into the channels that surrounded the plantings. I was impatient and wanted to see immediate results but vegetable growing was as slow as a school term. But by the time we were ready to return to school, the tiny green tops of the radishes had appeared in clumps rather than the neat lines I'd expected to see.

'You'll see the fruits of your labour next holidays,' said Dad. 'When you come home, the beds will be bursting with veggies.'

By December, the pumpkin vines were splendid, having sprouted from the compost and spread over the weeds, grass and footpaths. They covered the rock pile and had commenced their journey across to the Spider Shed. Pumpkins bulged from crude frames and dangled in Betty's old stockings, stretched to capacity. The watermelons, sheltered beneath their leaves, grew along the ground with equal determination in their resolve to overthrow the pumpkins and dominate the back yard. Radishes and carrots had been crowded out by the creeping vines and one tomato plant struggled to maintain its position in the centre of the patch. At least they hadn't invaded Ross's Tarzan Tree, but the cow pen was in danger. Dad had to move my wooden cubby-house with its lookout tower and Woman's Weekly wallpaper because the vines, climbing up the fence and across to the empty chook pen, had engulfed it.

'Needed the room,' muttered Dad when I complained. I was not impressed.

Over the weeks, Dad inspected and measured the pumpkins, most of which survived. The watermelons were treated with equal reverence as he stepped between each, tape measure around his neck, notebook in hand whispering to each, tapping and measuring his charges waiting for them to ripen. More often than not, it was all at the same time, causing a glut of pumpkin meals followed by a healthy slice of watermelon. Our moans of *not again* were greeted with comments about starving Africans. The only vegetables Dad ever had success with were pumpkin and watermelon. As we ate our way through them, the discarded seeds filled an empty Milo tin inside the back door. We couldn't match Dad's enthusiasm each time he presented *another home grown watermelon.*

Hot weather, poor rainfall and our declining interest were conditions more favorable for weeds. They flourished while the vines withered and died, so horticulture was abandoned in favour of chickens.

ROUGHING IT

In 1959, my two-week, mid-year holiday from boarding school was spent at the *Queen Bee* mine, twenty miles outside Cobar, where Dad had the lease. Ross had left school the year before and worked for Dad. There was no house, just a caravan and kitchen shack in the middle of the bush. Each time I came home from school, things changed. This time, it was the move to Cobar. Betty remained at Mount Hope until the house was built and a clothesline was more than throwing the clothes over the bushes to dry.

Ross opened the door to the caravan.

'Here we are. I had a bit of a tidy up. Your bed's over there.'

'We're sharing?'

'This is it,' said Ross. 'Welcome to your hotel accommodation.'

I stepped inside to disarray. Machinery parts dotted the floor. Work clothes hung from doorknobs on the overhead cupboards and opened textbooks cluttered the bed. The rumpled top sheet hung over the edge.

'Where can I put my things?'

'Can't they stay in the suitcase? You're only here for two weeks.'

The caravan was parked alongside the one-roomed shack that served as our kitchen. We had been sharing a bedroom since we were small. Now we were older, we would have preferred privacy, but our preferences were not a consideration in this secluded and isolated place.

'Where's Dad sleeping?'

'In the shed up at the mine.'

'At least his snores will be muffled.'

'I think Dad expects you to do the cooking and cleaning while you're here.'

Cooking was not on the curriculum at boarding school. In Girl Guides we once barbecued a snake and that caused an influx of patients in the sick bay.

A series of linoleum scraps dotted the ground the short distance from the caravan to the kitchen. Nailed across the doorway was a torn plastic curtain I recognised as one from the Mount Hope bathroom. It failed to prevent the blowflies, dust and mice from invading. Utensils were basic. Cutlery with missing handles, bent prongs and irregularly shaped spoons, occupied a cardboard box on the table beside the glass salt and pepper shakers. One large pot with a mismatched lid had a home under the rickety wooden bench. Sitting on top, was an enamel basin used for washing faces, hands and dishes. The rationed water, with a muddy film covering the bottom, became grimy as the day progressed. It was replaced in the morning for washing faces and in the evening for washing dishes.

Stacked wooden crates stored tinned food, cups, plates and utensils, and a small kerosene fridge provided warmth for brown snakes. I was certain they knew when it was my turn to fill the fridge with kerosene because each time there was one, curled around the lighted wick. My screaming was ignored. At night, we stuffed our boots with newspaper to prevent the horrors from curling up inside. When I was nine, Dad once chopped one up into many bits with the axe and, as the pieces kept bouncing across the dirt, Ross informed me each one would grow back into a full-sized snake. I had nightmares for years.

However, it was the ants that caused more problems than any other creature. Their black trails ran down the sink, across the floor, over the table and any other obstacles. Despite the necessity for airtight tins to thwart the marauding beasts, they succeeded in locating the tiniest infringement or spillage, providing evidence of sloppy housekeeping. Leaving the lid off anything was an offence.

'Who left the lid of the bloody sugar off, again.' Dad would bang the tin on the table and ants would dislodge, scrambling across the formica and over the side.

'You're not at boarding school, young lady.' He waved the tin in front of my nose. The remaining ants crawled down his fingers and across his watch.

'Sorry, Dad.' I didn't know where the sugar tin was kept at boarding school. In fact, my relationship with the kitchen was to deliver the dirty dishes.

'We don't waste food. Food costs money.'

'Yes, Dad.'

'Looks like you get to pick all the ants out of the tin. Perhaps you'll be more careful in future.'

'How will I? ...'

'Ross'll show you. He doesn't leave the lid off anymore.'

'Nothing to it,' said Ross, leading me outside. 'You flick 'em out one at a time.'

On Monday, Dad made a stew for dinner and it lasted until Friday. He came down during his lunch break and chopped vegetables, meat and onions. He threw them into a huge pot with a handful of flour and seasoning, then left it on the stove to cook all afternoon. This was my cooking lesson because I would be making the stew the following week.

'Someday you will have to cook for your husband,' said Dad. 'Men love stews.'

'When I get married,' I said with conviction, 'I'm going to have a cook.'

'Well, good luck with that, girlie.'

The first serving of Dad's stew, with thick fresh bread dipped into the gravy, was scrumptious. We weren't allowed second helpings; the pot was stored in the fridge then reheated each evening. However, as the days went by, our farts didn't diminish as much as the flavour of the stew. Dad added curry powder, tossed in chopped potatoes and onions and added more water. No longer thick and tasty, the salt and pepper shakers passed around the table with increased frequency. By Friday it was stale bread and coloured water. I sat at the wobbly table with a three-pronged fork bent out of shape watching as my father raised his plate to his mouth and slurped the remaining gravy. My brother followed his example. I was appalled by their disgraceful manners. Then, Dad poured his tea into the saucer and slurped the hot liquid.

'Dad?'

'What?' He looked at me over the rim of the saucer, brows furrowed, his specs halfway down his nose and foggy from the hot tea. He took another slurp. Tea dribbled down his chin and onto his shirt.

'Nothing.' I shuffled my feet, embarrassed at the lack of manners in my family, then remembered it was a dirt floor. Dust particles drifted upwards, settled on the table and floated on the top of our watery stew. Both punctured me with their stare.

'Thanks for the extra flavouring, Bonnie,' said Ross.

'Sorry about that.'

I was conscious of being in a family with etiquette at odds with the teaching at school and becoming less of a tom-boy and more a girl.

The dusty floor, trailing ants and watery stew were petty inconveniences in comparison to the bathroom facilities.

'Is there a curtain?' I asked Dad, when he took me down with Ross to show us how the shower worked.

'I can have the builder come out and put a fancy sliding door on for you if you like,' said Dad. 'When I was a boy we had to bathe outside ...'

Oh no, not again.

'... sometimes we'd go days with just a flick of water because it was so scarce.'

Dad turned and stared at me over the rim of his specs and I couldn't tell if he was cross or disappointed.

'What else can I help you with little lady?' Eyebrows raised, chin tilted upwards, his delivery resembled Laurence Olivier. 'Fancy soap? Large bathtub? Perhaps a maid?'

I was an old hand at these discussions. This one was going nowhere. 'No thanks, Dad.'

The three of us stood in the doorway of a concrete bunker once used for the storing of explosives. It was bigger than the kitchen. In the furthest corner, a four-gallon drum dangled from a butcher's hook. In its base was a series of random holes, a dozen or so, no doubt made by Dad with a hammer and nail. Underneath was the upturned half of a forty-four gallon drum which served as a seat, a step and, flipped over, a laundry tub.

This was the bathroom. There was no plumbing, no power and no door. The light from outside highlighted the word *Gerry* etched into the rough concrete wall in childish scrawl. Dirt was embedded in the coarse surface and the air smelt like the aftermath of a rainstorm; a combination of damp and dust. I stared up at the bucket and wondered if I'd survive in such primitive conditions. It was bad enough with a dirt floor in the kitchen where a film of dust covered everything and the meals had a touch of added grit.

'Good,' said Dad. 'You can have one with your brother.' His voice bounced off the walls with a soft echo.

'Share with Ross?'

'Something wrong, girlie?'

'Aw gee Dad, I can't ...' Ross shuffled his feet and found a crack in the concrete to poke his toe in.

'She can't lift a full bucket on her own, okay? This is not a hotel. Now grab your towels and get on with it. It'll be dark soon and I'm not wasting money on lights in here.'

Through the open doorway, I glimpsed a kangaroo in the shadow of a distant tree as I shuffled around the humiliating fact that I had to share a shower because I couldn't lift a bucket.

Dad headed off to the kitchen. In between his laughter I heard him comment, 'Curtain indeed.'

The demonstration had looked easy. At six feet, Dad was tall enough to reach without stretching. He'd hoisted the water bucket up to his shoulder and tipped it in with one fluid movement. Large sploshes descended through the holes and hit the concrete. In three-seconds it was all over. Boarding school had taught me the discipline of speedy showers. I could wash in one minute ... but three seconds? I shook my head to throw off my apprehension and maintain some composure.

The kangaroo I spotted was joined by another. They stared at me as if impatient for a show to begin. The doorway gave a panoramic view of the adjacent paddock and beyond. The few stumpy bushes close by did nothing to provide any privacy and with one bound over the fence they could be within handshaking distance.

'Don't take any notice of them,' said Ross. 'They're practically pets.'

'Oh, right smarty-pants. They won't come too close, will they?'

'Nah. As long as you don't feed them they won't bother you. Come on, let's get the water.'

We filled two buckets with heated water from the large copper boiler beside the kitchen and Ross carried his with ease as I struggled to cart mine twenty yards down the hill to the shower. By the time we got there, it was cool enough for us to wash. On the way, I'd sloshed some over the rim, leaving a wet trail in the dirt behind me and mud on my shoes.

'That's yours, remember? I still have a full bucket.'

The wind howled around the entrance, chilling the inside of the thirty-foot square bunker. We undressed fast, uncomfortable and embarrassed by the situation and our naked bodies. His tanned arms and legs contrasted with my pale skin. Shared bathing was once of no consequence for us. In the months of separation, he now working with Dad, me at boarding school, the distance between us had widened. We'd lost the ease of being together as brother and sister. We both felt awkward, so we tried to maintain eye contact, project indifference and not look down.

I stood underneath, naked, covering my privates.

'You won't get far like that. Soap all over first, then I'll pour. You'll have to be quick.'

He stepped on the upturned drum and as he hurled the full bucket up to his shoulder, I noticed he'd developed muscles in his arms from days of heavy work. After years of struggle with a chest expander, without success, he must have been pleased.

'Get on with it,' he said.

With experienced ease, he heaved the water up and over without a dribble wasted. I rubbed as fast as I could. When the stream stopped as abruptly as it began, I had soap in my ears and my hair felt like straw.

'My turn,' said Ross. My teeth chattered and my body shook as the draft through the doorway hit my wet skin.

'But I'm still covered in soap.'

'Too bad. Hurry up. It's cold.'

The bucket was heavy, but Ross offered no assistance. I stood on the step struggling and grunting as I heaved and wrestled to get the bucket up and over my head. Most of the water went in. The rest unloaded on me and not only removed some of the residual soap, but warmed my cold body.

Ross worked frantically as the water slopped over him. He had more success than I at removing all the soap. There was white froth in our ears and my skin was starchy from the bore water.

'That was terrible.'

'You'll get used to it.'

'These must be the oldest towels Betty could find.'

Thin, faded and frayed, they were as useless as a tea towel.

'Yeah, nothing but the best for us.'

'How can you stand it here?'

'It's quiet and I'm away from ... all that stuff. Dad goes back to Mount Hope on the weekends and I have the place to myself.'

'Yeah. I know what you mean.'

'Anyway, I don't mind being alone.'

'Maybe we could swim in the dam next time.'

'Sure, if you don't mind the two-mile walk.'

We stopped shivering, but my body was covered in goosebumps. I dried my feet with the saturated towel before putting on my sandshoes, trying to avoid the water that was running out the door. It cascaded across the planks of wood that formed a ramp over the hole created from the frequent water run-off. The puddle spread outwards into a lake of mud, reminding me of days at the dam in Mount Hope. My already grubby shoes got another coat. The line of kangaroos in the viewing gallery had swelled to front row size at the theatre – in the same spot, motionless. Eyes on us. We must have been their afternoon entertainment and I half expected them to burst into cheers and applause. A couple of kookaburras in a nearby tree began cackling but I didn't feel like laughing. I had no idea where I belonged. I was a mass of conflicted emotions.

I had few friends at school and none at home except Ross. The piano was still in Mount Hope and I missed being able to absorb myself in music. Relocating to Cobar felt a huge separation from my family. My mind was like the harsh, chaotic sound of the sulphur-crested cockatoos screeching into the dusk.

Without doubt, this was a holiday event I would not be sharing with my posh boarding school mates.

PINK CAR, GREEN SOCKS

It was Boxing Day 1960. Ross was thumping out *On Top of Old Smokey* on the piano with his one-chord-fits-all tunes left hand as the right hand fumbled over the melody. He had one year of piano lessons then decided he'd teach himself. Tippy was sprawled on his bed in the sleepout reading *Phantom* comics. Zilla and I had been making skirts and tops on the treadle sewing machine. We were snapping photos of ourselves in our newly-made outfits sitting on the top rail of the driveway gate when a pink sports car pulled up in front of the bowsers. The reverberating engine rattled a loose piece of tin on the roof as we all stopped to listen to the unfamiliar motor.

'That'll be your brother,' said Dad as he strode through the side gate over to the car.

'Brother?' said Zilla.

'Keith?' This was unexpected and exciting. 'Keith's here,' I shouted back to the house.

Ross flew out the front door, cleared the fence with Tippy following. Zilla and I dispensed with our modelling and joined everyone on the shop verandah. When the car door opened, I was dazzled by the green socks and white shoes that stepped onto the red, dusty gravel.

'Hello Dad. What do you think of my wheels?' said Keith in an unfamiliar deep drawl, peering over his sunglasses with a broad smile. He tapped the bonnet. 'Spent the last few months fixing it up.'

'Wow,' said Ross. 'Can I sit in it?'

'Tomorrow, buddy,' said Keith. 'I'll take you all for a spin.'

Keith wore a leather jacket, tight, white pants and a pink shirt the same colour as his car. His Elvis Presley hair style didn't impress Dad.

'You look like a bodgie with that hair style,' said Dad.

'It's the latest,' said Keith.

'You look cool,' I said.

'Yeah,' said Ross sweeping the sides of his hair back and pulling the fringe down over his forehead.

Zilla and Tippy gaped at a brother unrecognisable to them. The resemblance to Dad was unmistakable.

Dad and Keith shook hands. Polite, but quick.

'Staying long?' said Dad.

'A week,' said Keith. 'Back to work after that.'

'Best you move that contraption over to the house,' said Dad. 'Doesn't look safe.'

'Gosh it's good to see you kids,' said Keith slapping Ross on the shoulder and giving the rest of us a hug.

'Why are you wearing green socks?' asked Zilla.

'It's the latest thing,' said Keith, ruffling her hair.

'Can I carry your suitcase?' Ross asked when Keith had moved the car closer to the house.

Betty leaned against the post on the front verandah wiping her hands on her apron.

'Hello Betty,' said Keith.

'Your room out the back is ready,' Betty said. 'Then it'll be time for dinner.'

When we all crowded around the doorway in Keith's room he invited us in.

'I've got Christmas presents for you all,' he said, as he rummaged in his suitcase and handed each of us a box wrapped in brown paper.

To Ross, he gave a wristwatch. Zilla, a small, gold neck chain. Tippy received a Swiss army knife and mine was a gold heart-shaped ring with a tiny ruby in the centre. His choices were perfect.

'But we didn't get you anything,' I said. 'Because we didn't know you were coming.'

'That's all right,' said Keith. 'It's great to be here. Now, how about you let me unpack?'

Keith had a few beers with Dad and Betty before dinner on the first night of his visit and the rest of us sat on the back step with soft drinks listening to the conversation. Dad disapproved of Keith's work as a TV technician, his choice of car and manner of dress.

'I'm twenty-two Dad, not a child anymore. I work hard, my wages go on that car and I spend my spare time rebuilding it. I even fixed the body.'

'You should get a proper job,' said Dad. 'What sort of a job is it fixing television sets?'

'Why can't you be proud of me?'

The disappointment in Keith's voice was a contrast to the excitement of seeing us when he arrived. Their conversation was like two bits of sandpaper rubbing against each other. Ross, Zilla, Tippy and I went into the lounge room to listen to the serials on the radio while Betty clunked and banged about in the kitchen, stoking the fire and opening tins. Chops, mashed potato and tinned peas for dinner.

The following day at breakfast we bombarded Dad with '*Please, Dad, can we?'* and he grumbled but agreed that we could ride in Keith's car.

'All right, all right,' he said. 'No shenanigans, Keith.'

Betty mentioned paperwork at the shop and Dad went up to the mine for a couple of hours while we all scrambled to be first in Keith's pink car, fighting over who would sit in the front.

'Ross is the oldest, so he gets to sit in the front first,' said Keith. 'Everyone gets a turn.'

'Where's your green socks?' asked Zilla.

'Special occasions only,' said Keith.

There were no back doors. Keith pulled the front seat rest forward and we stepped into quilted leather seats and open sky. Zilla and I sat either side of Tippy and Ross hung his arm over the side of the passenger door. We were movie stars as we drove past the slag dump and turned off towards the racecourse. We stopped among the small bushes springing up on the racetrack so I could have my turn in the front seat. Our hair lashed against our faces as the wind churned, whipping dust around the open cabin. We spoke with hand signs as conversation was impossible above the sound of the motor and violent wind.

At the two-mile post we changed for Zilla's turn in the front seat. I walked to the fence looking beyond, into the memory of running away to find Mum when I was five.

'Do you ever think about her?' I said to Ross as he joined me at the fence.

'Sometimes,' he said. 'It's been so long since we've seen her.' He put his arm around my shoulder. A rare gesture of affection.

'I don't remember her,' I said.

'Me either,' said Ross.

'I wonder where she is.'

'I reckon if she'd wanted us, she'd have come back,' he kicked at the post.

'Come on you two,' said Zilla. 'It's my turn in the front.'

'You guys okay?' asked Keith.

'Yeah,' said Ross. 'We're fine. Can I drive?'

'Not this time, mate,' said Keith.

Off we bounced, back past the shop and along the bitumen strip across the front of the pub with its closed doors and empty car park, past the old post office, and empty paddock that once held Nancy and Sluggo. When the Mutton's moved to Forbes they were released and joined the other wild goats that roamed the hills. We stopped at the Euabalong West turn off for Tippy's front seat ride to return home. With faces stiff with dust and satisfied smiles, we came to a skid in front of the shop.

'Okay kids,' said Keith. 'That's it. I've got to fix a rattle in the motor.'

Zilla and I spent the day mucking about with duets on the player piano, singing at the tops of our voices to the piano rolls, showing off skills learned during the year. Ross helped Keith fix his car.

'How was the ride, kids,' said Dad when we sat down to tea. 'Keith's up the pub with some of the blokes.'

'Magic,' said Tippy.

'Bit windy,' said Zilla.

'We didn't go far,' said Ross. 'Past the racecourse and to the Euabalong turn off.'

'We all had a go in the front seat,' said Tippy.

'It was cool,' I said. 'All of us together. Cool.'

'Cool.' said Betty. 'What kind of a word is that?'

'It's the latest,' I said, echoing Keith.

'After dinner I want to record each of you at the piano.' said Dad.

'Cool,' I said.

Dad's latest gadget was a Grundig reel-to-reel machine. It resembled a small portable radio, with a handle and removable cover. Inside were two small reels. The tape was threaded through the playing head and the tiny speakers on the side played back his recordings. The recording was captured on a smaller, separate device that held a single reel and small microphone. Tinny voices, arguments during the washing up and us playing the piano in the lounge room were recorded, and we listened as the spinning reels played the shrill, squeaky sounds of our chattering. He recorded notes and letters for Betty to type, labelling the boxes and storing them in their room. Betty wasn't keen on working from the machine, so she abandoned it and resumed note-taking in shorthand.

Dad was still learning how to use the apparatus. 'Say something,' he said, shoving the microphone at Betty, who was darning socks, as he clicked and fiddled with the switches.

'I'd rather not,' said Betty, then snipped the thread with her teeth.

'What shall we play for you, Dad?' I asked.

'What's that one you both sing and play, something about wandering?' Dad said.

'*I love to go a-wandering, along the mountain track ...*' we both sang.

'That's the one.'

'We've heard it all through the holidays,' said Ross.

'What about *The Pub With No Beer*,' said Zilla. 'You play it all the time, Ross. Heaven help me, Slim Dusty.'

'What's wrong with Slim Dusty?' said Dad.

'Nothing,' said Zilla.

Slim Dusty was on the same pedestal as Bing Crosby and Richard Tauber. Dad's taste in music was confusing and not to be questioned but he didn't seem to mind what any of us played on the piano. His interest in our progress meant constant use of the piano during the day and concerts at night.

'Let's get this show on the road,' said Dad. 'I don't want to be all night.'

Dad adjusted and twiddled until he was satisfied. Zilla and I played *The Happy Wanderer* together as a duet, singing along in harmony. Tippy played one of his last exam pieces, a Bach Minuet, and Ross thumped out *The Pub With No Beer,* complete with left hand vamping out the same chord all the way through. Even Dad sang along. Halfway through the sixth chorus the tape ran out, but we continued singing at the tops of our voices, through to the eighth verse. Dad packed up his Grundig and we had an hour sing-a-long of British folk songs. Betty kept darning and tapped her foot, but didn't sing.

Keith walked in and leant against the door frame as we sang the final note of 'Molly Malone'.

'Dad's just finished recording us on the Grundig,' I said.

'Sorry I missed it. I was catching up with some of the locals.'

'Be nice if you spent time with your family,' said Dad.

'I'll be off to bed then,' said Keith. 'I'll listen to you guys in the morning.'

'Time for you kids to hit the sack, too' said Dad.

While Keith was visiting, I shared my bedroom with Ross. He had begun to shave and was conscious of our changing bodies. I was fourteen but still had the body of a girl. We found a routine the allowed space and privacy which avoided arguments. Our window opened on to the driveway and we heard the slamming car doors as the late drinkers from the pub drove home. I was in the middle of slipping my nightie on, still humming *The Happy Wanderer*, when Ross burst through the door.

'Hey,' I said. 'You're supposed to knock.'

'Listen,' he said. 'Yeah, sorry. Just shush and listen.'

He pulled me over to the window and stuck his head out.

'What?'

'Listen,' he whispered. 'Dad and Keith are having a barney.'

I put my head out the window and could hear their voices rising and falling against the sigh of the leaves brushing against the gutttering.

'What are they saying? Why are they fighting?' I listened, but the words were indistinct. A jumble of tones with attitude.

'I don't know, but it doesn't sound good,' said Ross.

A door closed. The scuff of slippers on the bricks petered out behind a closing door. Bed springs squeaked as Dad settled into bed.

My heart thumped to the receding night sounds so I closed my eyes and counted sheep in the hope I would forget.

At daybreak Ross shook me awake.

'They're in the driveway. I heard Keith toss his case on the back seat.'

'Is he leaving?' My foggy head cleared.

'Looks like it. Come on.'

Dad was striding over to the shed and Keith stood by his car, rubbing his chin.

'Hey, guys,' he said. 'I was just coming in to say goodbye.'

'You're leaving?' I said. 'But you only just got here.'

'I know and I'm sorry, but I can't stay, Bonnie.'

'But we haven't done anything together, yet,' said Ross.

'I know mate. Next time.' Keith squatted down and took both our hands. 'I can't stay here. You guys will just have to visit me in Sydney sometime,' he said with a cheery smile.

The front gate clicked and Zilla and Tippy walked over to us. We were a semi-circle of silence around Keith as he hugged each of us, ruffling hair and patting shoulders.

'I'm so glad we were all here together.' He jumped over the door without opening it, plopped onto the driver's seat, turned on the ignition then drove past the shed where Dad stood leaning against the wall rolling a cigarette.

'Bye,' Keith waved. 'See ya, kids.'

The pink car drove steadily across the bitumen strip and we caught a final glimpse of Keith, his arm relaxed along the door, his hair ruffled in the wind and a green sock flapping from the antenna.

LEAVE OF ABSENCE

'This will be fun,' said Aunty Ethel, crunching the gears as we left Dad, Ross and Betty waving at us from the front of the Mount Hope store. The VW Beetle had a full tank of petrol, five spare tyres loaded on the roof rack and luggage stored in the bonnet for the journey over to Western Australia in 1961. Zilla, Tippy and I were jammed in the back seat and the two fifty-something Aunties in the front. Aunty Ethel leaned forward, lips pressed, pouting with grim determination, her ample bosom squashed against the steering wheel. Her backside spilled over the sides of her seat. Aunty Dell was diminutive in comparison. She was cheerful, energetic and uninhibited. At five feet tall and slight-framed, she had room to spare on the seat.

'All set. Off we go.' Aunty Ethel let out the clutch and the car lurched forward in jerks as we spun on the gravel and headed out of town towards Cobar.

'For goodness sake, Ethel, let the clutch out slow-ly. You'll wreck the gear box.'

'You drive your way and I'll drive mine, Dell.'

'I've been driving a lot longer than you.'

'As you keep reminding me.'

'It'll get worse before it gets better,' Zilla whispered. 'They argue all the time.'

The fun dissolved as fast as the disappearing Mount Hope horizon and by the time we reached Cobar, 100 miles away, the sticky seats, dusty roads and endless games of *I spy* had dulled the adventure.

'Only 2,000 miles to go,' sang Aunty Dell, springing out at the service station to do a series of star jumps beside the car. The embarrassment was compounded when she sat in the middle of the concrete path and finished her exercise routine with a series of sit-ups and leg stretches. Traffic slowed to watch, but to Zilla and me, it was unseemly behaviour for someone her age. Especially a relative. We escaped inside the building and checked out the magazines. I pretended not to notice, but peered through the grubby windows while she pranced about outside.

'You'll get used to it,' said Zilla. 'She does this all the time.'

'I'm not sure I will.'

'She's a load of fun, though. Not afraid to try anything. One day she called to visit, riding a motorbike, decked out in leather pants and jacket. Aunty Ethel had a fit because she wanted to take her out for a run. Had an extra helmet and everything.'

'Did she go?'

"Course not. Not her style. I thought it would be a blast. But Aunty E wouldn't allow it. She doesn't visit often. Too busy driving all over the countryside with her boyfriends. She came with us to share the driving and because Aunty Ethel has only had her driver's licence for a year.'

Zilla and Tippy had been living with Aunty Ethel continually since 1955. They chatted about people I would soon meet and events I knew nothing about. I was leaving the familiarity of Mount Hope and boarding school to finish my education in Western Australia at a co-ed school.

I didn't like the clothes Betty ordered for me from a catalogue and envied the fashionable garments worn by others. Foolishly, I stole a cardigan from a fellow student and sewed my name tag over hers. My offence caused the headmistress to make snap inspections in my dormitory, open and read my mail and seek opportunities to reprimand me for my behaviour. It went from bearable to intolerable. I received the cane for the smallest infringement such as socks not even and scuffed shoes. The guilt I felt over the incident caused a lapse in my school marks. Dad offered me the choice of staying or spending a year in Western Australia. He was disappointed and said that Zilla would never behave in such a disgraceful manner. Betty said nothing. The choice was easy; I was excited to be living with my siblings for a year and away from Betty although I would miss Ross.

Our first tyre blow-out happened ten miles out from Broken Hill. Aunty Dell smashed Aunty Ethel's speed limit by ten miles an hour while we sang *Three Blind Mice* in rounds above the noise of the motor and din of the wind blustering through the open windows.

'I think you should slow down,' shouted Aunty Ethel, above the racket in the cabin. 'There's a truck coming in the opposite direction.'

'I'm within the speed limit,' said Aunty Dell. 'You drive at the same speed as a horse and cart.'

A loud BANG, followed by a thump, brought our singing to an abrupt end as the car began a lopsided jaunt across the road, down into the scrub.

'By the Hogan's Goat. Watch out, Dell!' said Aunty Ethel.

Aunty had a barrel full of weird sayings she would rattle off from time to time. We didn't know what most of them meant, but knew by the tone of her voice and her mood.

Aunty Dell brought us back to the side of the road with the skill of a racing car driver, skidded on the gravel and we came to a stop on the opposite side of the road. The truck whizzed past and the car gave another shake as our shrieks subsided. We were relieved to be alive.

'You'll get us killed with that kind of driving.' Aunty Ethel opened the door and pulled the seat forward so we could get out.

'We're okay, aren't we?'

'Nifty driving, Aunty,' said Tippy.

'That's number five,' said Zilla, checking the tyre. 'We had four on the way over.'

Blow-outs were a frequent hazard in our lives. Repairing punctures was something everyone in our family could do.

'Now. Whose turn is it to change the tyre?' said Aunty Dell.

'Bonnie hasn't had a turn yet,' said Tippy.

'But I wasn't with you on the trip over.'

'Bet you don't know how,' said Zilla.

'Of course I do.'

'Well, you'll fit right in,' said Aunty Dell.

'All this chatter is not going to get the job done,' said Aunty Ethel. 'Let's get cracking.'

'I think your Dad must've tightened these wheel nuts,' said Aunty Dell. 'They're as tight as Betty's purse.'

'Dell, there's no need for that sort of talk.'

We stayed at a Caravan Park in Broken Hill and again in Ceduna with the luxury of toilets, washrooms and beds. Aunty Dell continued her exercise regime every time we stopped and it was hard pretending I wasn't related to this strange lady. When we left the bitumen at Ceduna it was over a thousand miles of dirt until Kalgoorlie. Three tyres had needed to be fixed before the three-day challenge of driving across the Nullarbor Plain.

The car windows were closed to keep the fine powdery dust from swirling around the cabin. Toilet breaks were 'when one goes, everyone goes' with a dash to a small bush, checking for lizards, snakes and bull ants before squatting. Despite the lengthy view in each direction, the lookout for oncoming traffic was usually Tippy, who was frequently distracted by the surrounding sights and sounds.

The flat, arid earth stretched to the horizon, with a rare glimpse of rabbits, eagles and kangaroos. It was mostly saltbush. We played a game of guessing the colour of the next car, but hours might pass without seeing one. Relief came at the concrete, fresh-water tanks situated at regular intervals along the way. We filled our waterbags, splashed our faces to remove the grit and dust, and stretched our legs while eating as much fruit as possible before getting to the WA border where we had to discard it in the bins provided to prevent the spread of fruit fly.

At night, we camped under a marquee sky of flickering lights. The canvas wrapping from our roof rack became an envelope for our bed as we huddled together, wearing our day clothes. The overpowering heat of the day lessened as night brought a bitter chill. Wind snapped at the canvas and we held on tight with our feet and fingers to prevent its flight. I spent the night clutching the outer edge and listened to the sounds of the Nullarbor, feeling the uneven ground sharp against my buttocks. I heard the swish of wings overhead, the muffled thump of small creatures moving through the spinifex and the sound of an approaching car as headlights swept over the ground. Beside me, the others punctuated the air with their snores. I felt as alone as the vast expanse of the Nullarbor itself.

When we arrived at our destination, North Dandalup, fifty miles south of Perth, we hadn't bathed for three days and I declared that I would never do that trip again.

But I would.

Four more times.

* * *

North Dandalup had streets, a highway with traffic sounds and a railway station down the road from Aunty Ethel's house. The steam train rattled across the bridge twice a day jingling the ornaments on the mantel piece in the front room as it passed.

The front room had an upright piano, open fireplace, an armchair and a couch. Zilla and I shared one bedroom while Tippy slept in a room at the end of the back verandah. Our bedroom had a curtain across the doorway and opened into the kitchen where Aunty cooked daily. She rose at five each morning, trudged down the hallway from her bedroom, slippers slapping the lino floor as she hit the two steps leading down into the kitchen. The rustle of newspaper, strike of a match and smack of the kettle onto the iron stove signalled the beginning of another day. These early morning stirrings brought a warm, cozy mood through the curtain into our room. Compared to Betty's mean offerings, the food was wonderful. Fresh milk, butter and cream came from the cow, Blossom, who Aunty milked daily. We had home-made bread, jam and cream, fresh cakes and a variety of stews, vegetables and meat. It was even better than boarding school.

Aunty's children, Cecil and Beat, had married and moved out a few years before I arrived. Her youngest son Mel, was the same age as Keith and had recently become engaged. Their visits to Mount Hope were infrequent. Zilla and Tippy had lived here most of their lives but I had two weeks before school commenced to adjust to the routine. Over the years I had learned to keep my belongings in a contained space, but if I thought I was neat and tidy, I was wrong. Zilla was so organised, I felt sloppy. Each morning, her bedclothes stretched taut and wrinkle free with hospital corners and flattened pillow. I envied her ability to do so with minimum effort as I hadn't quite mastered eliminating the undulations from the kapok mattress and dithered in my attempts to imitate her finished look.

Each night, Zilla curled her hair with rags twisted around her ponytail. In the morning when the rags were removed, the hair coiled down her back in a twist. In contrast, my hair was a mess every morning and, depending on how restless my sleep had been, looked as if I'd been in a wind tunnel.

Aunty bought two second-hand shirts and tunics for my new school, the same as Zilla's. The tunic was re-dyed deep maroon in the boiler in the backyard. It was drab, despite the dip in the dye.

'You've got one year left of school,' said Aunty. 'I'm not wasting money on new uniforms.'

The thought of starting school terrified me. I'd been at an all-girls school and this was co-ed. Zilla was an A grade student. She was clever, consistent and excelled in everything except sport. I struggled to maintain a C plus, concentration was a major factor.

Aunty required tidy drawers, neat room and clean shoes and since Saturday was cleaning and washing day it was the designated day to tackle those tasks. I had my paltry collection of underwear strewn across the bed. They included bras that failed to produce the desired perky uplift and baggy bloomers worn over the top of my panties, should I break into a spontaneous handstand in public. My method of stuffing everything into the drawer and rummaging when needing something was unsatisfactory to both Zilla and Aunty. I was laboriously folding these items when Aunty called us into the kitchen.

Tippy arrived through the door with the shoe brush in one hand, shoe in the other.

'How long does it take to polish shoes?' said Zilla.

'As long as I want,' said Tippy.

'Is that from Dad?' I asked Aunty. She was holding a telegram smoothing the creases with shaking hands.

'Yes. It is,' she said. 'Sit down, children. I have bad news.'

Crikey. I bet Ross has finally killed Betty.

'Your brother Keith was killed in a car accident today.'

'No. It can't be true,' I sobbed. 'We saw him at Christmas. He was there, at Christmas.'

'I'm sorry, Bonnie,' said Aunty. 'He was driving his sports car.'

'It was pink. He'd just fixed it up.' I was unprepared for the crushing effect of this news. 'I want to go to the funeral. I want to go home. I want Ross.'

Zilla and Tippy stood in embarrassed silence.

'I know you'd like to but that's not practical,' said Aunty. 'It's too far.'

I'd adored Keith from a distance. He'd dodged Betty's cruelties because he was already at boarding school when she came into our lives. He was my connection to life outside Mount Hope and my escape when I finished school. *You'll have to visit me in Sydney sometime.* I threw myself on my bed and sobbed, regretting that his visits had been so irregular and so rare I was finding it impossible to believe I would never see him again.

'I know you two didn't know him as well as Bonnie,' I heard Aunty say to Zilla and Tippy. 'So let's leave her alone for a while.'

I fell asleep to the rattle and clinking in preparation for the evening meal. Zilla shook me awake for dinner and I noticed my underwear had been put away.

'Did you do that?' I said to Zilla.

'Didn't take long.'

'Thanks.' Her small display of kindness soothed my grief. Even Tippy was sympathetic and handed me a matchbox with a beetle trying to negotiate the cotton wool in a confined space.

'Found it in the wood pile,' he said. 'It just crawled into my hand.'

'Thanks, Tip. Would you take care of it for me?'

'Perhaps we can put him on the shelf in the bathroom,' said Aunty as two front legs poked through the end of the box. 'Right now it's dinner time.'

'Do I have to go to school on Monday?' I asked Aunty.

'I think it would be a good idea,' said Aunty. 'It'll take your mind off things. Zilla will help.'

The high school in Pinjarra was a nine-mile bus journey that took 45 minutes as it picked up students along the way. The racket on the bus was deafening. It was my first experience at travelling this way. Bodies leaned over the seats and voices shouted to each other as if they were in the next street. As each passenger boarded, it brought a fresh surge of greetings and the bus driver threatened to offload his charges if they didn't pipe down.

I clutched my brown leather satchel as protection against the assault on my senses. Bad breath, youthful body odour and diesel mixed with the various kinds of chewing gum that flavoured the air as the bus lurched its way towards Pinjarra. Zilla renewed friendships, offered sporadic introductions and quick explanations for my attendance.

'This is my sister, Bonnie, blah, blah, blah ...'

The day proceeded in a fog: assembly, finding students in my year, following them from one classroom to another, and listening to teachers welcome us for another year. By the end of the day I had textbooks and a timetable and a headache from the constant disruption by the boys. Focus eluded me. In the week following, the resident bully made me her target.

'Hey, four eyes,' she jeered at me from the centre of her followers. 'You deaf? Nah, just stupid.'

I avoided the playground at breaks because there she was, her face in my face, poking my chest, threatening me with a beating through toothless gums. I chose to remain silent and walk away, mainly because I was trembling inside. My grades moved from B minus to C minus.

Music became my solace. I joined Zilla and Tippy in having lessons with Mrs Inkpen. Although she was serious and strict, I had already been learning for six years and was proficient enough to appreciate her disciplined schedule. A timetable hung on a nail in Aunty's kitchen and on Saturday mornings, we'd have theory and aural lessons in the lounge room with all of Mrs Inkpen's local students. Despite my being the older sister, Zilla excelled. She was the academic, Tippy and I were the dreamers. Tippy's piano practice consisted of a quick run through of his pieces, often with multiple errors, then a dash out to the woods at the back. He'd become distracted with his games and arrive in a panic for the evening meal, often with dirty face and hands.

Aunty could get cranky. Cheekiness, unfinished chores, lateness and untidiness resulted in the removal of her shoe and a hefty whack across whichever part of the body she could reach. At first, I escaped her wrath, being new to the fold, as the other two were clobbered. Aunty would stomp after Tippy, waving her shoe shouting, *By the Hogan's Goat,* as he scarpered out the back door and headed for the trees. Often, he didn't return until after dark, an action which doubled the punishment. Aunty grabbed him by the ear, dragged him down the hallway as he howled in pain, then took him out the back and thrashed him with her shoe. Zilla, less prone to breaking into a run, stood her ground and received her whacks with dignity. Aunty took to giving me a severe scolding comparable to Dad's lectures. It must've run in the family.

The shock of Keith's death lessened and I adjusted to the routine of living in North Dandalup. In addition to cooking, cleaning and baking, we had chooks and a veggie patch in the backyard with a good supply all year round. Aunty also sewed all our clothes, including my bras which, considering my lack of breasts, were less of bra and more something to cover my nipples.

Aunty worked in the Post Office which was located in the corner of the General Store, during school hours, and to keep me occupied on weekends and in the holidays, got me a job there. Having spent considerable time assisting in the Mount Hope store, I felt confident no task was beyond my abilities. I developed a crush on the dreamy, blond boss's son and had heart palpitations and brain freeze whenever he was around.

'You've got no chance,' Zilla said. 'He's seventeen, for goodness sake.'

'I do believe he's courting a girl from Pinjarra.'

'Yes Aunty, he is. It's embarrassing,' said Zilla.

'I don't, I mean he ...' I said.

'You've only made it obvious with your googly eyed look every time he walks past.' Zilla strutted around the kitchen with exaggerated hip movements.

'Bonnie's in love, Bonnie's in love.'

'Shuddup, Tippy,' I said.

'I'm afraid it's common knowledge, dear. Now what about that nice boy who lives across the railway line? His parents are lovely.'

'Yeah,' said Zilla. 'He's already asked you out.'

'You mean pimple face?'

'Not nice, Tip,' said Aunty. 'We don't talk about people like that.'

'Oh heck. I'm not talking about this anymore. I'm going to study for the exams.'

***

One day I arrived home from school when Aunty called me into the kitchen.

'I think you should see this. It arrived this morning. It's from your Dad.'

She handed me a newspaper cutting from the *Sydney Morning Herald*. It was dated November 8, 1961.

'This is horrible. There's been a shooting at my old school. Wendy Luscombe's dead. She was in the class below me. Red hair. I liked Wendy.'

'That's terrible,' said Aunty. 'Her poor parents.'

A man had held the girls hostage in the chapel and Wendy was hit by a stray bullet when the Headmistress wrestled the gun from the gunman. There were 150 pupils in the chapel at the time.

'Poor Wendy,' I said.

I thought of Wendy's family, my school mates and the teachers and how terrible it must have been. For six years it had been my home and I knew all the girls who would have been in the chapel. For three years, I'd been one of the organists. Who was playing that day? If I'd been there maybe it would have been me. I could picture the rows of girls, the choir, seniors and teachers at the back and juniors in the front.

In November, I sat for my Intermediate Certificate, taking the necessary number of courses required to pass. Maths, Art, English, History and Music. My exam preparation was dismal. I couldn't concentrate. I hadn't felt part of the school all year. Zilla's results climbed and mine fell. My name didn't make it into the paper. I'd failed Maths and History. Maths was essential to obtain an Intermediate Certificate. My year with my youngest siblings was over and I'd be returning home to Cobar, already longing to escape, but with no idea how to achieve it.

JUNK

The smoke from our incinerator, a forty-four gallon drum, pricked my eyes as I approached. Heat burned my cheeks. Flecks of black, grey and white swirled in the updraft. The warmth reminded me of dry winter days with Ross, rubbing our gloveless hands, and while the rubbish burned, we chased mice as they abandoned their lair and escaped from the heat. I thought of the post-Christmas burn, when Zilla and Tippy were with us, as those gift wrappings unclaimed by Betty for re-use filled the drum. Ross was always prepared with a bucket of water for safety from flying sparks, which were inevitable due to his and Tippy's compulsive stirring.

I'd arrived home to pack up for my move to Sydney. Leaving Mount Hope had been easy for me. Despite the years Betty had been with us, none of us kids regarded her as our mother. She remained detached and inflexible throughout our childhood, tolerating us, we believed, as a condition of her relationship with Dad.

My escape was to Sydney to begin nursing at the Prince of Wales Hospital in Randwick. Since I'd spent years at boarding school living in a dormitory, sharing bathrooms and crowded dining rooms, it was a move from one institution to another. I would miss Ross, but we had spent so much time apart, our paths had diverged years ago.

Betty was clearing out the house in preparation for the move to a mine outside Cobar and incinerating anything she considered junk and unimportant to her. My room was now bare except for the bed and suitcase. My time there erased.

Peering into the drum, I stared open mouthed at the sight of my autograph book sitting on the top of the pile of scattered papers. It was the one my father had bought when he'd paid a rare visit to my boarding school. I'd pressed him to buy the one most of the girls at school owned. Choosing had been difficult.

'Plain cream cover will do,' Dad said as I'd cautiously held up the blue embossed one for his approval.

'Too expensive,' he'd said. 'Can't see why you want one of these. Waste of money, if you ask me.'

Many of the girls owned beautiful books with leather covers in rich colours of red, green and blue with gold cursive lettering carved on the front. They carried them everywhere – a fashion accessory designed to evoke envy and admiration. Most of my pages were empty with a few random sayings scattered throughout.

Algebra is tough
Geometry is hard
It tickles me and makes me laugh
That you want my autograph

The short rhyme appeared through the flames then disintegrated. I wondered who'd written it. Forming relationships didn't come easily for me, so there were no sentimental lines about friendship and love. As for the nasty ones, I'd ripped them out.

You're so ugly, no-one ...

There were a few like that. As the pages burned, a photograph was revealed. Five girls in uniform, sitting on the lawn outside the cottage in the grounds of the school, arms locked around shoulders. The recollection of those few happy occasions made me smile, then the corners curled inwards as heads and shoulders changed into waves of fluttering embers. Despite my dislike of boarding school, I was saddened to see the book destroyed.

The tip of my tennis trophy, won in a singles match against the school champion, poked through the ash and flame as it melted. It'd been a tough game with fourteen deuces in the final set and an abundance of skids across the clay court. I'd been certain the umpire was biased, calling in favour of my opponent. Not wishing to create a scene, it had always been my habit to succumb to pressure and stop trying, often running to hide in an empty corner and cry with frustration. This time, as my name moved closer to the top of the ladder, and I eliminated the competition to reach the finals, my desire to win burgeoned into fierce determination. I had wanted to keep the trophy to remind me of my sole win.

The coloured ribbons stored inside the cup began disintegrating. A blue one for hurdles, two red for hockey, and three green for basketball, but nothing for athletics. Sport had been compulsory and competitive, segregating those with talent and those without. I participated with an attitude and willingness that seldom produced the required results. Apart from tennis, the ribbons had been a significant achievement in my mediocre sporting efforts. Tree climbing didn't count and prowess on the monkey bars was considered frivolous. Evidence of sporting feats combined into a brief mix of melted colour before sinking into the growing remains of my treasures.

The edge of a cardboard folder caught fire, revealing a collection of my music certificates. How could Betty possibly think this was junk? *Australian Music Examinations Board ... Honours in Pianoforte Grade F...* I tracked the fragmenting of my Piano Certificates as name and grades were devoured. This, of all the things burning, was something that celebrated my persistence and tenacity. Daily practice of techniques had gradually developed my skills over the years and produced gratifying results.

I'd been studying piano for a year when, during the Preliminary exam in a draughty hall in Bowral, I conquered nerves that travelled down my arms to my foot by curling my toes to stop my foot from shaking on the pedal. The examiner wore a large buckled belt and full black skirt, didn't smile, and was stern and unfriendly. The table seemed yards from the piano and I was so anxious it was difficult to hear her softly spoken instructions. Afterwards, when the results were announced, my honours grading gave me a thrill I'd not experienced before. I wrote a letter to Dad and waited for his reply of congratulations. By the time I returned home for the holidays, the achievement was forgotten and the certificates were filed along with reports and reprimands from the headmistress. Was that letter also in there amongst my years of effort, perishing in a greedy, forty-four gallon drum?

I bit my bottom lip to squash my distress at the personal possessions being destroyed. I took the metal pole and jabbed at the contents. With smoke up my nose and tears in my eyes, I turned over unburnt pages and revealed forgotten drawings. These were my artistic attempts at five years old, not long after Mum left. No masterpieces but nothing, it seemed, was missed in this clean-out of prized mementos.

A gust of wind circled the rim, agitating layers of half burnt paper reviving weakened flames. A slow-moving corkscrew flaked upwards.

I stirred the fire again, not wishing to see reminders, or make new discoveries. The burn was obliterating tangible evidence of my childhood. At fifteen, I was moving to the city.

'You're not here and I'm not carting your junk to Cobar,' Betty had said. 'There isn't room.'

Junk? These were *my* things, *my* possessions and Betty had decided to burn everything without consultation. Tears spilled as I thought of my emptied bookshelves and drawers, my dolls and scholarly endeavours alike reduced to a pile of ash. The drum crackled as the metal cooled. The flames receded and the embers settled. My resentment magnified. As much as I was prepared for new adventures, pain would always tether me to this outback town.

CLASSIC JAUNT

A small number of people alighted when the train pulled into Cobar Station. I searched amongst those on the platform for a familiar face without success. One by one, suitcases were loaded into cars until only the station master and I remained. When he returned to his office, I was alone.

I was sixteen and my job as a nurse in Sydney had distanced me from my family in more ways than geography. Returning home filled me with dread and since the permanent move to Cobar, it didn't feel like home anymore. The older I became, the less Dad trusted me. He was work-driven and a strict disciplinarian. Mining copper was labour intensive and the hours fluctuated depending on production.

My pondering was interrupted by the sight of Dad's black Oldsmobile racing into the parking area. It skidded to a stop sending a hail of gravel peppering the side of the red brick building. The ensuing dust obscured my view of the driver, but the trademark artistry was discernable. Out tumbled Ross, Tippy and four of their mates.

'Hi Sis. Sorry I'm late. Been working on the Ols for a couple of weeks and we thought we'd take if for a run,' said Ross.

The words tumbled out in a breathless rush as he chucked my suitcase in the boot, gave me a quick hug that left a lingering aroma of oil on my clothing then clambered back behind the wheel revving the engine.

'Hi Bon, good to see ya,' said Tippy delivering another aromatic oil and grease hug.

'Hurry up. Get in,' said Ross.

'How are we all going to fit in?' I asked.

'You can sit in the front with Tip, the rest in the back.'

We pulled out in the same sweeping turn, a volley of gravel hit the wall below the stationmaster's window and narrowly missing the fresh water tank. He then fishtailed on to the main road and roared out of town. When Ross drove, it was a nerve-wracking experience.

'Just gonna take it for a bit of a run before dropping these guys home,' said Ross as the occupants peppered me with questions and comments.

'So, you're Ross's sister ...'

'You staying out at the mine ...?'

'How long for ...?'

'You're a nurse, aren't you ...?'

The Oldsmobile had been with us since Dubbo. It had a split-front windscreen, leather bench seats, running-board and column gearshift. I remembered the three of us, Ross, Zilla and myself, climbing on the running-board as Dad backed out of the driveway and we'd hang on the doorframe of the open window screaming *faster, faster,* until the car reached the gate.

'We've been fixing her up for weeks,' said Tippy.

Dad had decided that Tippy would finish high school in Cobar, so he lived in a hostel during the week and spent the weekend out at the mine. Tippy found it difficult adjusting after being with Aunty Ethel for so many years, but he and Ross were great mates and both were adventurous. If there was a boundary, Ross would ram through. His enthusiasm was infectious and contagious.

The Cobar road had been recently graded but the edges were still soft and powdery and there was a steep camber either side. No cars could be seen in either direction of the long, straight stretch of road.

'Let's open her up a bit,' said Ross to cheers from all the passengers except me. 'I need to test the motor.'

His foot pressed the accelerator while mine pushed into the floor. I squeezed my knees together as the Ols reached a speed of 45 miles an hour. The testosterone in the confined cabin reached alarming levels and cries of *Go Ross ... Pedal to the Metal,* and *Whoa, man,* pumped out from youthful voices.

'Right. Everyone left,' Ross shouted. 'Two wheels.'

The ancient glass scraped as windows were wound up. One boy removed his spectacles and put them in his pocket.

'Nobody fart,' said Tippy.

Four bodies in the back crammed together against the side door on the left as Ross drove off the road into the camber.

'Hang on,' said Tippy leaning hard against the door.

'Get ready,' Ross swerved to the side of the road, drove down an eighteen inch dip and pushed hard against the accelerator as the car tilted.

'What are you doing?' I screamed. 'You'll kill us all.'

'You've gone soft, Sis,' said Ross, grasping the wheel and listing left.

I reached for the dashboard but slid against Tippy who threw his arm around my shoulders and pulled me against him. The road disappeared as the car began to turn.

The right wheels lifted from the road and we remained at a 45 degree angle for about 20 yards. We could hear the sound of the wind, the crunching gravel and the roaring engine. Everyone was silent, holding our breaths as Ross struggled, and failed, to maintain control. The momentum he'd created wasn't enough. The car overbalanced as it tumbled over rocks and branches, bodies fell against each other as flailing arms sought traction. I was sliding and bouncing on the leather. My glasses flew to the floor well as the car skidded on its roof along the ditch. Grunts, groans and yelps accompanied the grating, creaking and banging from outside, as arms and legs became entangled. The thin roof offered little protection from the rough terrain we were flying over. Ross, upside down, still maintained his vice-like grip on the steering wheel.

The car came to rest on a patch of spinifex beside the fence. There was a moment of silence; shock at having survived the ordeal. Moaning from the various occupants soon confirmed everyone's survival as we all squeezed through Ross's open window. He limped over to inspect the car while the rest of us checked for broken bones, relieved to find that bruises, scrapes and minor cuts were the extent of our injuries.

Our relief exploded into spontaneous laughter.

'Ross, you are one crazy fella.'

'... That was some stunt.'

'... Geez, some ride.'

'... You got a death wish, brother.'

'You're bonkers, the lot of you,' I said. 'Someone could've been hurt.'

'Well, it's a good job we've got a nurse with us,' laughed Ross.

'Come on Bon,' said Tippy. 'It was just a bit of fun.'

I'd missed the fun and mischief of my brothers. Both were larrikins who sought entertainment and adventure in unexpected ways. Danger was a huge part of it.

'I know,' I said. 'I miss you too.'

'Okay let's get the car on its wheels,' said Ross. 'Hope the engine still goes.'

With all hands pushing and shoving, we got the car upright. I was surprised how much greenery we'd collected on our chaotic ride. It was attached to mudguards and jammed in the front grill. The roof, mudguards and bonnet had indentations, paint chips and scratches and the destruction on the right side was minimal compared to the left with its squashed-in doors and broken window. A tree branch had penetrated the driver's side windscreen, a lethal arrow pointed directly at where Ross had been sitting.

'Crikey, Ross,' said Tippy. 'That was close.'

'Yeah. Now I've got two windows to replace,' said Ross.

Ross presented an indifferent exterior, camouflaging his concern with wisecracks and nonchalance. I knew his private relief would have been immense.

The twisted bonnet failed to dampen the energy of these lads. My mechanical knowledge was meagre when it came to cars, so I sat against the fence and watched them tackle our transport problem. Tippy joined me.

'I think there are enough noses in the engine,' Tippy said as he flopped down beside me. 'They can do without me.'

'How've you been? I know it must've been hard with Zilla staying over in Western Australia.'

'I miss her. You know, I left all my mates behind because Dad said it was time for Ross and me to be brothers.'

'I've heard you're a tennis champion.' I said to Tippy. He shuffled his feet.

'Yeah. I play a bit.'

'What are you going to do when you finish school?'

'Work for Dad, I guess. Same as Ross.'

'That's gotta be hard.'

'Ross is getting his pilot's licence this year and when I'm old enough, I'll get mine.'

'Wow.' Zilla and I would've liked the opportunity to learn to fly an aeroplane but for Dad, there was one role for boys and another for girls. Flying was not a girl's role. Pixie Dust was a childhood fantasy, fuelled by imagination and stimulated by a desire to break free. Being in control of an aeroplane, doing it the conventional way, would have been fun.

Ross tried to start the motor but it spluttered and died. More discussion came from heads lowered beneath the deformed bonnet.

'How long will you be home?' said Tippy.

'This isn't home. Mount Hope was home. Cobar is just a place where Dad works and I visit.'

'I know what you mean.'

The Oldsmobile coughed, spluttered then roared. Ross pumped the accelerator a few times and the motor settled to a steady hum. The boys cheered as they punched the air then congratulated each other with back-slapping and hugs.

'I thought we'd be hitching,' I said.

'Not with Ross around. He's a genius.'

With a hefty push, grinding gears and revving motor, we got the car back on the road and were headed back to Cobar, when a dust cloud appeared around the bend and a familiar car stopped alongside.

'Hello Dad,' said one of the boys, 'What are you doing here?'

'Had a job over at Robbo's,' he said, leaning out the window. 'Looks like you've had a bit of a run in with something, Ross.'

'Ran off the road,' said Ross, 'Just heading into Cobar to drop these fellas off.'

'Anybody want a lift?'

'Yeah, thanks Charlie, that'd be great. Drop off Tippy at the hostel?'

'Sure. Hop in.'

'Bye Sis, see you next weekend.' Tippy gave me a hug and climbed in with the others.

'Nice meeting you nurse,' was shouted from the window as they drove away.

'We'd better head out to the mine,' said Ross. 'Let's keep this jaunt to ourselves, okay?'

'The rules haven't changed,' I said. 'I'll leave any explaining to you.'

* * *

'Things have changed since you were last here,' said Ross when I climbed back into the car after closing the last gate into the mine. 'There's a bathroom, for one thing.'

The Queen Bee mine was four miles in from the main road, crossing through a few gates. Visitors were either anticipated or the dust trail and engine sounds announced their arrival. Beyond the mine was scrub and trails, but no road.

'I'm glad,' I said. 'Roughing it is not my style anymore.'

'It's Dad,' he said as we rounded the final corner and I could see the house in the middle of the clearing.

'He does love those Nissen huts,' I said. 'What about Dad?'

'He's been a bit weird since Keith died.'

'Okay. I'll be nice.'

Still standing, was the concrete bunker, the site of many nightmares from two years ago. The toilet was perched on a new mound down the back and the old kitchen shed had various pieces of machinery spilling out from the opening. The caravan had been moved up the hill. Building paths always seemed to be way down on the 'to do' list as far as our family was concerned as indicated by the bits of masonite leading to the front door. Ross reefed my case out of the ute and dumped it on the ground.

'Gotta go. See you at dinner,' he said as he slammed the door. 'Plonk your stuff in the back room,' he shouted as he drove off in the rattling Oldsmobile that no doubt would be out of action for a while.

Dad was working up at the mine and Betty was somewhere around, but didn't come to greet me. I was disappointed. A cloud of dust would have announced our approach but there was no hello, no welcome – no nothing. If we hadn't been so far out of town, I'd have walked away.

This wasn't my home. Even the connection with my brother was beginning to fade. I was a stranger here. I stood in the dusty clearing in front of the house and wondered why Betty hadn't bothered to greet me.

I weaved my way across the path and placed my suitcase inside the doorway and was struck by my trepidation, as if trespassing. Instead of locating my room, I decided to explore. A squark from above the kitchen cabinet startled me. Perched on top was a galah. He flapped wings and squarked again. I left him and walked around the back of the house where I spotted Betty at the clothesline. She turned.

'Well, hello Bonnie,' she said continuing to toss clothes into the basket. 'You made it then.'

'Ross picked me up at the station.'

'How was the trip?'

'Okay. House finished?'

'Not quite.'

'Where's Dad?'

'Working. He'll be down for tea.'

'There's a galah on the kitchen dresser.'

'It belongs to your father.'

The conversation was interspersed with awkward silences and her lack of interest in me was obvious. It was reciprocal. As her hands unpegged garments and threw pegs into the bucket, a glint from her left hand hit me like a physical backhand.

'You're wearing rings?'

'Your father and I were married last year.' She smiled.

It was a smile of triumph.

Despite the length of time she and Dad had been together I'd foolishly hoped that as long as they weren't married we had a chance. A chance she would leave. Her wedding ring was a defeat. Dad had betrayed us.

Betty picked up the basket.

'Come on,' she said. 'I'll show you where you're sleeping.'

'What's the galah's name?'

'Cocky.'

We walked through the kitchen. Newspaper covered the floor below the kitchen cabinet and layered the table. Cocky side-walked along the top of the cabinet watching, as we dodged bird droppings along the way. The furniture was familiar. Formica table and chairs, lounge chairs and glass cabinet containing Dad's collection of rock samples. The space inside the Nissen hut was bigger than the last one.

'This is the spare room,' said Betty taking me to a room at the front.

A faded candlewick bedspread covered a lumpy kapok mattress. The sagging wire base showed evidence of years of trampoline abuse and I recognised the wardrobe with its chipped edges and rattling drawers as the one I'd wrestled with in Mount Hope. Replacing the furniture would have been impractical in the harsh surroundings.

'Ross and your father will be home soon,' she said. 'Why don't you unpack?'

When she left the room, I noted the lack of decoration. No photographs or paintings. Ornaments were impractical and required dusting. I left my unopened suitcase on the floor and heard Ross enter through the back door. His hair was wet and he was wearing clean shorts and shirt.

'Where's Bon?' I heard Ross ask Betty.

'Here I am.'

'Come on, let me show you my room.'

His room was the same size as mine and both had the same furniture. Beside the wardrobe was an empty bookshelf built from slats of wood supported on bricks. I was puzzled by the stacks of books in the corner, each with a brick stitting on the top. There were books on science, geology, and aircraft maintenance together with his large collection of Phantom and Superman comics, but none in the bookshelf. The unmade bed was strewn with bits of clothing which he grabbed and tossed under the bed as he straightened the blankets. The mess was not unusual, but the bricks were.

'What's with the bricks?' I asked.

'You'll see. Have a seat,' he said as he slumped into the bed. I dropped into the gully created by the sag of his weight.

'What on earth is that?' I asked pointing to the enormous propeller inserted in the back wall.

The opening which housed the propeller encompassed the entire wall. A metal casing supported the circumference with a central shaft connected to a motor on the outside of the house. It was difficult not to be impressed with the sheer grandeur of it. I wasn't certain if it was a really elaborate wall decoration or functional machine. Knowing Ross, it was the latter.

'How do you like my air conditioner? ' he said. 'This room gets a bit hot.'

'Where did the blades come from?

'Old generator fan. Pretty good, eh?'

I was processing the visual architecture.

'Watch this.'

He flipped a switch attached to the one remaining space on the wall and the propeller began to rotate. The air swirled as the revolutions and noise increased. I was fascinated by the building rhythms all around me as the speed and velocity escalated to an alarming level. The vibrating floor tickled my feet as I listened to the polyrhythms the motor and propeller created resisting the temptation to join in with a syncopated drumbeat. Conversation was impossible with all the racket bouncing off the walls and because of my distraction, I was unprepared for the blast of air that pushed my cheeks upward, straightening my hair and pinning me to the wall. Comics flapped and bits of clothing swept across the floor. The gyrating monster subsided when Ross turned his air-conditioner off and conversation became possible.

'That's your air conditioner?' I said, touching my wind-blown cheeks and re-styled hair.

'Well, maybe a few problems to solve yet,' said Ross. 'There's only one speed and it's a bit noisy. I can only have it on for a few minutes at a time because of the vibration and it's impossible to have anything on the shelves because it just gets blown off. Apart from that, it's better than the sweltering heat, and it's a beaut clothes drier and vacuum cleaner.'

Through the gap between the blades, I saw Betty standing outside under a wattle tree, twenty yards from the house. One hand cupped her elbow, in the other arm she held a cigarette away from her face. Smoke drifted into the air. That pose transported me to the day she had arrived, eleven years before, standing in the doorway of another Nissen hut on the hill in Mount Hope.

'In all the years Dad and Betty have been together, I've never seen them hug or kiss in front of us.'

'I gave up trying to figure them out, years ago.'

'Did you go to the wedding?' I asked him.

'Me invited to the wedding? That's a laugh. She and Dad went off one week and came back married.'

'Well, I haven't been included in family things for a long time.'

'At least you got away.'

'Yeah, but it is strange being here. It's like I'm an unwanted guest.'

'Don't worry about it. You get to leave.'

Betty crushed the cigarette butt into the dirt and went over to Dad as he walked down from the mine. They chatted for a few minutes, Betty with animated gestures, Dad casting brief glimpses at the house. I went out to say hello.

'Hi Dad.'

'Hello Bonnie,' Dad gave me a hug. 'Nice to see you could pay us a visit.'

Ouch. Letter writing had always been one of my lazy traits.

'Time for a whisky,' he said, standing aside to allow Betty inside first. 'How long are you staying?'

'Couple of weeks, then back to work.'

Betty sat three glasses and a bottle of whisky on the table and Dad went over to the kitchen cabinet.

'Whisky, Ross?'

'Thanks,' said Ross as he pulled out a chair and sat down.

'Who's a pretty boy? Who's a pretty boy?' Dad cooed. As the bird hopped up to his hand Dad clicked his tongue.

Ross rolled his eyes. I sat down.

Cocky hopped onto the back of a spare chair with deep gouges and peeled vinyl that had left the surrounding metal exposed.

'Cocky wanna dance, cocky wanna dance?' chimed Dad, dipping his head up and down. He put a peanut between his teeth which Cocky removed with surprising care.

Ross rolled his eyes again and sipped his whisky. I'd been indulging in underage drinking for some time but knew I would not be offered any alcoholic drinks here.

'Lemonade, Bonnie?' said Betty.

'Yes, thanks,' I said, hoping I would not be expected to perform tricks with the bird. It stepped from the chair to the edge of the table, strutting towards me dropping dollops of poop along the way.

'He won't hurt you,' said Dad.

'I'd just prefer a bit of distance,' I said giving tentative flicks with my hand in a shooing motion. I covered my glass.

'So, what have you been up to, Bonnie?' Dad repeated the peanut trick and held out his whisky glass. Cocky stuck his beak inside and flicked his gristled tongue into the liquid. He then hopped on the sugar bowl. It was difficult to have an intelligent conversation while an incontinent bird sashayed all over the dining table.

'Oh, fetching bed pans, folding bandages, making beds, delivering meals. That sort of thing.'

'Sounds thrilling,' said Ross. 'What do you do on your days off?'

'Go to the beach, movies and study.' I decided not to mention my nightclub visits, parties with army guys and discovering boys. 'Oh, and I've bought a piano.'

'A piano?' said Dad.

'I keep it at Mum's and I'm paying it off.'

'Well it's good to know all the years we shelled out money for piano lessons were worthwhile,' said Betty putting out the dinner plates with devon, tomato and mashed potato on them. Her cooking had remained uninteresting.

'What happened to the piano at Mount Hope?' I asked Dad.

'Gave it to an old folks' home in Cobar,' he said. 'Nobody was playing it.'

That was disappointing. I'd spent hours on it when I came home on holidays and imagined that it would always stay in the family.

Cocky waddled over and leaned into my plate. I shushed him away and he jumped onto the demolished chair.

'You got a problem, little lady?'

'I'd just prefer not to share my dinner with a bird.'

'She's not used to him, Dad,' said Ross. 'He's not usually that friendly with strangers,' he said to me. 'He likes you.'

'Sorry, Dad.' I muttered shoving a spoon of potato into my mouth as I received a friendly kick under the table from Ross.

Two weeks of meals with newspaper on the table shared with a galah that received the full attention of my father. Would I survive?

On the second morning of my visit, it was obvious that in the division of affection amongst those seated at the table, Cocky rated highest. Each meal, my tolerance dwindled until it resembled the wrecked chair. I wandered around outside, inspecting the old kitchen and bathroom avoiding Betty and Cocky. The bird delighted in attacking my toes with his beak whenever I walked inside. I longed for the clatter of cutlery and babbling nurses back at the Prince of Wales Hospital.

During lunch on the third day, Cocky meandered between the condiments and plates, fed by Dad and Betty while dropping his usual messages around the table as he pierced my eardrums with intermittent shrieks. I refrained from making any comment – until he dipped his beak into my food.

'I'm sorry, Dad, but can you put Cocky in his cage during meals?'

'I beg your pardon?' Cutlery poised mid-air; eating ceased. The bird froze, a lump of devon on his beak.

'I'm finding it difficult with the bird wandering all over the table while we are eating.'

Betty covered her lips. Ross sighed and raised his eyebrows. Dad placed his knife and fork on his plate in a steady, deliberate movement.

'When did you get so high and mighty? If you don't like it you can leave. In fact, you can leave now.' He extended his arm and Cocky stepped on, flipped the devon, caught it and swallowed. I expected the bird to add a *humph*.

'This is my house, you understand,' he said. Was the bird frowning too?

'Leave?' I said with an ache of sadness that frayed the fragile, tenuous connection between us. 'Now?'

'Yes. Leave now. Ross will take you to the station.'

He stood, put Cocky back on the top of the cupboard and walked to the bedroom.

Betty came to the door as I was clipping the suitcase closed. She handed me twenty pounds.

'This'll pay the fare back and give you some spending money,' she said. 'You should know better than to antagonise your father.'

Antagonise?

'Thanks for the money,' was all I said.

I walked back through the kitchen and heard the door of Dad and Betty's bedroom open and the creak of their bed. Muffled voices came from it. Cocky was on the top of the cabinet, head tilted, eyes following my exit.

'I'm so sorry, Bonnie,' Ross said as he threw my suitcase into the ute. 'Dad's become bit ornery about Cocky. I tried to warn you.'

'I'm sorry too.'

'Dad can be difficult sometimes.'

'That's not my fault.'

We entered the carpark at Cobar station in a more dignified manner than the previous time, the excitement of my arrival three days ago now negated by the backlash from my father.

'You're in luck,' said Ross returning from the Station Masters office. 'Train will be along soon.'

'I'm sorry about all this. I was really looking forward to spending more time with you.'

'It's okay. I'll pay a visit to Sydney, then we can have a good chin-wag.'

'How can you stand it here?'

'Don't you worry about me. I'll be fine. You keep doing what you're doing by making a life for yourself away from here. You've done the right thing. You've escaped.'

The choice to become a nurse had been a good one. The discipline, the routine and the patients. I loved it all. Working with a team gave me a sense of belonging I hadn't experienced before. Although awkward initially, the relationship with my mother and Gerald had become less reserved and I enjoyed living in the city with the anonymity of large crowds.

I wondered if my brother would ever have the courage to leave as well.

'Ross, are you going to be okay?'

'Yeah. I'll get away one day. See the world and all that.'

'I know Mum and Gerald would love to meet you and Tippy.'

'Yeah, I'd like that. One day.'

He shoved my suitcase on to the train and we hugged. I climbed aboard.

'See ya, Sis. Love ya.'

'Love you too. Bye.'

He turned and walked along the platform; head down, shoulders slumped. When he reached the corner he hesitated. Without turning, he raised his hand and waved then began twirling the curl on his forehead.

MOVING ON

Ross was right. For the next three years, I learned how to enjoy myself without the rigid restrictions of school and the friction at home. This was a different discipline. One with a strict purpose. The imperative to save lives.

For the first eight months I was a nurse's aide and in the chain of command somewhere between the delivery guys and cleaners. Matron terrified me and rarely spoke to the nurses unless they were summoned to her office. All communication was at a senior level and the inspections were worse than school. Beds, tidy uniforms, clean nails and spotless autoclaves were mandatory for the daily checks. The ward was a whirl of activity each morning as beds were made to a standard of which Aunty Ethel would have been proud. For ten minutes the patients were instructed not to make a mess or call for attention during Matron's or doctor's rounds. Any such interruption to their rounds reflected on the nurses and pointed to defects in performance.

I started my first duty at 8am on the female geriatric ward where the majority of patients required hip surgery or were recovering from an operation. At 10.30 am, I was horrified when after having delivered a patient a cup of tea and a biscuit, I returned to collect the cup and discovered her dead. When the Sister and senior nurse confirmed this, I learned discovery meant bathing the deceased, cleaning and inserting false teeth and dressing the body in a shroud then walking with the gurney to the morgue. Due to the age and condition of the patients, this would be a regular occurrence, but I had not expected to experience it on my first day. That same day I found out that two hours of sterilising bedpans was the best alone time on the ward.

I learned how to give a bed bath, the skill in making a bed when still occupied by the patient, where to put a thermometer and how to take a pulse. My bedside manner improved when I figured out personalities and took a moment to chat. It wasn't long before I became familiar with my duties and settled into a daily routine. Having spent so many years at boarding school and Betty's cooking, I had no trouble surviving on institutional food.

Formal nursing training could not begin until I was sixteen and a half and had obtained my Intermediate Certificate. So along with regular shifts on the wards, I attended Sydney Technical College at night. When I passed and was old enough, I became a student nurse. Training was in blocks of six weeks at Prince Henry Hospital at Little Bay where we learned the more detailed and intricate side of nursing. My bookshelf became jammed with books on Infectious Diseases, Anatomy and Physiology and Orthopaedics, and my walls were plastered with diagrams of the human body. I had moved up in the chain of command.

Although I was the youngest of the group, colleagues became friends and during off-duty times they introduced me to city life. One of our frequented spots was the Randwick movie theatre and when our meagre wages permitted, we saw a newsreel and two movies. On Saturday nights the ringing phone in the nurse's quarters was often a request for a group to attend a party. These could be anything from a social night at an army base to a party at Coogee Bay. Those of us not working or without a boyfriend, took advantage of the free drinks, food and transport to and from the hospital. The doors to the nurse's home was locked at 10pm and the only way to get in after that was at the back, navigating shrubs, bushes and long grass on the way to the night nurse's quarters, finding an open window, then climbing through the narrow gap at the top of the bars endeavouring not to burst into a fit of the giggles. Breaking curfew incurred a black mark on your record and a lecture from Matron. Three black marks meant termination of employment. I was fortunate never to get caught but dived into bed fully clothed on several occasions when footsteps approached my door.

By the time I was sixteen, I'd been introduced to alcohol and cigarettes by my mother, and Kings Cross night life by friends. Bouncers with huge chests and bulging biceps allowed us in without asking for identification. I found the congested streets uncomfortable and clubs dingy. Conversation was impossible, the drinks were watered down and it was so crowded, dodging groping hands became an art form. *Surf City* attracted a younger crowd where live bands performed to a decibel that hurt my ears. All we wanted to do was dance.

After zigzagging in and out of clubs one Saturday night, we wandered down William Street towards the city. Half-way down was a club called *The Sound Lounge*. A gigantic Maori outside encouraged us to enter through a doorway beneath a car sales showroom. We followed the curved staircase down into a dark room with booths, flashing lights, a wooden dance floor and Elvis Presley blaring through speakers in the ceiling.

There was no cover charge and they served coffee, tea and light snacks but no alcohol. Despite having been on our feet all day, we danced until it closed at 3am then wandered back up William Street to a small café, where we ate crepes and crashed at Mum's afterwards. This became a regular hangout on Friday and Saturday nights when I wasn't working.

When I could I would visit Mum and Gerald. Mum worked permanent days at Crown Street Women's Hospital and Gerald was a chauffeur for the PMG, driving politicians around Sydney. Gerald taught me how to drive in the city and Mum showed me how to cook.

In September 1963, Zilla turned sixteen and worked in the Perth Telephone Exchange as a telephonist. Ross was nineteen and still at the Queen Bee mine with Dad and Tippy at fourteen attended school in Cobar. Although correspondence between us was spasmodic, they were inspired that I had initiated contact with Mum first and discussed the possibility of all getting to meet her.

Zilla flew over from Perth to celebrate her birthday with us and stayed for a few days. Although we were the same height, there was a confidence and purpose in her that I lacked. She had goals and direction. I drifted, allowed others to choose my course. She was colour co-ordinated and stylish; her long hair a wonderful combination of spirals and kinks. I was a miss-match of garments and my hair behaved only when tucked under my nurse's cap. Both of us had returned to our music as organists at our local church. I did it for the money, she as a community service.

Ross and Tippy arrived by train from Cobar the day after Zilla. The last time we had been together was 1960 Christmas holidays at Mount Hope when Keith had been alive. Ross was serious with intense dark eyes and wide shoulders. We each received a quick superficial hug with a short pat on the shoulder, but he wrapped his arms around Mum and held tight. Tippy did the same. It was a rare display of affection from both of them.

We girls did not feel the same bond as the boys. It was evident in their relaxed and effortless conversation and friendly banter. We struggled to find the same casual ease as the years of her absence had left a cavity difficult to fill.

Ross was uncomfortable in the city. He remained in the safety of Mum's flat rather than suffer noisy traffic to view the sights. During TV advertisements, he would do pull-ups on the door frame and push-ups in the hallway to the amusement of the other tenants. On the three mornings he was in Sydney, he stood with Gerald on the footpath and discussed VW maintenance. Gerald nodded politely but preferred to leave such things to his mechanic.

Tippy was fit from playing tennis and football, still skinny, had a cheeky grin and quirky sense of humour. Leaving Ross with Mum, the three of us would take walks in Moore Park, a couple of blocks away from the flat. Between us, we'd fill in details about Cobar and Dad, WA and the Aunties and our plans for the future. We'd prick the surface of our emotions, then back away.

When my siblings left, Mum became sullen and silent, Gerald worked extra shifts with the PMG. I returned to a six-week study block and immersed myself in studies, parties and dancing. I didn't want to miss anything. I sampled everything, yearning for affection and connection in the people I met, unfamiliar with giving and receiving. Then, for the first time I fell in love.

I was flying without Pixie Dust.

Acknowledgements

Fresh Milk and *The Veggie Patch* (abridged) were finalists in the *Newcastle Herald* Short Story Competition in 2018 and 2020 respectively.

This book would have remained embryonic without encouragement from my daughter, Rachel Walker and niece, Jody Adams.
Thanks to Marc Walters and Maureen Fitness for getting me started. The journey in becoming a better writer has been possible because of various writers' groups at The Hunter Writers Centre with Karen Crofts, Lake Macquarie FAW and workshops with Ed Wright at The Creative Word Shop.
In bringing this book to publication I thank my regular editors specifically, the East Maitland Writers' Group, Megan Buxton, Patricia Green, Rebecca Trowbridge, Ellen Shelley, Deb Arthurs, Rosemary Bunker.
Thanks to Jill Ferguson, Louise Clayton-Jones for proof reading.
Special thanks to Ed Wright for the final editing.
I thank Rebecca Trowbridge for her valuable and generous assistance in helping me prepare this book for publication.
My thanks to family and friends who put up with my fluctuating emotional barometer during this entire process.
Any and all mistakes are mine.

Biography

Bronwyn MacRitchie is a retired music teacher who lives in Lake Macquarie and when not writing, dabbles in watercolours, acrylics, photography and gardening. During her working life she has been a nurse, governess, cleaner, waitress, punch card operator, creative costume designer, secretary and for a brief period – a cook on the Nullarbor.

She has three adult children and six grandchildren.

This is her first book.